ACTIVE CITIZENSHIP IN SCHOOLS

a good-practice guide to developing a whole-school policy

JOHN POTTER

KOGAN
PAGE

To Val, my wife, whose own book inspired me to write this one

First published in 2002

Kogan Page Limited
120 Pentonville Road
London N1 9JN
UK

Stylus Publishing Inc.
22883 Quicksilver Drive
Sterling, VA 20166-2012
USA

© John Potter, 2002

British Library Cataloguing in Publication Data

A CIP record for this book is available from the British Library.

ISBN 0 7494 3618 2

Typeset by Jean Cussons Typesetting, Diss, Norfolk
Printed and bound in Great Britain by Clays Ltd, St Ives plc

Contents

Foreword

This book represents the culmination of many years' work by CSV Education for Citizenship on promoting the concept of 'active citizenship' and on helping and advising schools on its implementation. Under the directorship of the author, CSV Education achieved a major breakthrough in 1995, by becoming a collaborator in the UK's largest education sponsorship, Barclays New Futures, which provided opportunities for schools to become actively involved in their communities through cash awards, advisory support and the receipt of resources, all managed by CSV. Many case studies drawn from these pioneering schools appear throughout this book.

Much has happened since at a national level to establish citizenship at the heart of the curriculum and September 2002 is a landmark for secondary schools as they begin to implement the subject of citizenship. Sir Bernard Crick's seminal report in 1998 led to a response by CSV on active citizenship and the curriculum: this was inspired by Peter Mitchell whose thinking is reflected in the pages of this book. More recently a report by Derry Hannam, in collaboration with CSV, has looked at the relationship between schools which involve their pupils in 'participative activities' and standards of achievement as well as effects on attendance and exclusion.

John Potter has drawn intensively on examples from these initiatives as well as those which have become known to CSV through their notable and innovative practice in involving pupils and giving all of them an entitlement to active citizenship.

In 2000, CSV published *Active Citizenship*, a toolkit for supporting classroom teachers in developing models of community involvement. This book both complements and extends the scope of that resource by being directed at those with responsibility for managing the implementation of citizenship. There is also much here that will help teachers, trainers, advisers and other educators think deeply about the values of active citizenship and how they can best prepare young people for their future lives and their rightful place as genuinely empowered citizens.

Peter Hayes, Director, CSV Education for Citizenship

Acknowledgements

I am indebted to:

My two indefatigable readers Peter Hayes and Peter Mitchell.

The heads, citizenship teams and students in the schools to which I refer in the text for their vision, creativity and sheer hard work in demonstrating that citizenship education is not only possible but fast becoming a felt reality in many schools.

Elisabeth Hoodless, CSV Executive Director, and my colleagues in the CSV Education team who over 10 years have worked to make active learning in the community a reality in British education. In particular I value the contributions of Peter Hayes, Peter Seaden-Jones and the Barclays New Futures team; Elaine Slater-Simmons and the university student tutoring team; Melanie Elkan for her contribution to community partnerships, peer mentoring and adult volunteering in schools; Jim Mulligan for his writing and training programmes; Maralyn Lewis and Rachel Masika for the CSV Millennium Award projects; my many American colleagues who have been so generous in sharing their experience of service learning; and Delphine Garr and the teams of CSV administrators who helped keep it all together.

William Plowden and the CSV Education Advisory Council for encouragement and clear thinking.

The many staff in government and the voluntary sector who over recent years have proved real partners and friends in moving citizenship education from the statute book to the classroom.

David Blunkett and Professor Sir Bernard Crick for their vision and strength of purpose in making citizenship education a reality in schools.

Introduction: the big picture

We aim at no less than a change in the political culture of this country both nationally and locally: for people to think of themselves as active citizens, willing, able and equipped to have an influence in public life.
(Education for Citizenship and the Teaching of Democracy in Schools, para 1.5[1])

> **Aim:** Here we set out the purpose and approach of this book in the context of the big picture embraced by the Citizenship Order.

Citizenship education is now on the statute book; it is part of the national curriculum, and teachers across England are working to make it a daily reality in schools. Behind this recent addition to the national curriculum lies a crucial challenge of our time. The idea is audacious in its apparent simplicity. It is that through education we should aim at 'no less than a change in the political culture of this country both nationally and locally: for people to think of themselves as active citizens, willing, able and equipped to have an influence in public life'. The challenge behind citizenship education stems from a range of related concerns, particularly the fear that our democratic and social capital is being eroded.

Purpose of the book

The purpose of this book, therefore, is to show how education for *active* citizenship gives schools greater prominence as centres of social and civic renewal. The emphasis in these pages, therefore, will be mainly upon the *active* dimension of citizenship education rather than the knowledge content of the programme of study. This is dealt with admirably by others[2] and should, of course, be given due weight in planning the citizenship curriculum.

Active citizenship uniquely links learning with the development of healthy communities in and beyond the classroom. Citizenship education, therefore, is a challenge not only for teachers and pupils but also for all who have a stake in the quality of our democratic way of life. What follows, therefore, is intended primarily for those who are actively involved in leading, implementing and supporting citizenship education in English schools. Headteachers, senior management teams and curriculum advisers are clearly in the front line of providing citizenship education. There are, however, other people including governors, local government officers, employers and people in voluntary sector organizations who have a key role in contributing to the 'common core of civic education'.[3]

Last, and perhaps most important of all, there are the students, the people who – as consumers of citizenship education – will be in the best position to reflect and comment on what is offered to them. This book is not a student textbook, but it contains material that is relevant to students' role as partners in the creation and practice of citizenship education.

Structure of the book

The book is set out in such a way that readers can go to the parts most relevant to their interests. Each chapter – like a lesson plan – starts with a brief statement of intent. Each part concludes with a short summary of key points and a brief set of questions for participants: teachers, governors, students and community partners.

Part I: WHAT – What is education for active citizenship?

This part explores what citizenship education is about. It sets out the bare bones of the Citizenship Order, its three defining strands, the outline programme of study and the immediate circumstances of its introduction. The first part concludes with an exploration of three issues: 1) the immediate concerns of teachers; 2) the relationship between the standards-based and values-based approaches to education; and 3) the ways in which the New Labour Government is seeking to support the introduction of the Order in schools.

Part II: WHY – Why is active citizenship important?

This part explores reasons why citizenship education has come about, including falling turnout at the polls, the condition of young people today, and crime. After a brief review of the recent history of citizenship in England, we explore the political ideas – particularly those of the Third Way – that are shaping our understanding of citizenship today. In this part, therefore, we trace the connection between the social, economic and political imperatives of our time and the implications for education in general and citizenship education in particular.

Part III: HOW – How schools are meeting the challenge

This part – substantially the biggest in the book – is written chiefly for practitioners and participants, particularly for those who are responsible for planning, implementing and promoting the citizenship agenda. We begin by identifying the challenges posed by the Order and review briefly CSV's experience from working on these challenges with the CSV Lighthouse Schools.[4]

Citizenship education presents heads, teachers, pupils and governors with a challenge. It requires schools to develop a whole-school strategy that embraces a new subject, existing subjects and the school ethos. It also expects schools to develop opportunities for students to engage in active learning in the local community. The large challenge of citizenship education will be broken down into 10 separate, albeit related challenges: 1) whole-school strategy; 2) leadership; 3) curriculum: planning; 4) global citizenship; 5) pedagogy – active learning, new insights on learning and service learning; 6) assessment, evaluation and research; 7) professional development; 8) student participation; 9) management and structures; 10) context – governance, finance, buildings and partnerships.

This part, in particular, will draw on CSV's work with schools on active learning in the community throughout the UK. The chapters on the challenges will be interspersed with case studies, descriptions of schools that are already making a distinctive contribution to citizenship education. Many, but not all, of these illustrations are taken from CSV's work with Barclays New Futures and with the CSV Millennium Awards scheme. Barclays New Futures is the biggest single educational sponsorship in the UK and offers competitive awards to schools in the form of cash, materials and advice to schools. There is an annual bidding round in the autumn and award winners are announced in the following spring. CSV is the education partner in the scheme. The CSV Millennium Awards projects ran for three years (1998–2001) and provided cash and personal support for young people who successfully bid for help with a project designed to bring schools (and universities) and the community together for their mutual benefit.

Part IV: Community matters

In this part the reader is given the opportunity to reflect further on key themes that link citizenship education to social, political and community development. The chapter explores our changing sense of national identity, and the challenges we face in seeking to find and live by a framework of shared values. We examine the idea of social capital and the need to strengthen the fragile networks of trust and mutual cooperation that bind communities together. We explore the role and possible future of volunteering and corporate citizenship. These themes open up a consideration of the changing role of local government, the current emphasis upon community partnerships and the involvement of young people.

Appendix

This provides a list of useful resources.

Citizenship at the crossroads

It is the central thesis of this book that citizenship education stands at a crisis – a crossing point – in the development of our political and educational culture.

Terrorism

We live in a state where, until 11 September 2001, we had imagined that we no longer faced external enemies. The collapse of the Soviet Union had brought to an end the bipolar world that had defined and dominated international politics during the past century. The enemy is now the terrorist who no longer plays to the old rules and the old politics. The assault on the twin towers of the World Trade Center in New York has given greater urgency to our need to understand what we mean by democracy and what it is to live in a global society that is shaped by both economic and cultural imperatives.

Erosion of social capital

During the last decade sociologists such as Robert Putnam[5] have pointed to the erosion of social capital. The networks of trust that bind communities have become weaker and, in significant respects, we have lost our sense of community. The erosion of social capital is treated as directly associated with the growing alienation of people, particularly young people, from the formal processes of democracy. In 2001 there were riots involving significant numbers of young people in traditionally ordered and seemingly peaceful cities such as Oldham and Burnley. Furthermore, there is growing tension between town and countryside, sharpened by the depredations of BSE and foot and mouth disease.

Young people

Young people are increasingly the focus of suspicion and concern. They are violent and criminal; they have no interest in democracy, and prefer street protest to reasoned argument. They take drugs and have abandoned the canons of traditional sexual morality. This malign caricature of young people is sufficiently widespread to trigger alarm in the media and among sections of the electorate. Where society is experienced as coming apart at the seams, young people are seen as the agents and victims of this unhappy state of affairs. In reality, of course, nothing is simple and it is easier to vilify young people – or asylum seekers, or the Euro – than it is to wrestle with the underlying causes of these alarms and panics. Nonetheless, it is evident and inevitable that education is called upon to help tackle these challenges. Citizenship education is a response to our growing and pervasive unease about the way things are.

Politics in the melting pot

Political ideologies are in the melting pot and there is widespread disenchantment with the politicians. At the last election more people joined the 'No Vote' party than voted for the present government with its landslide parliamentary majority.

It seems as though the glue that once held society together is dissolving and our world is falling apart. The dismal state of the nation's railway system – with its accidents, disruption, strikes and chronic battles over private and public ownership – symbolizes for many the parlous state we are in.

Together these themes form the backdrop of challenge to education for active citizenship, the call for a 'change in the political culture of this country both nationally and locally'. In this book I explore the implications of this challenge under three headings – the what, why and how of citizenship education – and invite the reader to reflect upon their chances for success.

Painting the big picture

Epic moments in our island story were once shown in oil paintings depicting the signatories to a great treaty or the protagonists in the debate over a Reform Bill. There is no such portrait of the process leading up to the Statutory Order for citizenship education. However, if there were such a picture, it would almost certainly be a vast collage, composed (by students) around the solid and reflective figure of David Blunkett, Secretary of State for Education and Employment during the first Labour administration of the new century. In his hands is a copy of the now-familiar pale blue and white document labelled simply *Citizenship – the National Curriculum for England*. He is pictured in the company of his erstwhile university tutor, Professor Bernard Crick, who is holding a bright red report, more elaborately entitled *Education for Citizenship and the Teaching of Democracy in Schools*, commonly called the Crick Report.

Around the central figures are pictures – mostly drawn by children and young people – of teachers, young people, parents, school governors, members and officers of the local authority, businesspeople and a sizeable contingent from the voluntary sector. A knot of journalists, in grainy black and white, clusters by the door at the back of the hall, suspicious but intrigued. In the entrance way is an unexpected, but all-too-familiar figure – the reader of this book.

The foreground of our collage shows pictures of people cut from a variety of group photographs. They are members of the Advisory Group on Education for Citizenship and the Teaching of Democracy in Schools. They are a cross-party gathering of notables, including the previous Tory Secretary of State for Education, Lord Baker, the political journalist Michael Brunson and representatives from teaching, think tanks and the voluntary sector, including Elisabeth Hoodless, the Executive Director of CSV. Next to them stand teams of civil servants who are working round the clock to keep pace with the growing pace of events. Among them is the tall, laconic figure of David Kerr, the professional officer for the group and responsible for pulling together the final documents.

On one side of the room hang portraits of historical figures who have contributed to our present-day identity as British citizens. There is the usual scattering of kings and queens but only William the Conqueror, Henry VIII and his daughter Elizabeth I have been given much prominence. (There's a nice shot of Queen Victoria on horseback with Billy Connolly.) There are some postcards of the more famous politicians and social reformers, but these people are in the minority. Most of the pictures are of people known personally to the artists, and include farm labourers, miners, machine workers and railwaymen. Many of them are

British Africans, Asians and West Indians. There are explanatory notes beneath some of the portraits, in over 70 languages.

On the opposite side of the hall, the young artists have inserted a vast plate glass window that fills the whole side of the room. Through the window among the hills and vales, streets and housing estates are the towns and villages from which the young contributors to our collage have come. Here and there are graffiti, some witty, others angry. It is clear that not all who have contributed to this vast picture feel that they live in a green and pleasant land.

Feelings as well as thoughts

Most of us respond to pictures with our feelings and to words with our minds. Education for active citizenship is as much about feelings, a sense of belonging or of its opposite, alienation, isolation and anger. Above all citizenship education is about people. Knowledge of laws, rights and constitutional arrangements are important only in so far as they affect the lives of people. Throughout this book, therefore, it is important to keep in touch with our hearts as much as with our heads. Nowhere is this more important than when we address traditionally cerebral activities such as assessment and evaluation. Citizenship education requires us all to *act*, *reflect* and *change*. It is about learning from shared experience and contributing to public life in and beyond the classroom. We also have to record this experience. Most methods of recording educational achievement are statistically heavyweight and emotionally (and morally?) lightweight. In citizenship education we need research and assessment methods that 'measure what we value, rather than teaching us to value what we can easily measure'.

Portraiture

One such research method is called *portraiture*. It has been developed by a group of US academics and is increasingly used to discern the impact of initiatives such as citizenship education and service learning. This method offers a framework for research that can be used both in school and also as part of a larger initiative to develop and share good practice across the country.

The challenge

The (then) Speaker of the House Betty Boothroyd is depicted near the centre of our collage. From her mouth is drawn a large speech bubble:

I have become increasingly concerned that citizenship as a subject appeared to be diminishing in importance and impact in schools – this despite a number of governmental initiatives over a long period of years. This area, in my view, has been a blot on the landscape of public life for too long, with unfortunate consequences for the future of the democratic process.

All that is about to change. Citizenship education is an idea whose time has come.

Summary

1. **Aim of citizenship education:** 'We aim at no less than a change in the political culture of this country both nationally and locally: for people to think of themselves as active citizens, willing, able and equipped to have an influence in public life.'
2. **Learning linked with the development of communities:** Active citizenship uniquely links learning with the development of healthy communities in and beyond the classroom.
3. **Structure of the book:** The book is set out in such a way that readers can go to the parts most relevant to their interests. Each chapter – like a lesson plan – starts with a brief statement of intent. Each part concludes with a short summary of key points and a brief set of questions for participants: teachers, governors, students and community partners.
4. **Citizenship at a crossing point:** It is the central thesis of this book that citizenship education stands at a crisis – a crossing point – in the development of our culture: terrorism, rural/urban tension, politics in the melting pot; and young people.

Notes

1. DfEE (1998) *Education for Citizenship and the Teaching of Democracy in Schools*, DfEE, London, hereafter referred to as the Crick Report.
2. The Citizenship Foundation and The Institute of Citizenship (in the Appendix).
3. David Hargreaves described this in pp 31 and 34, *The Mosaic of Learning*, Demos, London (1994). 'The problem of Britain as a pluralist society is to find some social cement to ensure that people with different moral, religious, and ethical values as well as social, cultural and linguistic traditions can live together with a degree of harmony; and to discover the contribution that the education system should play in generating social cohesion.' 'There should be a requirement that all schools, religious or secular, should provide a common core of civic education.'

4. CSV (Community Service Volunteers) was founded in 1962 by Alec Dickson to provide young people with an opportunity to volunteer away from home in the UK in a range of challenging circumstances. Subsequently CSV has promoted volunteering and community involvement through education, the media, training for work and local action projects throughout the UK. Further information is available on the CSV Web site www.CSV.org.uk.
5. Robert D Putnam, *Journal of Democracy*, **6** (1), January 1995, pp 65–78. Robert Putnam is Dillon Professor of International Affairs and director of the Center for International Affairs at Harvard University. He is now completing a study of the revitalizing of US democracy.

PART I:

WHAT – What is education for active citizenship?

1

Citizenship – an entitlement for all

We state a case for citizenship education being a vital and distinct statutory part of the curriculum, *an entitlement* for all pupils in its own right.

(Crick Report, para 3.1)

Aim: To set out the goals, requirements and key contents of citizenship education with reference to: 1) the Crick Report; and 2) the national curriculum programme of study.

It all happened so quickly. In scarcely more than 24 months after the election of New Labour to power, citizenship education had become a statutory part of the newly revised national curriculum in schools.

The Crick Report

The government had accepted the recommendations of the advisory group set out between the bright red covers of what became popularly known as the Crick Report.[1] Crick had recommended that citizenship education should become an *entitlement for all pupils* and that it should have *statutory force*, particularly in secondary schools. The Report had further proposed that as far as possible citizenship education should be *left to teachers to develop* and deliver against a simple list of learning outcomes for each age group. This was in marked contrast with other statutory subjects where the programmes of study are far more prescriptive and detailed about precisely what should be taught and learnt.

Definition

The definition of citizenship education in the Report drew strongly on the work of an earlier writer. T H Marshall had argued that citizenship comprises three distinct, albeit related dimensions: the civil, the political and the social.[2] 'The civil is composed of the rights necessary for individual freedom,' said Marshall, and went on, 'By the political element I mean the right to participate in the exercise of political power.' By the social element he meant 'the whole range from the right to a modicum of economic welfare and security to the right to share to the full in the social heritage and to live the life of a civilised being according to the standards prevailing in the society'. Since the 1950s there has been a growing emphasis upon citizens' responsibilities as well as their rights. Furthermore, welfare was seen to include what people can do for each other as well as the provision made by the state.[3]

Three strands

The Report[4] reinterprets Marshall's definition and describes citizenship education as comprising 'three things, related to each other, mutually dependent on each other, but each needing a somewhat different place and treatment in the curriculum: social and moral responsibility, community involvement and political literacy':

● **Social responsibility**
  'Firstly, children learning from the very beginning self-confidence and socially and morally responsible behaviour both in and beyond the classroom, both towards those in authority and towards each other. This learning should be developed, not only in but also beyond school, whenever and wherever children work or play in groups or participate in the affairs of their communities.

  'Some may think this aspect of citizenship hardly needs mentioning; but we believe it to be near the heart of the matter. Here guidance on moral values and personal development are essential preconditions of citizenship. Some might regard the whole of primary school education as pre-citizenship, certainly pre-political; but this is mistaken. Children are already, through learning and discussion, forming concepts of fairness, and attitudes to the law, to rules, to decision making, to authority, to their local environment and social responsibility, etc. They are also picking up, whether from school, home or elsewhere, some knowledge of whether they are living in a democracy or not, of what social problems affect them and even what the different pressure groups or parties have to say about them. All this can be encouraged, guided and built upon.

- **Community involvement**
  'Secondly, learning about and becoming helpfully involved in the life and concerns of their communities, including learning through community involvement and service to the community. This, of course, like the other two branches of citizenship, is by no means limited to children's time in school. Even if pupils and adults perceive many of the voluntary groups as non-political, the clearer meaning is probably to say 'non-partisan': for voluntary bodies, when exercising persuasion, interacting with public authorities, publicizing, fund-raising, recruiting members and then trying to acti-vate (or placate) them, are plainly using and needing political skills.

- **Political literacy**
  'Thirdly, pupils learning about how to make themselves effective in public life through knowledge, skills and values – what can be called 'political literacy', seeking for a term that is wider than political knowledge alone. The term 'public life' is used in its broadest sense to encompass realistic knowledge of and preparation for conflict resolution and decision making related to the main economic and social problems of the day, including each individual's expectations of and preparations for the world of employment, and discussion of the allocation of public resources and the rationale of taxation. Such preparations are needed whether these problems occur in locally, nationally or internationally concerned organizations or at any level of society from formal political institutions to informal groups, both at local and national level.

  'So our understanding of citizenship education in a parliamentary democracy finds three heads on one body: *social and moral responsi-bility, community involvement* and *political literacy*. 'Responsibility' is an essential political as well as moral virtue, for it implies: 1) care for others; 2) premeditation and calculation about what effect actions are likely to have on others; and 3) understanding and care for the conse-quences.'

The government moved swiftly following the publication of the Crick Report in September 1998. There was a period of consultation on the proposed general revisions to the national curriculum during the summer of the following year, and by November 1999 it was all done and dusted. Citizenship education became a formal and, in the case of secondary schools, statutory part of the newly revised national curriculum.

'A light touch Order'

In brief, the government ruled that every child in primary and secondary education should undertake citizenship education. In secondary schools citizenship was to become a foundation subject from September 2002. This meant that the Office of Standards in Education (OFSTED) would formally inspect citizenship. In primary schools citizenship education was immediately incorporated alongside personal and social and health education in a shared curriculum framework. A programme of study was published with learning outcomes for each key stage. These outcomes were defined in terms of young people becoming informed citizens and developing the skills of communication and enquiry through participation and responsible action.

It was, in the words of the Secretary of State, David Blunkett, 'a light touch Order'. The Government would set out the framework of what young people will be expected to learn, but it would be left to teachers to fill in the detail in ways that best meet the needs of their own schools and pupils.

A unique subject

Citizenship education was to be a curriculum subject in its own right, but it was unique and different from other subjects in three key respects:

1. **Linked with other subjects:** Schools were explicitly encouraged to link citizenship education with other subjects across the whole curriculum.
2. **A way of life:** Citizenship education was – to borrow a phrase from television – 'not so much a subject, more a way of life'. Citizenship education had to be rooted in the ethos and way of life of the whole school.
3. **Participation:** Citizenship education requires young people to learn through participation and real experience.

These three requirements form a mutually reinforcing cycle. Pupils are expected to develop their knowledge, understanding and skills *through participation and responsible action*.

It was clear from the start that citizenship education has profound implications for curriculum planning, pedagogy, and the relationships between students and staff, and between schools and their communities.

Notes

1. QCA (1998) *Education for Citizenship and the Teaching of Democracy in Schools*, Final Report of the Advisory Group on Citizenship, QCA, London.
2. T H Marshall (1950) *Citizenship and Social Class and Other Essays*, Cambridge University Press, Cambridge.
3. See B. Crick (2000) *Essays on Citizenship*, p 7, Continuum, London.
4. Crick Report, paras 2.10–2.12.

2

Background to the Order

The Crick Report was not the first attempt to introduce citizenship as a named activity into schools. The failure of the initial attempt is worth recording as it contains instructive lessons about the link between politics, culture and education. It also has something to teach us about getting things right in the future.

Subjects not citizens

Until the mid- to late 1980s the general view in and out of schools was that citizenship, like patriotism, is something that is 'caught not taught.'[1] In Britain, during the post-war period citizenship was narrowly defined in terms of the rights of the individual. The 'good citizen' was someone who enjoyed the protection of the law and the benefits of state provision in return for which he obeyed the law, paid *his* taxes and, if necessary, performed military service. (The citizen was most often conceived of as male.) The issue was clouded by the fact – of which we were reminded whenever we raised the subject – that the British are 'subjects' not citizens. Citizenship is for other people like those in France and the United States. In retrospect it seems extraordinary that such arguments held sway for so long.

Social and political concerns

During the late 1980s, however, the political debate had moved on, as had our understanding of the potential importance of citizenship and citizenship education. Politicians in particular were becoming increasingly worried about two things. Firstly, people, particularly young people, were becoming increasingly alienated from society and democracy. In other words they were less and less interested in voting and more and more likely to engage in anti-social behaviour. Secondly, the networks of trust and personal relationships that bind society together were perceived as wearing thin. Put crudely, there was a growing fear that society is falling apart. These crude fears, which obscured the complexity of the underlying facts, nonetheless proved potent in public debate. (We explore them further in Part II.) They led to fresh talk about the need for citizenship education.

The 'active citizen'

Douglas Hurd, when he was Home Secretary, talked publicly of the importance of the 'active citizen' rather than the 'good citizen'. Active citizenship would step forward and volunteer to fill the gap between growing personal needs and the necessarily limited provision of the state. In this context active citizenship became an extension of Victorian philanthropy, and voluntarism was seen as the mark of moral citizenship.[2]

Speaker's Commission

It was against this backdrop that Bernard Weatherill, Speaker of the House of Commons, was invited to be Patron of the Speaker's Commission on Citizenship. It was no accident that the Commission arose from a voluntary sector initiative. CSV with support from Esso established a series of consultations with a view to identifying the challenges and opportunities posed by revisiting the notion of active citizenship in the closing years of the 20th century.

The Commission's report *Encouraging Citizenship*[3] captured the changing mood of the time. The thrust of the report was simple: the bonds of mutual responsibility that make for the good society are, for a variety of reasons, growing weaker and less effective. Therefore something must be done, consciously and deliberately, to remedy the situation.

The authors of the report, drawing on evidence from distinguished academics, lawyers and politicians, called upon all sections of the community to play their part in fostering a more civil, and a more neighbourly, society. There was plenty about volunteering and community service, but there was no mention of political literacy. Politics was the business of the politicians, elected by the citizenry to act on their behalf.

In particularly the report proposed that citizenship education should be taught in schools.

Alienation of young people

At the time that the report was in preparation, however, there was growing concern about the alienation of young people from mainstream society. The poll tax riots had in March spread from Scotland and reached London where there was violence in Trafalgar Square. The riots probably fuelled the Commission's concern about young people and the importance of leaving politics to the politicians. The Commission had further made use of two pieces of research concerning young people and citizenship education. The first had elicited the views of young people about citizenship and the other surveyed the extent and nature of citizenship education in schools.[4] The young people for the most part were vague about the notion of citizenship, and when probed many of them thought that citizenship should have been included in their own education. The survey of schools merely underlined the fact that there was little evidence of any systematic citizenship education.

Cross-curricular themes

No sooner had the Commission reported than a further and quite separate document, *Education for Citizenship*,[5] was published by the National Curriculum Council. This was the body that had been set up to advise the government on the implementation of the newly created national curriculum. The 1988 Education Reform Act had established something that was quite new in England, a national curriculum. This curriculum is based on subjects. There are three core subjects – English, maths and science – and seven foundation subjects – history, geography, technology, music, PE, art and a modern foreign language. Across these solid vertical divisions were then pasted a set of cross-curricular themes and dimensions. The themes are or were – they have since been allowed to 'wither on the vine' – economic and industrial understanding, health education, careers education and guidance, environmental education and education for citizenship. The dimensions included multicultural education, gender issues and special educational needs. Thus, in theory at least, children and young people from 5 to 16 now had a statutory entitlement to citizenship education. It might seem that Bernard Weatherill's fine ambitions were realized almost as soon as he had given them voice. The reality, however, was very different. Citizenship as a cross-curricular theme was dead in the water from the moment it was launched, in spite of the imaginative efforts of a minority of schools to make something of it.

Failure of citizenship as a theme

This initial attempt to make citizenship education a part of the curriculum failed for clear reasons. Three conditions are necessary in a democracy for a new movement to be successful. First, it must be built around a coherent idea. Second, the idea must have sufficient support. Thirdly, there must be people, resources and systems to make it happen. In the case of the early experiment with citizenship education these conditions were not in place.

No coherent 'big idea'

First there was no coherent big idea that could be commended to educators and the public. There were plenty of ideas but they did not yet add up to a major project that would seize the imagination of politicians, educators or the public, let alone young people.

Politically the citizenship agenda was one-sided and weak. There was much about young people understanding their responsibilities and behaving 'nicely', but there was little or nothing about young people exercising their rights or flexing their political muscles around issues about which they feel strongly. For example,[6] 5- to 7-year-olds were encouraged 'to participate in decision-making by identifying jobs that need to be done', while 11- to 14-year-olds were invited to assume 'collective responsibility for an aspect of school or community life, e.g., keeping the school litter free'. These are the words of a conformist charter not a rallying cry for serious civic engagement.

Conceptual confusion

Secondly, the initiative foundered on the fact that the themes and dimensions – and few could understand the difference between them – were conceptually at odds with the main body of the national curriculum. The national curriculum framework was based on a 19th-century model of knowledge and teaching. The task of schools is to fill the heads of children with the knowledge that has been carefully accumulated in the past. This knowledge has clear boundaries and is most effectively approached through separate subjects. The teacher empties the jug of his or her learning into the empty glass of the student's mind. The strength of this model of education is its clarity and its longevity. It is simple and rooted in the way things have been for a very long time. The problem with this approach is that it is fallacious. Knowledge does not exist independently of the knower, nor does it exist outside contemporary culture.

Lack of support

Thirdly, as a cross-curricular theme, citizenship education failed to enjoy serious support from beyond the tiny circle of those who championed it. It certainly was deprived of political endorsement. No one spoke up for it, although a significant number of individual teachers in particular schools and local authorities pioneered some excellent and ground-breaking practice. But from the Cabinet and the Department of Education and Science there was a palpable silence. Meanwhile in the staffrooms and classrooms around the country most teachers felt so overloaded by the new priority demands of the national curriculum and the local management of schools (LMS) that they had little time and energy to pursue cross-curricular themes even where they wanted to. In this context it is no surprise that citizenship education failed for the most part to excite the interest and support of young people.

Lack of resources

Finally, no resources were made available to promote citizenship education in schools let alone in teacher training institutions. Policy initiatives that pay no regard to budgets, management and staff training are bound to run into trouble.

A different prospect

This time round, however, the situation is significantly different and the runes more encouraging. Citizenship education is now a statutory subject that enjoys support from the top of the (now) Department for Education and Skills (DfES). There is a ministerial working party served by a cross-agency group of civil servants and professional officers behind the programme. Furthermore, there are sustained efforts to meet with and support those in schools who have the responsibility to make the whole initiative happen. Above all, and the importance of this may be slower to emerge, political literacy is a key strand of the Order. It is not enough for children to form themselves into a clean-up team or to collect money for a famine-struck region. Now they – and we – must ask ourselves why these situations happen, and how – politically and practically – the problems we face can be alleviated, even removed.

Citizenship education has the built-in capacity to reflect on itself, to make new connections within and beyond the school, and to ask the larger questions that lie behind the issues of our time. Introducing citizenship education will encourage reflection on educational and social reform.

Notes

1. C L Hahn (1993) Preparing citizens: a preliminary report of a cross-national study, Nashville, TN, Conference paper, November, NCSS.
2. See Ch 6 pp 99 ff, Bernard Crick (2000) *Essays on Citizenship*, Continuum, London.
3. Speaker's Commission on Citizenship (1990) *Encouraging Citizenship*, HMSO, London.
4. K Fogelman (1990) *Citizenship in Schools*, Fulton, London.
5. NCC (National Curriculum Council) (1990) *Education for Citizenship*, NCC, York.
6. See Ray Derricot (1998, 2000) *Citizenship for the 21st Century*, p 30, Kogan Page, London.

3

Reactions

In a national context where so many secondary schools are tempted to treat citizenship as an initiative too far, the only way to promote this theme is to demonstrate how it can contribute to a school's success. We believe that it is absolutely essential that those schools who are well placed to pioneer aspects of citizenship education and provide tangible examples of manageable good practice are given the funding to develop citizenship education as a specialism.

(Deptford Green School)

In the wake of the announcement that citizenship was to be made a statutory subject many teachers were enthusiastic – but cautious about the additional demands on their time. During the conferences and consultations that took place around the introduction of the Order, teachers expressed particular concern over five issues:

1. the perceived tension between the standards agenda (driven by league tables and cash) and the values agenda (driven by no such imperatives) (see Chapter 13, under The benefits of a whole-school strategy: The contribution of citizenship education to standards);
2. the struggle to find *space* in the curriculum and *time* for the teachers to tackle the new subject, particularly community involvement (see Chapter 14, The curriculum: Creating learning experiences);
3. the matter of assessment and accreditation – whether pupils can fail citizenship (see Chapter 14, under The curriculum: Assessment);
4. increasing democratic student involvement (see Chapter 14, under The curriculum: Involving students in school);
5. sufficient training, resources and support for citizenship education (see Chapter 14, under Professional development; Management; and Context).

These concerns continue to dominate staffroom discussions up and down the land and are explored in the chapters that follow. These challenges require whole-school strategies, leadership, management, teaching styles, training and access to appropriate resources. These issues are addressed in Part III.

'Less bricks through windows'?

There were those who asked the larger, more strategic questions. There was, for example, some controversy about whether lessons on the 'proclivity to act responsibly' really lead to 'less bricks through windows'[1] or whether the whole agenda is around indoctrination. In response to such questioning there were those who were developing a vision of the positive role that citizenship education could play in their schools. Teachers at Deptford Green School in Lewisham commented, 'Our belief is that providing pupils with opportunities to become involved with their communities provides new and important learning experiences.'[2] The previous head of Highfield Primary School in Plymouth pointed out that citizenship education – in the form of student participation in decision making – did indeed lead to less bricks through windows. The windows of the school were regularly broken during the summer holidays until such time that the pupils were given real respon-sibility, under the supervision of staff, for the good order of the school.

The teachers' remaining concerns – time, whole-school policy, curriculum management, community involvement, pedagogy, training and resources – came up regularly and systematically at every discus-sion about citizenship. A headteacher with a strong track record for encouraging citizenship education, especially through community involvement, summed it up when he said, 'It's easy to organise commu-nity participation for a class here and a class there, even occasionally for a whole year group. But to offer it as a systematic entitlement across the school is a major undertaking. In the meantime I have a Sixth-form Centre to set up.' Thus spoke a man who was deeply committed to his school, his students, his staff and his vision for education. He was also someone who wanted to measure the things he valued, rather than the other way about. Other teachers throughout the country have echoed his comment. The question is simple: how can we make active citizenship education an entitlement for *all* young people?

Link with other priorities

The answer is more complex and requires a clear vision, strong leadership, good teamwork and effective management and strategic planning. It was, however, clear – even at such an early stage – that education for active citizenship would be most effective in those schools where it could be linked directly with other priorities such as strategies for improved learning through student participation.

Teachers clearly have mixed feelings about the fact that they rather than the authors of the national curriculum are responsible for mapping the details of the citizenship curriculum. A minority of teachers warmly welcomes this fresh opportunity to create their own curriculum around the broad learning outcomes set out in the programme of study. They see this as an opportunity for teachers to win back their professionalism, which in certain respects they had lost through the introduction of the national curriculum. Others, though attracted by this idea, are worried about how much time this will take.

At the time of writing (summer 2001) there is relatively little systematic nationwide evidence about how schools are approaching citizenship education. As time passes, and particularly as major pieces of long-term research[3] are set in motion, much more will be known. A useful survey of 400 schools undertaken across the UK in the summer of 2000 gives a brief but useful snapshot of the situation in secondary and particularly in primary schools.[4] UNICEF staff contacted 1,000 schools and had 400 replies. This might suggest that the non-respondents were less interested in citizenship education than those who replied. The results are therefore likely to be optimistic. The results indicate a relatively high commitment among schools to including citizenship education in their mission statements (323 out of 400) and a similar intention to include it in existing subjects across the curriculum. There is a comparable commitment to developing citizenship through assemblies and cross-curricular themes, and in the school ethos. There is some reluctance to developing democratic decision making (276) and considerable caution about developing new subjects (133). There appeared to be general interest in community participation, which, as far as the authors of the report could tell, was chiefly about inviting people from the community into the school (364). Only just over half showed an active interest in community service (222).

Agreement about key challenges

Surveys of this sort give a feel for what is happening. It is clear that there is growing interest in citizenship education and a growing readiness to take it seriously and make it work. It is also clear that teachers are agreed about the challenges they face – whole-school strategies, leadership, management, teaching styles, training and access to appropriate resources.

It is much less clear how far teachers as individuals and as staff teams are seized by the big idea of citizenship education. Since the introduction of the national curriculum, OFSTED inspection, attainment targets and league tables, schools have felt themselves under overwhelming pressure to account in detail for what they are doing. With the arrival of the New Labour Government pressure has further increased on teachers to deliver fresh initiatives, particularly through the national literacy and numeracy strategies. The further expectation that they should provide citizenship education alongside a raft of additional requirements related to personal, social, health and careers education is seen by many as a burden too far. In this context it is no accident that some of the teaching unions are becoming increasingly militant about teachers' hours and workloads.

It is less clear whether most teachers are seized by the big idea of citizenship education. Decisions and attitudes tend to be shaped by day-to-day concerns rather than by wider considerations. There is some evidence that a growing minority of headteachers are interested in citizenship education as a route to educational reform. There are, furthermore, encouraging signs that policy makers outside the education system are taking these possibilities increasingly seriously. For example, local government is putting increasing emphasis on the importance of involving young people in local decision making through its Hear by Right campaign. There are now fresh approaches to volunteering, including corporate volunteering (see Part IV). In some places, particularly major cities such as Oldham, Bradford and Burnley, there are critical questions about the hopes and fears of the ethnic communities – not always minorities. In these situations young people have a vital role to play. For example, the Dream project in Oldham was set up by young people who are determined to do something to improve community relations (see Chapter 7).

The larger vision

However, there remains the danger that legitimate concerns about the logistics of citizenship education will distract teachers and administrators from keeping the big picture in view. The larger vision for citizenship education requires schools to educate and encourage an active and politically literate body of citizens. As an increasing number of teachers have pointed out, schools' capacity to respond to the enormous challenge will depend in large measure on the extent to which teachers feel they are actively supported by the values, behaviour and policies that are pursued beyond their gates. It is cynical to expect schools *on their own* to make good the glaring deficiencies of society. On the other hand, there is a body of teachers who are able and willing to contribute to what must necessarily be a larger campaign to change the political and social culture of our country.

Notes

1. *TES*, 17 July 1998.
2. See Chapter 14, Deptford Green School.
3. The DfES plan a longitudinal, eight-year research programme on the impact of citizenship education.
4. Aileen McKenzie (2000) *Citizenship in 400 Schools*, A baseline survey of curriculum and practice amongst 400 UK primary, middle and secondary schools in summer 2000, UNICEF, London.

4

Government action

David Blunkett, as Secretary of State for Education and Employment, set himself the task of controlling the direction of education policy through providing guidance and support at classroom level. He described the challenge in these words:[1]

> Previous Secretaries of State for Education had few real levers in the Department – particularly in the days when it was the Department for Education and Science. While civil servants did a good job getting legislation through, there was little that could be done to improve school standards beyond exhortation and inspection. Although the national curriculum and OFSTED inspections began to change that, the Department itself remained largely untouched by the change of culture these reforms signalled.

Under Blunkett's leadership the government set up mechanisms to foster and support new forms of educational provision. The argument was simple. If government expects teachers to meet targets – on numeracy, literacy and citizenship – the same teachers may rightly expect government to assist them in making the new policy work.

Points raised by teachers

The government and its agencies noted the points raised by teachers and developed a bundle of strategies to address their concerns:

- A Citizenship Education Working Party was set up to bring together representatives from the DfEE, QCA, OFSTED and the Teacher Training Agency (TTA).
- Guidance was offered to ease three major tensions that had to be managed from the start. These included the debates about:

– citizenship and personal, social and health education;
– summative and formative assessment;
– the place of citizenship education in the curriculum.
These tensions have not disappeared, but the fact that they were faced up to at an early stage proved helpful in clarifying for teachers what was to be expected (or not expected) of them.

- The Standards and Effectiveness Unit was identified as one source of funding and support for citizenship education.
- Voluntary sector organizations such as CSV were given some additional funding to fill the gaps in resources in the field of community partnerships, political literacy, school councils and global citizenship.
- A citizenship Web site was prepared.
- Resources for some initial teacher training were provided to a group of university education departments.
- Money was set aside for long-term research into the impact of citizenship education.
- Some efforts were made to join up thinking on citizenship education within the government, particularly between the DfES and the Home Office, where the relevant ministers would regularly refer to each other's work in the field.

Summary

1. **Citizenship education**
   (i) **Foundation subject:** In secondary schools citizenship is a foundation subject from September 2002. In primary schools citizenship education was immediately incorporated alongside personal and social and health education in a shared curriculum framework. A programme of study was published with learning outcomes for each key stage. These outcomes were defined in terms of young people becoming informed citizens and developing the skills of communication and enquiry through participation and responsible action. The Government set out the framework of what young people are expected to learn, but it is left to teachers to fill in the detail in ways that best meet the needs of their own schools and pupils.
   (ii) **A unique subject:** Citizenship education is unique and different from other subjects in three key respects:
   – It is linked with other subjects as well as being a subject in its own right.
   – It is a way of life rooted in the ethos and way of life of the whole school.

– Young people are to learn through participation and real experience.

These three requirements form a mutually reinforcing cycle. Pupils are expected to develop their knowledge, understanding and skills through participation and responsible action.

2. **Political and practical support**

   The 2000 version of citizenship education is more robust than its predecessor and enjoys more political and practical support.

3. **Teachers' concerns**

   Teachers have concerns about an overcrowded curriculum, assessment, training and resources.

Note

1. The challenges of improving schools: lessons for public service reform, The Rt Hon David Blunkett MP, Secretary of State for Education and Employment, 1 May 2001, Address to an invited audience at an IPPR seminar, London.

PART II:

WHY – Why is active citizenship important?

5

Why citizenship?

Young people do not become good citizens by accident, any more than they become good nurses or good engineers, or good bus drivers or computer scientists.
(Lord Bernard Weatherill, Patron of the Commission on Citizenship – Encouraging Citizenship 1990, Speaker's Commission on Citizenship)

Aim: To show the immediate concerns of politicians over citizenship and citizenship education in relation to: 1) the democratic deficit; 2) the erosion of social capital; and 3) the question of shared values.

By the late 1980s, politicians and many others had come to feel that something should be done about citizenship education. They were concerned in particular about the attitudes and behaviour of young people.

On 31 March 1990 there were riots in London over the poll tax. Police baton-charged a crowd of 300,000 people in Trafalgar Square and violence broke out on all sides and continued late into the night. The Government was visibly shaken and politicians on both sides of the house were afraid that increasing numbers of young people were against not just the tax from society.

The poll tax protests were directly linked to the concern about apathy at the polls because many young people refused to register for the vote for fear of being caught as a poll tax abstainer.

A small group of influential social scientists on both sides of the Atlantic pointed out that their research suggested that there were indeed connections between voting, general behaviour and social inclusion.

Public discourse – a precondition of active citizenship

Professor Ivor Crewe of Essex University worked with others to conduct a survey between similar communities in Britain and the United States (1996). The focus of the research was on attitudes towards politics and civic engagement. His study revealed that nearly 80 per cent of British pupils say that out of school they engage in very little discussion at all of public issues, including issues important in their own communities. Many reported strong social norms 'never to talk about religion or politics'. Those who had such an opportunity at school, however, were shown to be more likely to talk at home or in the community. Crewe concluded that *'talk' or discourse is a precondition of active citizenship.*

Crewe goes on to argue that 'civic engagement' is the necessary counterpart of 'public discourse'. He then makes the connection between general community involvement and political participation: 'There is now ample evidence that electoral turn-out, attention to political and public issues in the media, involvement in election campaigns and demonstrations are all strongly and consistently related to motivations that are reinforced through participation in informal groups and voluntary associations.'[1]

It may well be that political activity is reinforced by community involvement of various kinds. It is not, however, the case that people, particularly young people, who engage in voluntary or community action necessarily take an interest in formal politics. When the British sample of interviewees in Crewe's study were asked to give examples of good citizenship only 10 per cent mentioned voting or exercising political rights, whereas 70 per cent 'talked about civic engagement in some form – for example, working in local voluntary associations, doing something beneficial in the local community'. A central concern among politicians is the fact that young people are becoming ever more distrustful of politics and politicians.

The erosion of social capital

In parallel with the work of Ivor Crewe on public discourse and civic engagement, a US academic, Robert Putnam, has developed the idea of social capital. In his seminal article, 'Bowling alone: America's declining social capital',[2] he opens with these words:

Many students of the new democracies that have emerged over the past decade and a half have emphasized the importance of a strong and active civil society to the consolidation of democracy. Especially with regard to the post-communist countries, scholars and democratic activists alike have lamented the absence or obliteration of traditions of independent civic engagement and a widespread tendency toward passive reliance on the state. To those concerned with the weakness of civil societies in the developing or post-communist world, the advanced Western democracies and above all the United States have typically been taken as models to be emulated. There is striking evidence, however, that the vibrancy of American civil society has notably declined over the past several decades.

Citizenship education as a source of new social capital

Social capital refers to those stocks of social trust, norms and networks that people can draw upon to solve common problems.[3] The argument runs that where stocks of social capital are high, it is more likely that communities can develop vital democratic institutions and respond positively and effectively to social and economic challenges, particularly in the inner cities. Citizenship education is one means by which schools can help replenish the nation's depleted stocks of social capital. It is, however, not the only means. School-based initiatives need to be matched by equally determined efforts to promote neighbourhood renewal through community development and 'strategic partnerships' between local government and community-based organizations (see Chapter 16).

Shared values

The Crick Report was clear about the importance of shared moral values at the heart of citizenship education. The report stresses the importance of:

> children learning from the very beginning self-confidence and socially and morally responsible behaviour both in and beyond the classroom, both towards those in authority and towards each other. This learning should be developed, not only in but also beyond school, whenever and wherever children work or play in groups or participate in the affairs of their communities.
>
> Some may think this aspect of citizenship hardly needs mentioning; but we believe it to be near the heart of the matter. Here guidance on moral values and personal development are essential preconditions of citizenship.

The Report goes on to list quite precisely the values that underpin a modern, participating democracy.[4] Among those detailed are:

- concern for the common good;
- belief in human dignity and equality;
- practice of tolerance;
- courage to defend a point of view;
- determination to act justly;
- commitment to equal opportunities and gender equality;
- commitment to active citizenship and voluntary service;
- concern for human rights and the environment.

Of these values the ones that touch on *equal opportunities* and a *concern for human rights* are likely to prove the most contentious and, by the same token, important. Over recent years there have been reports of racist attitudes in many of our major institutions, including the police and the health service. Economic injustice and racist attitudes are believed by some to underlie the riots in places like Oldham, Burnley and Bradford during the summer of 2001.

This clearly poses a challenge for citizenship education. There is a significant difference between: 1) a form of citizenship education that simply encourages decency and good behaviour; and 2) one that is rooted in political awareness and a commitment to social justice and equal opportunity. The words of the Crick Report clearly encourage the second and more radical approach.

Citizenship education stands at the confluence of the political, moral and social developments of our time. It is not bending language too much to refer to this as the 'crisis – the crossing point – of citizenship'. The crisis of citizenship calls for a holistic vision, shared values and a political framework capable of promoting these at every level.

Notes

1. I Crewe, D Searing and P Conover (1997) *Citizenship and Civic Education*, Citizenship Foundation, London.
2. Robert D Putnam, *Journal of Democracy*, **6** (1), January 1995, pp 65–78.
3. Carmen Sirianni and Lewis Friedland, Social capital and civic innovation: learning and capacity building from the 1960s to the 1990s. This essay, originally presented at the Social Capital session of the American Sociological Association in August 1995, focuses on civic innovation in the environment and community organizing.
4. Crick Report, p 44, Fig 1: Values and dispositions.

6

Apathy, anger and commitment

'Hurrah!' wrote Darcus Howe in June 2001:[1]

> We non-voters easily won the general election... In Brixton where I live, an area largely home to working-class Caribbeans, not voting is taken for granted. I did as I have done for years, and stayed away from electoral politics. At the start of the campaign, I asked at my local pub who the sitting MP was. Nobody knew, and, more than that, nobody thought they were missing out on anything.
>
> The following day, I approached about half a dozen kids, aged 15–16, who were equally ignorant and appeared quite pleased that they did not know. All this led to one huge fact: that we 'no-voters' won the election, but the Labour Party seized the power.

For Howe the moral of this tale was that politicians, despite their noisy protestation, don't listen to the voters. In Kidderminster Dr Richard Taylor beat the Labour candidate at the poll because he knew what people wanted, and furthermore he knew what they did not want. They did not want a new private-sector hospital that was being built in Worcester at the expense of downsizing their old facility in Kidderminster. 'The decision', Howe pointed out, 'ignored the needs of local people. The planners executed their plans because they knew what was best and the masses did not. They had their comeuppance.'

Howe links this theme with the feelings and attitudes of young people on his Brixton estate. The link is instructive and touches the heart of citizenship education, or what could be citizenship education:

> We [the voters] are treated as pigs to be fattened, fed from a trough (the public services) through which our betters pump the swill. Increasingly in my little village in south London, young people from 13 upwards hate

school, literally hate it. We parents wonder what is going on. I think it is simple. *What is being taught has no bearing on their lives, their expectations and their interests* [my italics].

In a single sentence Darcus Howe puts together the issues of politics, young people and education, and he does this in the context of an article that is about the relationship between the *adult* electorate and their politicians. He ends his article with a sobering comment:

The mass of the population is much more advanced than half a century ago. It is not that the election campaign was especially boring, or that we were especially apathetic. The people are more developed, wiser, much more certain about what the politicians lack and what they have. Both parties have sensed that now. The new slogans are 'We must listen' and 'We are humble'. Trouble is, they are not trained to hear, and they cannot interpret what they see.

Howe was not alone in his comments and feelings. There is mounting evidence that politicians and the political process are increasingly distrusted in the West. In the United States 76 per cent of people in an opinion poll in 1964 said that they trusted politicians to do the right thing for all or most of the time. A similar poll 30 years later showed that the proportion of trusting people had dropped to a mere 25 per cent. In Western Europe confidence in politicians – and authority figures in general – has also, in many countries, declined. Only one in four young voters turned out to vote in the 2001 UK general election. Citizenship education in England lays great stress on the importance 'of playing an active part in the democratic and electoral processes'. It remains clear, however, re-engaging the electorate, particularly the young electorate, is likely to prove a challenging task. Behind this debate there are three issues, each of which impacts on the way citizenship education is to be developed in schools.

Apathy

The first issue is 'apathy'. It is true that on election night there was a television shot of people in a pub just opposite a polling station, and, when asked why they didn't vote, the reply was simply, 'I cannot be bothered.' There are, perhaps, growing numbers of people who accept that they are apathetic about politics. But apathy is not the right word to describe the feelings of the majority of non-voters. Darcus Howe is not apathetic about politics; he is disillusioned and angry, perhaps, but not apathetic. He is clearly deeply unhappy about the way things are going and points out that young people round him can make no connection between politics and life as they know it. They cannot even see any connection between what goes on in school and life as they live it, let alone what goes on in government. That is not apathy; it is alienation.

There is a similar reported pattern in the United States.[2] Among students there is clearly active interest in volunteering in the community: 60 per cent of college students are or have been involved in community service of some kind over the past year. Only 16 per cent have joined government, political or issues-related organizations, however. Only 7 per cent have volunteered or plan to volunteer in a political campaign. College students in the United States, a country with a good record of public participation, are disillusioned about and disconnected from the political system: 64 per cent do not trust the Federal Government to do the right thing all or most of the time; 74 per cent of college students believe that politicians are motivated by selfish reasons; 87 per cent say they need more practical information about politics before they get involved; 86 per cent agree that volunteering in the community is easier than volunteering in politics. Almost all of them (97 per cent) believe that 'enjoyment of the activity' is an effective factor in motivating them, but only a tiny proportion (7 per cent) agree that 'political activity' is enjoyable.

It is clear that disillusion with politics is not something that is found only in Darcus Howe's backyard in Brixton. It is also clear that young people are interested in solving local and national problems, but they have no faith in the political process as a way of achieving this: the US survey showed that 85 per cent prefer community volunteerism to political engagement as the better way to solve important issues facing their own communities, and as many as 60 per cent prefer community volunteerism to political engagement as a way of solving important issues facing the country.

The situation among young people in Britain is much the same. A recent article on the youth vote suggested that 'depending on who you speak to, the growing number of young people with no interest in conventional politics can be seen as a threat to democracy or a cause for celebration'.[3] But perhaps the challenge lies in explaining why the political process is such a turn-off for so many of the younger generation:

> For the statistics suggest that youth and politics just do not mix. In 1992, 68% of 18–24-year-olds voted in the general election. At the last election in 1997, this figure fell to 60%. Only three in five young people aged between 18 and 24 are on the electoral register. Young adults are less interested in politics today than they were five years ago, according to a survey of British attitudes, and the trend looks set to continue.

For ministers and politicians this is bad news. But for young radicals the disillusionment of young people with mainstream politics is a cause for celebration. The comedian and journalist Mark Thomas suggested that young people were not interested in mainstream politics 'because politicians by and large are uninterested in them'.[4] They considered politicians to be, among other things, 'lying, self-serving, greedy pigs'. But far from regretting this disillusionment, Mr Thomas said it was 'absolutely brilliant' that young people were not interested in mainstream politics. Instead, he said, a 'grassroots approach is beginning to come through, operating outside mainstream political structures'. While effecting change through party politics was a lengthy and often futile process, the immediacy of direct action and 'creative dissent' increasingly offered people 'a real chance to feel empowered', he claimed.

Alison Park, research director at the National Centre for Social Research, speaking at the same debate disagreed and disputed the rise of young people taking to the streets, saying it was 'not very common'. But she cautioned that any analysis of political apathy needed to make clear that 'people do get involved more in politics as they get older'. Young people, she said, were generally 'no more cynical about politics than anyone else'.

This surely is the point. Disillusion with politics and political processes is by no means confined to young people. During the Thatcher years we were positively encouraged to think of ourselves as citizen consumers; it was part of government policy that we should do just that. It is therefore hardly surprising that the editor of trendy style magazine *Dazed & Confused*, Rachel Newsome, issued the starkest warning to anyone trying to tempt the young into politics. To cheers from the audience, she said: 'Young people see themselves more as consumers than citizens. They make a difference through the consumer choices they make, and perceive government to be "part of the problem".' It was, she said, 'a case of idealism being replaced by pragmatism'. She then added, 'Young people do have a voice but it is outside the political system… not by fighting the political system but by ignoring it.'

It is, therefore, clear that something is amiss at the heart of our democratic processes. The No Vote party is the biggest party. Young people are even more disillusioned and alienated than their elders, but among older people too there is a sense of frustration, even anger, that people are not being listened to. Either we must conclude that politicians are getting worse at their jobs – and there is no particular evidence for that: most of them are honest, hard-working and genuinely committed to doing a good job according to their lights – or we must take notice of the fact that we all need to do something about the way we handle our democracy, because it isn't working. For this reason alone citizenship education is the more important, because it can be a part of the process of discerning where we need to go. This is not the same thing as saying that citizenship education will instruct young people in the answers. The fact is that there is no agreement about the answers, but a growing awareness of the problem.

The subversion of politics

The second issue stems from Mark Thomas's point that increasingly young people who do care about the way things are turn to direct action to get something done. Some will argue that this is simply political ignorance, that if young people understood the process better they would use democracy to work for them. This may be true, but it is also the case that increasing numbers of thinking, articulate people believe that direct action is the only form of effective political lobbying. What is branded as electoral apathy is in reality protest against the subversion of politics by big business. 'Corporations', argues Noreena Hertz:[5]

> are taking over from the state, the business man becoming much more powerful than the politician, and commercial interests are paramount. Political answers have become as illusory as the rows and rows of homogenised clothes, standard T-shirts and cardigans, folded in your local Benetton store. High street conservatism and conformity par excellence... Politicians continue to offer only one solution: a system based on laissez faire economics, the culture of consumerism, and the power of finance and trade. They try and sell it in varying shades of blue, red or yellow, but it is still a system in which the corporation is kind, the state its subjects, its citizens consumers.

Criticism of consumer politics is not coming only from disenchanted voters on the left. Elements of the right are equally dismayed. Peregrine Worsthorne argues that capitalism was always a greater threat to old authority than socialism.[6] Capitalism with its wholesale attack on the culture of deference that was once rooted in our traditional institutions has, so to speak, dissolved the glue that holds society together. Worsthorne claims that historic conservatism has always been flexible about changes in the distribution and patterns of power, but that it has had this flexibility because beneath these changes it retained the tradition of an open-ended ruling class:

> No longer. For the first time since 1688, Britain's political institutions are trying to operate without even a lingering aura of that old aristocratic class by whom and for whom they were created. No wonder the body politic today is suffering such dire withdrawal symptoms. At long last its life support machine has as near as damnit been switched off.

Worsthorne concludes with a ringing condemnation of the party he once supported:

> What we must fear in the future is the rule by successive classless and unprincipled factions whose access to the levers of power will depend largely on the sophisticated demagogic manipulation – their new way of acquiring acquiescence. Slightly more hopeful would be the slow and painful development over generations of a new governing class with its own, very different and (judged by present indications) very inferior set of people's institutions. Either way, it is surely understandable that many upper- and lower-class old Tories have little stomach to play much part in the next chapter of our island's story. Hence our abstention in the recent [2001] election.

Young people are acting as a kind of litmus test for political change, a change that has now reached a point where two such articulate and politically different people as Darcus Howe and Peregrine Worsthorne find themselves members of the winning party at the election, the No Vote party.

The challenge

In this context citizenship education faces a huge challenge. It is not simply a new curriculum subject put together around the tick boxes of a list of learning outcomes. It is a move to involve young people consciously and positively in playing their part among the profound changes and fundamental disagreements and frustrations that make up today's society. It is easy to see how a classful of kids can discuss the rights and wrongs of changing the age of consent or the arguments for and against genetic modification of crops. It is harder, however, to see how even the most imaginative citizenship initiatives can address the deeper issue of the alienation of not only young people but older people too. The fact is that increasing numbers of people from very different political backgrounds believe that the political process has been hijacked by corporate agency over which there is hardly a shred of democratic control.

This point – the need to offer young people the chance to take part in an effective democratic process – is at the heart of citizenship education and is the third issue arising from the matter of so-called apathy. Citizenship education requires us all – including young people in school – to have ready access to opportunities whereby together we can create, sustain and develop healthy and democratic communities. Part IV of this book provides case studies and examples showing how young people, their schools and their local communities have already developed programmes and projects based on these principles. If we are not able to encourage democratic participation on a wide scale, Peregrine Worsthorne's nightmare will be realized and society will come apart at the seams. In this context citizenship education is not so much a subject – with all the fuss and palaver about assessment criteria and inspection – as one small, but vital, means to create and sustain a vibrant and genuinely democratic society for our children and grandchildren.

Notes

1. *New Statesman*, 18 June 2001, p 21.
2. A national survey of college and university undergraduates, conducted by the Institute of Politics of Harvard University and reported in the *Harvard Political Review*, Spring 2001.
3. Winning the youth vote, an article by Andy Tate, *BBC News Online*, 13 May 2001.
4. At an IPPR debate on politics and young people, 2000, quoted by Andy Tate.
5. Noreena Hertz (2000) *The Silent Takeover*, quoted in *New Statesman*, 14 May 2001, p 4.
6. The slow death of Tory England, *New Statesman*, 25 June 2001.

7

Who are we?

A main aim for the whole community should be to find or restore a sense of
common citizenship, including a national identity that is secure enough to
find a place for the plurality of... cultures found in the UK.

(Crick Report, para 3.14)

Identity: The rapid social, political and cultural changes that are transforming most societies throughout the world are compelling us to ask
ourselves questions about our identity as a people.

In politics today few questions are as vexed or as elusive as that of
national identity. The issue of Englishness and Britishness erupts in
passionate disagreements about the place of Britain in Europe. But it is
wider than that. It touches on race and the visceral fears of what it is to
be alien and to experience not the richness of diversity but the threat of
difference.

Who are the English?

For the English the sharpening identity of the people of the other three
countries that make up the United Kingdom of Great Britain and
Northern Ireland underlines the question about what it is to be English
rather than simply British. It is possible to highlight the points through
satire, as Michael Bywater does. He begins his piece on 'Englishness –
who cares?'[1] with a hefty slice of English middle-class angst:

I am English. And ashamed of what it means. I am ashamed to be white;
ashamed to be middle-class; ashamed to have been educated at an elitist

university, to speak Received Pronunciation, to be emotionally constipated. I am ashamed of my violent history, my rape of the globe, my racism, my ego-phallo-ethnocentricity. I am ashamed of the unspoken discourse of supremacy that lies at the heart of my foundation myths and my literature. I am ashamed of the atrocities that have been committed in the name of my (established) religion and the entrenched interests of my ruling class. I am ashamed that bad food, bad sex and bad weather led to my disenfranchise-ment of so many peoples, the enslavement of some, the obliteration of a few. I am ashamed of our stroppy proles, white-van men, thugs, oiks and geezers.

He then changes gear:

I am English and proud of what it means. I am proud to be a member of the most innovative, creative people in history; proud to belong to its middle class, known throughout the world for fairness, discretion, a respect for privacy, for the cultivation, not of flamboyance, but of decency. I am proud of the way my people have fought as often for dignity, freedom and justice as for power and self-interest. I am proud that my people were immune to tempest and drought, to the lures of gluttony, to narcotic flesh and the sodden tumble of bedsheets. I am proud of my nation's established religion, tempering mysticism with fair play, infusing clear-eyed thought into excitable Italianate transcendentalism. I am proud of our working class, neither slaves nor aspirant bourgeoisie: culturally coherent, ironical, resourceful, uncowed and uncorrupt. I am English...

Finally, he changes tack one more time: 'I am English. And, frankly, I couldn't care less...'

Things that have changed us...

Such issues of identity are elusive. They depend so much upon attitude and personal history. They tend very often to generate more heat than light. It is clear that over the past 50 years the English have had to come to terms with huge changes in the environment that shapes their sense of national identity: the loss of Commonwealth, the loss of Empire, the creation of the European Union and the current moves to devolve power within the United Kingdom. The fact that we remain a country from whence many emigrate and to which others immigrate from elsewhere adds to our sense of continuous change. For some this generates a profound sense of uncertainty and the need to reach out and touch the symbols of our continuity and self-respect. The pound sterling, the monarchy, even the Church of England are for many such symbols; but for others, equally British subjects, these things mean little or nothing;

they may even represent all the negatives that Bywater lists in his opening paragraph.

Schools are crucibles of national identity

All this is of more than passing interest to schools, particularly those where there may be as many as 50 different first languages spoken in the school by British pupils. Schools more than any other single institutions are the crucibles in which national and cultural identities are explored by people who are old enough to be aware of the issues, but young enough to escape, partially at least, many of the rigid attitudes of the adult world. Furthermore, there is no escape for those schools where most staff and pupils are white and where only English is spoken. 'It doesn't affect us, really. You see we are an all-white community. Except of course for Mr Singh and his family; and Mr Singh is a college lecturer.' It is precisely here, where children are not regularly involved with real cultural diversity, that the most subtle but pervasive racial and national stereotypes can – almost accidentally – be nurtured.

Multiple identities

Most British people and, by inference, most English people have learnt to live with multiple identities. Nationhood in a global society produces fuzzy sovereignty and fuzzy political identity. It is increasingly common to meet people who were born in one country, to parents from another two countries, who are now more or less permanent residents of a fourth country – England. We are learning to wear multiple identities, often with pleasure and family pride. The idea that there is a simple Tebbit test of English consciousness – like which cricket team do we support? – is both fatuous and impossible. Children in particular are good at wearing more than one identity. The problem only comes when others, particularly adults, present those identities as being somehow wrong or in conflict. The way in which some people, following the New York tragedy, have branded all Muslims as unacceptable or dangerous has been all too dreadful an example of this.

Many schools are extremely good at fostering attitudes of mutual respect for the multiple identities that we carry. Where this respect is lacking, there need to be strategies to address the issue. Peer education can provide one highly effective means of enabling the students to take responsibility for addressing matters of attitude and behaviour, particularly in relation to racism, bullying and issues around sex and relationships.

There are also opportunities to explore issues of difference in formal lessons. Different perceptions of personal and social identity can be dealt with powerfully in history, English, drama and PSHE. A school like the Anglo-European School (see Chapter 14, under The curriculum, The global dimension) deliberately sets its teaching and learning experiences in a world rather than a purely national context.

All this having been said, it remains the case that our personal sense of identity is often elusive and not necessarily the most useful way of approaching questions of political identity. Professor Linda Colley asks whether, after so many changes, it is any longer possible successfully to redesign and refloat a concept of Britishness for the 21st century.[2] She suggests instead that we should leave intransigent issues of Britishness to look after themselves, and focus instead on an area where we can all make a substantial difference.

Distinction between identity and citizenship

'I propose to you', she argues:

> a crucial distinction that is often insufficiently understood: that between identity and citizenship. Instead of being so mesmerised by debates over British identity, it would be far more productive to concentrate on renovating British citizenship, and on convincing all of the inhabitants of these islands that they are equal and valued citizens irrespective of whatever identity they may individually select to prioritise.

Her suggestions impact directly upon the agenda for citizenship education, and are therefore worth pursuing.

Five recommendations

Colley makes five specific recommendations, each of which has implications for education for active citizenship:

1. **More accessible definitions of citizenship.** Colley suggests a new millennium charter or contract of citizen rights. This would in one form take the shape of a major and complex document incorporating European, English and Scottish law as well as fundamental but currently unwritten ideals. But this charter or contract of citizen rights should also be available in a much briefer, more accessible version, which every schoolroom, every home, every place of work could have on hand. If citizenship is to function well and to excite and unite, then citizens themselves must feel they have direct access

to some of the answers to these questions. This would certainly set a context in which class rules are negotiated and school rules developed in consultation with students.

2. **Equality.** The essential equality of the people needs to be more clearly marked. The symbolism and public culture of this new citizen nation would need to acknowledge the essential equality of the people of these islands far more than at present.

3. **Diffusion of power from centre.** Diffusing power – a process that devolution has already initiated – recognizes the plurality of national identities contained in these islands; but it is also a way of nurturing active citizenship. The more you diffuse and localize power, the more you increase the number and type of people playing some kind of active political role. This can apply to schools, especially large schools, as much as it does to the nation as a whole.

4. **Ethnic minorities.** We need further to work with the ethnic minorities to improve their position. Colley suggests that in some respects the position of ethnic minorities in this country 'is a powerful argument for the enduring utility of Britishness. Unlike Englishness, Welshness, or Scottishness, Britishness is a synthetic and capacious concept with no necessary ethnic or cultural overtones. Consequently, large numbers of non-whites seem reasonably content to accept the label "British" because it doesn't commit them to much.' The Fourth National Survey of Ethnic Minorities found that two-thirds of the Indians, African Asians, Caribbeans, Pakistanis and Bangladeshis questioned, though only half of the Chinese, felt themselves British at some level; and, as you might expect, these proportions were higher among the young and those born here.

The recent riots (2001) in Oldham, Burnley and Bradford underlined the importance of community relations and of equal economic opportunity. Projects such as Dream in Oldham (see p 52) demonstrate ways in which young people are taking direct and personal responsibility for addressing these questions. The work with refugees in Forest Gate in London (see below) also demonstrates how students and pupils are getting involved.

Forest Gate Community School: refugee club

In autumn 1999, 20 pupils at Forest Gate Community School set up a club for refugees. They involved three staff members and representatives from the Newham Refugee Council, and Somali and Kosovan support groups together with the Emmanuel Church, which is providing a regular member of staff. A member of the learning support team also offered help, as did a

Somali interpreter. They involved some parents and were further supported by a Barclays New Futures award along with advisory help from CSV.

Members from around the world

The refugee club was soon going from strength to strength with a membership of around 25 pupils from all over the world. Activities centre on games, learning support (one to one), IT and the preparation of banners for a vigil that some of the group were going to at the Home Office to protest at the suicide of a Lithuanian at a detention centre. This is a real example of active citizenship – and with the blessing of the headteacher.

Teamwork

The atmosphere is friendly, obviously multiracial, empowering and extremely positive. The youngsters are growing as a team, their English is improving, friendships are being made and self-worth is being re-established. On a recent visit I saw some 50 pupils, together with representatives from another East London school, working on ideas to help a number of the club who had recently received deportation orders. A group role-playing a previous situation that had resulted in a positive outcome set the scene. Thence the students were divided into groups to brainstorm possible courses of action.

'It was a most humbling experience that reflected student empowerment with a citizenship emphasis par excellence. It also put the quest for a multitude of GCSE's into perspective as here not only were like skills to the fore but possibly human survival' (Peter Seaden-Jones, CSV adviser, Project visit notes).

5. **Equal opportunities and rights for women.** These offer a platform on which to build a clear, strong sense of mutual and legally recognized citizenship in Britain.

A citizen nation

Colley summarizes her points in a sentence: We need 'a renovated Citizen Nation, with a Charter of Rights, with a more open, less hidebound public culture, with a different brand of monarchy, with a broader diffusion of power and a more comprehensive vision of politics, equal opportunities for minorities and women positively and persistently pursued'.

Celebrations

The Reform Act of 1832, the first step towards achieving universal suffrage
The Catholic Emancipation Act of 1829
The end of Jewish disabilities in the 1850s
Votes for women in 1918
The independence of India in 1947

Figure 7.1   *Suggestions for celebrations*

In short we have here an agenda that could sharpen and strengthen the basis of our shared citizenship and provide a framework within which other institutions including schools can develop programmes of active citizenship. Colley ends by suggesting a set of shared moments in the past that we might helpfully celebrate together (see Figure 7.1). They could easily be adopted in schools and presented by young people.

Dream, Oldham

Dream, in Oldham, came together in January 2000, following discussions about the pros and cons of Youth Council. Dream set out to be innovative, concentrating on representation, inter-community conflict and the provision of 'young-people-friendly' services. They chose the title 'Dream' from Martin Luther King's speech: 'I have a dream that one day this nation will rise up and live out the true meaning of its creed: "We hold these truths to be self-evident: that all men are created equal."'

Structure

Dream currently consists of 25 young people aged 15 to 26. Although it is supported by local authority youth workers, it is an independent body: 'We are run by and advocated by young people. It's not a group with adults sitting around trying to work out what young people want. With Dream the young people have control, which is one of our unique selling points.'

Investors in Young People awards

Dream is currently promoting the Investors in Young People award (IiYP), which aims to help any organizations acting for or working with or on behalf of young people to ensure that their services reflect what young people want.

Influencing Connexions

IiYP has allowed young people to help shape Oldham's pilot Connexion Service, which is an enthusiastic supporter of Dream and IiYP. They experimented with various different models of involving young people in influencing Connexions, including young people evaluating the role of personal advisers, through which they engaged with senior managers.

Addressing inter-community conflict

Dream is also a force behind a powerful think tank addressing inter-community conflict. Presently in the research stage, Dream intends to focus on resolving local conflict in unusual or innovative ways, perhaps involving sport or the arts. It is currently researching methods of addressing friction between local Bengali and Pakistani groups, developing an anti-racist advertising campaign and creating a music CD. Its focus is on identifying shared issues and goals, in order to bring people together, rather than simply discussing the issues that divide communities.

Key features

The key features are:

- It is led by young people.
- It retains independence from the local authority while valuing the authority's support.
- It is an alternative to the youth council model.
- Rigorous IiYP standards are developed.
- There is a focus on bringing communities together.

Notes

1. *New Statesman*, 3 April 2000.
2. Professor Linda Colley, Britishness in the 21st century, LSE, December 2000, in an address arranged in conjunction with the Foreign and Commonwealth Office.
3. Project quoted from Local Government Association/National Youth Agency (2001) *Hear by Right*.

8

Young people now

In the end it is the involvement and experience of young people that counts. Neither Statutory Orders, however splendid, nor advisory groups, however wise, will achieve anything worth while without the ready involvement of young people. Earlier we pictured a formal portrait of the kind of people who inspired and developed the Order. What follows is a brief pen portrait of the young people who were, so to speak, passing the door of the committee room when the collage was created.

'Britain's young people are the best qualified, and most mobile, defiantly single and sexually liberated young generation ever raised in Britain,' wrote *Guardian* journalist Paul Kelso in his description of the way young people are now.[1] He was drawing on the evidence of the National Statistical Office 1998 survey of Britain's 8.7 million young people between the ages of 13 and 24.[2] He then went on to paint the other side of the picture. Young people are also the least well-paid group in society, suffer high rates of unemployment, are the most likely victims and perpetrators of crime, take more drugs than any other age group and are sicklier than previous generations.

This portrait of young people offers us a starting point for developing citizenship education from the point of view of the young people who are not only the recipients but also the chief agents of citizenship education. The way they live and the perspective that they have on the world will prove the biggest single factor in what they and others can achieve.

Family life and sexual activity

As far as sexual activity is concerned, young women are – perhaps contrary to popular belief – more active than young men of the same age, with 37 per cent of 16- to 19-year-old women having one sexual partner in the past year, compared with 24 per cent of men, and 33 per cent having more than two, compared with 28 per cent.

As far as their family life is concerned the majority of teenagers still grow up in families headed by a couple, although just under a quarter of the age group come from single-parent families. But while 71 per cent still grow up in a married family environment, this has done little to stem the decline in marriage rates. In the 1950s young couples were four times more likely to marry than they are today, and young people are no longer marrying as early as they did then.[3] More of them, however, are living together than in the past.[4] More than half of all 20- to 24-year-olds have moved out of the family home.

There is a continuing debate about how far personal and family life can be regarded as a part of citizenship education. Are motherhood and fatherhood on the citizenship agenda? Perhaps the simplest answer is that motherhood and fatherhood are citizenship issues as and when they influence public behaviour and attitudes that affect public life.

Health

Young people today are in certain respects less healthy than their predecessors at a comparable age. An increase in asthma and muscular complaints is thought to be responsible for one of the report's more worrying findings: that 20 per cent of young people suffer from long-standing ailments, an increase of 8 per cent since 1975. Five times the number of people went to the doctor's suffering from asthma in 1994 than in 1976, indicating an illness that seems to be an increasing by-product of modern life.

Eating disorders are another big 'plague' for young people, most notably among girls. Young women are increasingly bothered about how they look. Almost one in four teenagers aged 13 to 15 said they thought they were too heavy. This figure increased to 28 per cent among 16- to 19-year-olds and 38 per cent for those aged 20 to 24. By contrast, more than half of all boys said they were the right weight.

The study reveals a marked difference in the experiences and attitudes of boys and girls in relation to health, sex and education.

Girls are more likely than boys to be regular smokers by the age of 15.[5] By contrast boys and men are far more prodigious drinkers than women.[6] The 20 to 24 age group contains society's heaviest drinkers regardless of gender, with regular extreme alcohol consumption tailing off as people pass into their mid-20s.

Around a third of all young people (16- to 24-year-olds) have taken an illegal drug. Young men are more likely to indulge compared to young women. The most commonly used drug is cannabis, followed by amphetamines and ecstasy. Cocaine use is much lower than in older age groups, where drug use as a whole is less prevalent.

Mental health

Young people's mental health is also a cause for concern. One in five young people suffers mental health problems, and an equivalent number of young people show signs of disturbed behaviour arising from emotional disorders.[7] Older teenagers are likely to be even more widely affected. A third of 18-year-old boys and almost half (42 per cent) of 18-year-old girls have emotional or psychological problems. In an average population of 100,000 boys and the same number of girls, six boys and one or two girls commit suicide and the situation has been growing worse over recent years.

Education

Here again young women have bucked the trend of previous generations. Educationally girls perform better than their male counterparts. In 1998–99, 54 per cent of girls achieved five or more GCSE grades A to C or equivalent, compared with 44 per cent of boys. At A level, 25 per cent of girls have two A levels or more, 4 per cent more than boys.

More people than ever stay in full-time education and for longer, with 2.4 million people – around a third – staying on beyond the minimum age of 16.

Employment and earning

Young men, however, continue to earn more than young women in full- and part-time employment, although the gender discrepancy increases in the above-25 age group. This is probably a reflection of the way employers regard young men rather than objective grounds for believing that young women are less competent than young men. Average weekly wages for 18- to 20-year-old women are around £20 less than for young men. Unemployment rates are high, with 19 per cent of young men not in education out of work, and 29 per cent of young women.

Those who have gone into work after taking a degree can expect to earn £100 a week more than their fellow workers with GCSE qualifications. But as a whole, the age group is coming under increasing financial pressure as the introduction of student loans forces most full-time students into part-time work to make ends meet.

Couch potatoes

Young people in Britain tend to watch a lot of television, according to the study. Teenagers spend an average of 12 hours watching television each week, while spending only five or six hours with family or doing school work. When they do venture outdoors, the survey finds boys more likely to participate in sport than girls. Three-quarters of boys aged up to 16 frequently play a team game, compared with only 42 per cent of girls. The biggest out-of-school sport played by boys is football, while girls tend to favour more individual activities such as swimming and keep fit.

The conclusions that we may draw from this survey should be set beside the further information in the chapters on political attitudes (Chapter 6) and on crime (Chapter 9). It is clear that the experience of young people today is significantly different from what it was a generation ago. In this sense it is less easy for the parents to draw on the reserves of their own experience to guide and support their children, particularly during the teenage years. This point, however, is easily exaggerated. Many of today's parents, even grandparents, who grew up in the 1960s may well have experienced a more turbulent time as young people than do their children today.

Perhaps the main differences between then and now stem from the fact that we now live in a more developed consumer society. The Web really has changed the global feel of the age and – with a touch of irony – the Net has made many people less rather than more convivial. Young students are under pressure to run up large overdrafts in a way that never happened in the 1960s, and sexual attitudes have shifted. The 1960s witnessed the birth of the 'new morality', a morality that now, in many respects, has become 'old hat' and widely accepted as the norm.

A more developed consumer society has generated not only consumer politics, but also consumer education. New Labour appears to have stolen the Tories' clothes as far as choice is concerned. Choice is seen as good and variety of opportunity is prized, hence the rush towards specialist schools and opportunity of potential. But choice is born, in part at least, from competition; and competition can provoke stress. The distressingly high levels of emotional disturbance shown by young people may be a symptom of the increasing pressure under which they are expected to live their lives.

High standards in education can often lead to a sense of achievement and self-respect among those young people who prove themselves good at what is expected of them, particularly in the field of academic achievement. But one person's high standard is another person's occasion for misery and failure.

It is at least arguable that the tension between the standards agenda and the agenda for social education is a major cause of emotional and mental ill health among teenagers. Furthermore, it does not take a genius to work out that, where young people are pressured into activities in which they fail or do badly, they will become anxious and distressed. The normal human response to such pressure is to fight or flee. The more robust young people will resort to anti-social behaviour, if they feel that they are being treated badly. The less robust will attempt to find safety by hiding away. There is nothing strange or unexpected about these reactions; they are a well-understood part of the human condition. Increasingly schools are taking stress seriously by involving young people as a part of the solution rather than treating them as the cause of the problem. Teenagers and children are being helped to support each other. The mentoring movement in schools, linked to mediation programmes, listening schemes and systematic peer learning (in sport as well as in academic subjects) is a sign of returning health in our schools.

It is worth mentioning that the same attention needs to be paid to teachers' feelings as to those of young people. In recent years teachers have experienced ever-increasing pressure to deliver against new targets and tests. In itself this is no bad thing. In most walks of life people are increasingly expected to account for the quality of their work. Teachers, in common with so many other 'public servants', have become increasingly vulnerable to abusive, even violent, behaviour by young people and their parents. This is clearly unacceptable. It is even less tolerable for a parent to abuse a teacher than for a child to do so. However, incivility does not go away through being ignored; if anything it grows worse. A colleague who has taught in Botswana returned in recent years to teach in London. What shocked and depressed her was the extent to which chronic disrespect had somehow become acceptable and was simply regarded – rather like traffic pollution – as unpleasant but perfectly normal. At the heart of citizenship education is the expectation that fellow citizens will treat each other with respect. Common civility is an essential not an optional item.

Our portrait of young people now presents a challenge to schools, pupils and their families and local communities. First, young people and adults need to be treated with respect. It is essential that young people in our schools are helped to feel that they matter as individuals, that their emotional and academic needs will be taken seriously and that the contribution they can make to others will be treated as a priority. It is usually easy to treat academically gifted children with respect; and this respect brings further rewards in terms of effort and achievement. It is less easy to treat less able children with respect, particularly when they lack the social skill to explain their difficulties and seek help for their problems. Mentoring can provide just these additional elements of respect and encouragement. In a later chapter we shall examine how peer mentoring and adult mentoring can have a profound, even transforming, effect on young people's self-image, motivation and achievement.

Secondly, it is important to take the symptoms of an unhealthy community seriously. It is not acceptable that so many girls and young women should be so deeply unhappy about their appearance. Nor is it tolerable that more and more children should suffer from asthma, a disease that clearly has a psychosomatic dimension. These indicators of the breaking points in our society are opportunities for us to improve the way we do things, including the way we treat young people.

Thirdly, in a world where more is expected from personal relationships but where there are fewer institutional frameworks to help people manage these relationships (eg marriage or religious norms), it is ever more important to help young people cope both emotionally and intellectually with the everyday demands of living, working and being together. At last it seems that emotional literacy is beginning to be taken seriously as something more than an optional extra in education.

The fourth point concerns the ownership of what is done. Young people – like most other people – respond to being asked to help, particularly when that help includes the opportunity for their attitudes, feelings and experience to be taken seriously. We need in education, as in other dimensions of life, to foster a culture of mutual help and of ownership of what is done.

It is sometimes said that young people are cynical and unwilling to become involved in community activities. Cynicism is neither healthy nor natural in the way that caution and self-preservation are natural. Cynicism is the fruit of bitterness and chronic disappointment. The cynics will not normally admit this in public; they will prefer to wear their protective coat of cynicism with style, even panache. Too often young people are asked to help with some project or other on other people's terms, usually adult terms. Those old enough to recall the 'You, you and you' approach of 'volunteering' for unpleasant tasks during military service will remember also the stratagems that soldiers developed to avoid such volunteering. 'Always carry a clipboard or a shovel and look busy. That way you'll be left alone.' It usually worked. Soldiers, however, when they were taken seriously for their courage and their skill in times of war regularly volunteered to undertake tasks of epic heroism. The same principles apply today. Young people will make astonishing efforts to help others if they feel their contribution is important and that they can have a say in what they do and how they do it.

The portrait of young people drawn from the *Social Focus on Young People* survey is accurate in so far as it goes; but it does not go far enough. It paints a picture of young people out there as though they were some strange island people subjected to the scrutiny of anthropologists. In truth, however, they are nothing of the sort. They are our children, our brothers and sisters, our pupils or neighbours. They do not want to be treated as though they are from another planet. But they, like the rest of us, do want to be taken seriously; they resent being patronized and like to have as much control as possible over shaping their own lives. In this sense, they are the ideal partners for serious (but fun) ventures in citizenship education.

Notes

1. Paul Kelso, *The Guardian*, 29 June 2000.
2. National Statistical Office, June 2000, *Social Focus on Young People*.
3. The mean age at which people marry has steadily risen since 1971, from 24 to 30 for men, and 22 to 28 for women. Only 3 per cent of men and 7 per cent of women under 24 were married in 1998, the period of the study.
4. In 1998, 9 per cent of unmarried 19- to 24-year-old men and 18 per cent of women of the same age were living together.
5. 29 per cent against 19 per cent. The situation changes as people reach the 20–24 age group, with 42 per cent of men and 39 per cent of women smoking regularly.
6. 44 per cent of 18- to 20-year-old men claim to drink more than eight units (4 pints) daily, compared with 29 per cent of women claiming to consume more than six units daily.
7. National Children's Home, 1996.

9

Preventing crime

Our portrait of young people today omitted an important characteristic of their behaviour that usually stands prominently in the statistics about youth. It concerns crime and the fear of crime. It features regularly and dramatically in speeches by politicians and articles by journalists. Crime figures tend to come in one of two kinds of wrapping. First, there are those data that illustrate long-term trends and are usually presented to show how much worse things are now than they were 50 and – even more remarkably – 150 years ago. The second type of data gives us a snapshot of the type and number of crimes committed by a given group within the population. Both approaches are relevant to citizenship education.

We shall start with a recent snapshot of crime committed by young people. A recent survey showed that nearly 21 per cent of victims of violent crimes are young men, while 35 per cent of all offenders are men aged between 16 and 20.[1] Furthermore, 10 per cent of juvenile offenders were responsible for nearly half of the crimes admitted by the sample. The remaining survey findings were summarized briefly as follows:

- Almost half of the 12- to 30-year-olds involved in the survey admitted committing at least one offence at some point in their lives.
- Women were less likely to have offended (11 per cent had done so) than men (26 per cent) in the last year.
- The average age at which offending began was 13.5 for boys and 14 for girls.
- There were marked differences in the nature of crime committed by men and women at different ages:
  - Girls under 16 were most likely to be involved in criminal damage, shoplifting, buying stolen goods and fighting, while over the age of 16 they were committing less criminal damage and shoplifting but were increasingly involved in fraud and buying stolen goods.
  - Comparatively high rates of offending by 14- to 15-year-old boys

    reflected their involvement in fights, buying stolen goods and criminal damage.
- A similar pattern of offending was shown by 16- to 17-year-old boys but they were less involved in buying and selling stolen goods and criminal damage. Over a third of offences involved fighting.
- The highest levels of offending were among 18- to 21-year-old men and involvement in fraud and workplace theft.

From this evidence, there is no doubt that a remarkably high proportion of recorded crime is suffered and perpetrated by young people. Furthermore those who turn to regular crime tend to do so at a very young age. Girls are involved as well as boys, although in rather different ways.

The Home Office Minister Charles Clarke said:

> Cutting juvenile crime, creating safer communities and restoring confidence in the youth justice system are at the top of the Government's agenda. We are determined to cut youth crime. This survey demonstrates why the Government was right to bring forward radical changes to the youth justice system. Both the Crime and Disorder Act 1998 and Youth Justice and Criminal Evidence Act 1999 tackle youth offending head on. By making our courts more effective, punishment more effective and by preventing offending and re-offending, we are building safer communities. The Government's pledge to fast track persistent young offenders by reducing the time between arrest and sentence from 142 days to 71 reached 93 days in July 2000 and helps ensure swifter justice. To tackle youth crime we need effective prevention, performance and punishment. The measures we have introduced such as youth offending teams, reparation orders, referral orders and action plan orders ensure criminal justice agencies have the tools to tackle juvenile crime and to address the issues raised in this survey.
>
> When we prevent youth offending, we cut youth crime and create a safer society.

New measures have now been put in place. Detention and training orders (DTOs) have been available from April 2000 and reparation orders, action plan orders, child safety orders and parenting orders were rolled out nationally from 1 June 2000. All the measures, except DTOs, have been piloted across 10 areas since September 1998 under the Crime and Disorder Act. In addition there are now 154 youth offending teams up and running across England and Wales, supported and monitored by the Youth Justice Board (YJB). These multi-agency teams coordinate the delivery of the youth justice reforms locally.

The principles are clear. Juvenile crime must be nipped in the bud by swift action that involves the young criminals making reparation (often directly with victims) for what they have done and being supported in developing more creative and responsible ways of living. The link with citizenship education in schools is evident. Young people need to learn at an early age that unsociable behaviour is not acceptable, and that it will be dealt with swiftly and clearly and will be followed by opportunities to make reparation and support for a fresh start.

The story of Highfield Primary School in Plymouth is just one example of a school that has been turned round by a swift, clear intervention from a new headteacher. The school is set in a housing estate on the edge of Plymouth, and reflects a community that has known hardship, relative poverty and increasing unemployment with the closure of the docks. The children's behaviour was out of hand; bad language and physical aggression were commonplace. During the summer holidays classroom windows were broken and the school buildings subjected to vandalism. The new head arrived and was promptly told to '.... off' by an abusive child who was clearly in the habit of such behaviour. Everything then changed. The new head, Lorna Farrington, introduced two golden rules and insisted that everyone kept them. There was to be no abusive language and no touching. The staff supported the new regime and before long behaviour had improved beyond all recognition. The teachers asked the children what they thought.

'We really like no bullying and name calling and things, Miss, but...' The child's voice trailed off uncertainly into silence.

'But what, Wayne?'

'But why do the teachers tell us what to do all the time? They keep telling us off,' the boy explained.

'Would you rather you told each other what to do, and not the teachers?'

'Yes, Miss, that would be much better.'

'Very well then, we'll try it. But you'll have to play your part. I expect a lot from you, Wayne.'

The child looked at her and grinned. 'OK,' he said. And so it was.[2]

The teachers set up a school council and the pupils agreed to take on front-line responsibility for children's behaviour in the public areas of the school. They also set a regular agenda of issues that needed to be tackled. It worked. Behaviour improved and with it the motivation to work and learn. This was citizenship education that permeated every aspect of the life of the school.

A couple of years later the school, which by then had become one of CSV's citizenship Lighthouse Schools, was presenting a workshop at a CSV Lighthouse conference for schools in south-west England. For those of us who attended the event, it seemed the most natural thing in the world that children from Highfield Primary School should be playing a leading role in setting the tone and behaviour of the school. The lesson they shared was that, given a firm framework, clear support and the trust and encouragement of teachers, pupils were capable of exercising real responsibility with enthusiasm, good will and the kind of wisdom that children have when they are taken seriously.

There was another lesson, too. Many Highfield children go on to Lipson College, a Plymouth comprehensive school. Having learnt to accept responsibility for important aspects of the life and work of Highfield School, the children were surprised on arriving in secondary school that they no longer enjoyed these responsibilities. They raised the matter persuasively, and before long – to its eternal credit – Lipson too developed strategies to involve the students in taking more responsibility for the life of the school. There are three lessons here. First, children can undertake and build on real responsibility provided they are trusted and given appropriate support. Secondly, primary schools can have as great an influence on secondary schools as the other way about. Third, the transition between primary and secondary school offers invaluable opportunities for developing good work around citizenship education, mentoring and a sense of shared community.

These reflections on citizenship education and behaviour arose from exploring patterns of criminal behaviour among young people. There can be no doubt that crime and the fear of crime proved a significant motivating force behind some elements of the political support for citizenship education. Our perspective on crime has been to take a detailed snapshot of the behaviour of a group of self-reported young offenders in the last years of the 20th century. Another approach is to make historical comparisons drawing on large-scale aggregate data over long periods. This perspective suggests that there have been dramatic changes in the levels and experience of crime.

If we look at the crime figures for the period stretching from the middle of the 19th century to the end of the 20th century we are faced with a 'U-curve model of deviance', which applies equally to Britain and the United States.[3] The curve shows a drop in recorded crime, violence and illegitimacy, and alcoholism in the last half of the 19th century, reaching a low at the turn of the century, and a sharp rise in the latter part of the 20th century. Even if we take the period of the 1850s when 19th-century crime figures were at their highest and compare it with the last years of the 20th century, the increase in crime is staggering. The crime rate then was about 500 per 100,000 of the population in comparison with 10,000 per 100,000 now.

It is possible to produce a whole range of arguments why the figures are not strictly comparable. The recording of crime will almost certainly have improved. It may even be the case that we are now more sensitive to crime and include incidents in the statistics that would not have been considered worthy of inclusion 150 years ago. The blunt fact remains, however, that crime is running at what for most people are unacceptable levels. It is also the case that increasing numbers of people, particularly older people, are living their lives in the fear of crime, and this fear is reducing the quality of their lives. They go out less, they will actively avoid the streets that they once enjoyed and, particularly if they are living on their own, they may live in fear of violent intruders.

It may never be possible to make pure comparisons between crime now and crime in some previous time. It is often tempting to vilify or glorify a previous age. The statistics are cause for serious concern. The US sociologist Myron Magnet cast a fresh eye over the figures:[4]

> By 1970 a baby born and raised in a big [US] city had a greater chance of being murdered than a World War II GI had of dying in battle. Today [1993], a twelve-year-old American boy has an 89 per cent chance of becoming a victim of violent crime in his lifetime... In mid-1989, one of every four black American males was either in jail or on probation – a larger proportion than was in college.

This vignette of life in the United States may be removed from that in Britain. Maybe the incarceration of black rather than white males is linked with racist policing. Maybe life in Britain is more orderly and less dangerous. But there have been shootings in British schools and teachers are stabbed, even killed, by violent pupils armed with weapons. Teachers increasingly report violent incidents with pupils, and the exclusion of such pupils is increasingly a bone of contention between teachers and governors. More than that, there is what can only be described as the chronic background of hassle between teachers and pupils in so many schools, particularly those in large cities. The story of Highfield School when the children were at their most violent and aggressive is repeated in other places. As worrying, perhaps, is the fact that aggressive and disrespectful behaviour – road rage, air rage and any other sort of rage that captures the headlines – is increasingly accepted as a part of our modern way of life. In schools the situation is particularly sharp where teachers daily face what can so easily become the nightmare of dealing with chronically disruptive young people. It is easy to paint too black a picture – not every school suffers aggression and disruption – but where there is an atmosphere of suppressed violence or even muted alienation everyone will have a bad time. The teachers' lives are a misery and the pupils – like the pupils at Highfield – hate the widespread bullying and name calling. Citizenship education involves interventions that set clear boundaries about behaviour, insist that the boundaries are observed and – just as important – subsequently involve the pupils in accepting real responsibility for maintaining a positive ethos throughout the school. In Chapter 6 we heard from Darcus Howe about the hatred that local children have for being at school. Citizenship education offers one route (and potential strategies) to create a culture that will enable those children to value and be valued by their schools.

All this is more easily said than done. The starting point, however, which has been proven in schools that have successfully tackled the issue of behaviour, must be to recognize a problem where it exists. Problems that are ignored tend to come back and haunt those who have ignored them. It is necessary to be clear about what is unacceptable behaviour and to be equally clear about offering children and young people the opportunity, respect and encouragement to be part of the solution rather than a continuing part of the problem. In this, citizenship education is at the heart of the school improvement agenda.

Notes

1. Youth crime: findings from the 1998/99 Youth Lifestyles Survey. The survey looked at the extent of self-reported offending by 4,848 young people aged between 12 and 30 living in private households in England and Wales. It is based on the Youth Lifestyles Survey carried out between October 1998 and January 1999. Further information is obtainable from the Home Office Web site: www.homeoffice.gov.uk/rds/index.htm.
2. This account has been written up in story form on the basis of a telephone conversation between the author and the headteacher. The outline of the account is accurate; the details of the conversation employ dramatic licence.
3. These arguments are set out in more detail in Gertrude Himmelfarb (1995) *The Demoralisation of Society: From Victorian virtues to modern values*, pp 224 ff, IEA Health and Welfare Unit, London.
4. Myron Magnet (2000) *The Dream and the Nightmare: The sixties legacy to the underclass*, pp 50, 231, Encounter Books, New York.

10

A cultural shift

Citizenship and the welfare state

Schools have always been shaped by the prevailing culture – including the politics – of their day. By the same token pupils have always been required to behave according to the expectations of the ruling classes. During the period immediately following the last World War a Labour administration had come to power on a mandate to create a welfare state. The new reforming government set out consciously and deliberately to transform the culture of the United Kingdom into that of a welfare state. The battle-weary citizens of Britain were given what in effect was a set of welfare rights.

These rights were originally defined and proposed in what was popularly known as the Beveridge Report.[1] Citizens, Sir William Beveridge argued, should be given protection by the state from the evil giants of want, disease, ignorance, squalor and idleness. These rights were rooted in the value of equal opportunity. Health care that was free on delivery, a massive public housing programme and Keynesian demand management created the culture of the welfare consensus. Freedom from ignorance was provided through a new comprehensive system of schooling that made a huge impact on the life chances of millions of children, in spite of the fact that in many places independent and grammar schools continued to select the more able children out of the comprehensive system.

Citizenship at that time was perceived mainly in terms of the enjoyment of state protection against the social evils of the pre-war years in return for a general levy of tax contributions linked to the capacity to pay. The word citizen was then scarcely used in Britain. We were and remain subjects of the Crown, not citizens of a republic. There were a few reminders of the obligations of citizenship. National service, whereby the vast majority of the young male population were called up for two years' military service, was not finally ended until the early 1960s. Citizens were called upon to do jury service, and, of course, citizens were expected to pay their taxes, obey the law and behave in a neighbourly fashion. Those who possessed a British passport noted that they enjoyed the 'National Status of British Citizen' and that 'Her Britannic Majesty's Secretary of State requests and requires in the Name of Her Majesty all those whom it may concern to allow the bearer to pass freely without let or hindrance and to afford the bearer such assistance and protection as may be necessary'. This was heady stuff, redolent of the Empire, but the daily reality though mundane was very different after the war from what it had been before 1939. The Beveridge reforms that together constituted the welfare state were based on a broad measure of consensus between all political parties. There had been a cultural shift towards equal opportunity, mutual protection, subsidized housing and free health and education for everyone. This welfare consensus remained unchallenged until the mid-1970s.

An end to consensus

Margaret Thatcher brought about an end to the welfare consensus after the Tory triumph at the polls in 1979. The emphasis was now upon removing the nanny state with its well-intentioned but blundering and expensive arrangements. There was now 'no such thing as society' and citizenship was increasingly equated with the need for volunteering and philanthropy. In schools the emphasis was upon 'standards, standards and standards'. The good citizen was seen as a successful meritocrat, and the state was increasingly modelled on the values and methods of the market economy. In schools there was a somewhat half-hearted attempt to introduce citizenship education but this failed for reasons given in Chapter 2. This fresh shift in the culture of the country ran deeper than the arrival of an iron lady at the head of the Conservative Party. Thatcherism was successful precisely because it tapped into a widespread public feeling that the corporatism of the welfare state had become tired, expensive and unable to respond to the fresh demands of an increasingly consumer-led society.

By 1997 the neo-liberal whirlwind that had changed the face of Britain over the 1980s and early 1990s had become a spent force, and Labour came to power in a landslide election from which the defeated Tories are still recovering. Once again the culture of the country was shifting, and once again this shift – though led by one political party – enjoyed public support far beyond the membership of that party. This latest shift provides the moral and social – as well as political – context of citizenship as it is now proposed and pursued.

New Labour – a new consensus?

Before the eyes of an astonished nation the Labour Party under Tony Blair shed its old skin and reinvented itself as a pragmatic party of the radical centre. Clause 4 – the socialist commitment for the state to own and manage the commanding heights of the economy – was ditched and the party given a new name, New Labour. It was no accident that the political transformation of the left gave rise to a fresh emphasis on citizenship – on the need for people to engage with civil society. Citizenship education in schools became one of the distinguishing marks of David Blunkett's time at the then newly titled Department for Education and Employment, and is documented in Part I of this book. Furthermore, England was not alone in its concern to develop and promote effective education initiatives for democracy. Indeed, in significant respects we came late to the matter in comparison with the rest of Europe.

Ideological crisis

During the early 1990s Western democracies – not only in Britain – faced an ideological crisis. The new right had exposed the endemic weaknesses in the old left. In its place the neo-liberals had imposed a market-oriented politics based on the individual rather than the collective. But by 1997 the Tories were no longer trusted, their ideology – even to their sympathizers – seemed narrowly meritocratic and the people wanted something different. New Labour were given a massive mandate around a programme that Tony Blair described as the 'third way', in his conscious attempt to provide an alternative to both old Labour and neo-liberalism.

A third way?

The political philosopher Tony Giddens, sometimes described as 'Tony Blair's favourite intellectual', wrote a book on the third way. Will Hutton, himself a New Labour guru, said that Giddens 'has done what many considered impossible; he has constructed a coherent and persuasive definition of the third way'.[2] He has, furthermore, set out to show that the third way 'rather than being beyond left and right... is a part of the left, a conscious attempt to renew social democracy. The overall aim of Third Way politics', wrote Giddens,[3] 'should be to help citizens pilot their way through the major revolutions of our time: globalisation, transformations in personal life and our relationship to nature.'[4]

The leading philosophers of the third way do not, of course, speak directly for government. Indeed the Government can be remarkably coy about setting out the philosophical framework behind its policies. It may also be that the Labour Party, having earlier impaled itself upon the rusty barbs of outdated socialist ideology such as Clause 4, is now determined to avoid raising similar hostages to fortune. It would, therefore, be a mistake to assume that government formally endorses the political principles set out below. Indeed, in many respects the new political thinking offers a critique rather than an affirmation of government policy. It also suggests – and only time will show whether this is true – a fresh cultural consensus that offers a setting for democratic politics over the coming decades. It is a consensus that is emerging around our developing understanding of modern democracy.

Modern democracy

Democracy is emerging as the favoured form of government throughout most of the world, although the shattering impact of the terrorist assault on the twin towers of the World Trade Center in New York on 11 September 2001 has given a fresh edge and urgency to democracy's sometimes-complacent view of itself.

The alliance between global capitalism and democratic government, though neither universal nor unchallenged, is evolving as the fittest and most adaptive political system. The 'third way' thinkers offer a valuable perspective on the way democracy itself must respond – under parties of both the democratic left and right – to the exigencies of the post-modern age.[5] This same perspective highlights the opportunities and the challenges of teaching citizenship in schools.

The context of modern democracies

Democracies today have to function in a world that is characterized by five post-modern dilemmas. These dilemmas affect schools as well as the society beyond their gates. The five dilemmas are: globalization, individualism, the left–right divide, political agency and the challenge of the environment. Each dilemma influences, in one way or another, the life of the school and is grist to the mill of citizenship education.

Globilization

The dilemma of globalism is to reconcile the conflicting demands of the region or nation state with those of an increasingly dynamic global community. Globalization means that we now live in a world where what happens in one place rapidly and radically affects what is happening everywhere else. This is most obvious in the economic sphere where international corporations increasingly dominate world trade. Globalization also affects politics, the law and, most obviously, popular culture. Modern mass communications mean that we live in a global village where every pupil might be given the chance to undertake shared ventures by fax, e-mail and the Web.

International capitalism

Globalization is in part an economic phenomenon. It is in significant part the product of international capitalism. There is clearly a debate about the benefits of international capitalism and its relationships with government, particularly democratic governments. There are those who claim that international capitalism distorts and damages the working of democracy.[6] There are, on the other hand, those who argue with equal passion and sincerity that international capitalism is a powerful force for good.[7] What is certain is that we have not seen the last of the debate, and it is likely – if present form continues – that many people around the world will argue and protest against aspects of global capitalism. It is a part of the task of citizenship education to create informed opportunities for students to discuss and reflect on these issues.

The identity and behaviour of nation states

Globalization is transforming the identity and behaviour of nation states. It 'pulls away' from the nation state in the sense that some of their traditional powers are shared with others through associations such as the European Union. However, globalization also 'pushes down' by devolving the central powers of nation states to local regions and constituent nations. In Britain we are increasingly talking of the United Kingdom comprising four nations, each with its own identity and governance. Regional government is already seeking new and more vibrant ways of relating to children and young people in and beyond the classroom.

Globalization also 'squeezes sideways', creating new economic and cultural regions that sometimes crosscut the boundaries of nation states. Barcelona, for example, which is part of both Catalonia and Spain, is involved in an economic area that spills over into southern France.

This three-way movement of globalization is affecting states across the world. Sovereignty is becoming fuzzier, but – as Giddens observes – there is no sign that the nation state is disappearing. The irony is that, as globalization proceeds, the scope of government tends to expand.

Young people, including those living in remote rural areas, will be more dramatically affected by globalization than their parents' generation. It is important that citizenship education anticipates and tackles the implications of these changes.

Globalization has, in recent times, been the context in which modern democracies have experienced a new kind of enemy. We live in a state where, until 11 September 2001, we had imagined that we no longer faced external enemies. The collapse of the Soviet Union had brought to an end the bipolar world that had defined and dominated international politics during the past century.

The implications of terrorism

The enemy is now the terrorist who no longer plays to the old rules and the old politics. The assault on the twin towers of the World Trade Center in New York has given greater urgency to our need to understand what we mean by democracy and what it is to live in a global society that is shaped by both economic and cultural imperatives.

The issues that have grown up around the threat of terrorism prompt fundamental questions about our understanding of ourselves as British citizens and world citizens. It also raises specific questions about a citizen's responsibility to support the democratic (and shared?) values of the country of which she or he is a citizen. This has immediate and significant consequences for citizenship education in schools.

Individualism

The changing relationship between the individual and society is a characteristic of modern democracy. Our expectations of life have grown in response to what is now possible. We have more choice in work, in leisure pursuits and in relationships than humans have ever had in times past. We live longer and so have more choice over what we can fit into our lives including serial jobs and, for some at least, serial relationships. The dilemma of individualism arises from individuals wanting ever-greater control over their own lives in a world where their needs and wishes have to be accommodated with those of others.

The new individualism:

is not Thatcherism, not market individualism, not atomisation. On the contrary, it means 'institutionalised individualism'. Most of the rights and entitlements of the welfare state, for example, are designed for individuals rather than for families. In many cases they presuppose employment. Employment in turn implies Education and both of these presuppose mobility. By all these requirements people are invited to constitute themselves as individuals: to plan, understand, design themselves as individuals.[8]

Democratic participation in schools

Schools are expected to help young people do this in a context where tradition and custom have largely retreated from our lives. The formal subjects of the taught curriculum along with personal and social education are a necessary, but not sufficient, part of the process. The schools that are effectively tackling the challenge of individualism do so by giving young people the opportunity to make decisions and to take actions in a supportive environment where they have also to take account of the needs of other people. Effective school councils, quality mentoring, tutoring and mediation programmes and practical projects provide such opportunities.

'We have to make our lives in a more active way than was true of previous generations,' argues Giddens, and adds, 'We need more actively to accept responsibility for the consequences of what we do and the life-style habits we adopt.'[9]

Left and right

The explicitly political dilemma here is between those who say that the left–right distinction no longer makes any sense and those who claim that it still has meaning. The former group point to the fact that New Labour has stolen so many of Thatcher's clothes particularly on privatization, public services and aspects of law and order that it is no longer possible to use the labels right and left. Their opponents, however, argue that politics is necessarily adversarial and that the terms 'right' and 'left' will always be useful, even though their context and content may change. Furthermore, at times when one party has an overwhelming majority, it is all the more important to remind ourselves that there are other points of view.

Schools can and often do equip young people with the capacity to see more than one side of a question and to acquire the habit of critically questioning the *status quo*. From the perspective of those in power – whether they are ministers, teachers or students' leaders – the informed and persistent critic may often be seen as a nuisance or worse. The alternative, however, could be the death of democracy. Students need experience of both offering and coping with opposition.

The chief distinction between right and left has been – and is likely to remain – a concern about equality. The Tories show little interest in equality; they value tradition (inherited wealth and power) or, paradoxically, the kind of liberty that fosters competition and meritocracy. Labour has traditionally nailed its colours to the mast of social equality; but New Labour speaks more about social inclusion than equality.

The issues of equality, inclusion, meritocracy and liberty do not necessarily sit easily together. They need debate. They are also caught rather than taught; and they need to be honoured through deeds as well as words. These, therefore, are citizenship issues and have as much to do with the way schools behave as what they teach.

Recently, however, new issues have come to the fore that do not belong specifically to the left or right. They include ecological questions and matters concerned with the changing nature of the family, work and personal and cultural identity. Giddens suggests that these might usefully be called 'life politics', which touch on life decisions rather than life chances. In the past emancipatory politics concerned *life chances* and were about people having jobs, health care, housing and education. Life politics is about 'choice, identity and mutuality. How should we react to the hypothesis of global warming? Should we accept nuclear energy or not? How far should work remain a central life value? Should we favour devolution? What should be the future of the European Union? None of these is a clear left–right issue.'

Giddens concludes that nearly all the questions of life politics require radical solutions, an active centre, rather than the middle ground of compromise. Schools can, and often do, provide a setting in which possible solutions can be explored and even tested.

Political agency

The dilemma of political agency is about the way in which social and political activists often distrust politicians, and are turning to direct action and single-issue campaigns rather than working through the existing democratic mechanisms such as the MP or ballot box. The recent protests against aspects of global capitalism are a case in point.

Schools, particularly if they can work in partnership with local government and community organizations, can offer young people active opportunities to work with local people on issues of their choice (see Chapter 16). Some well-informed young people, who have thought through their disillusion with current democratic mechanisms, may welcome the opportunity to challenge in debate those whom they oppose.

Ecological problems

The dilemma posed by ecological concerns such as global warming is how their management can and should be taken into democratic politics. On the one hand, there are those who argue that the future of the world is at stake, and that urgent and massive action by politicians is needed throughout the world. Those who worked for the Kyoto agreement on global warming would support this view. On the other hand, people like George Bush and the US right think either that the issue is exaggerated or that global warming is a natural phenomenon that can be left to nature to resolve.

Policy makers are struggling to establish clear and publicized principles against which to manage environmental strategies for handling issues such as BSE, foot and mouth and the wider challenge of developing and managing rural and urban social economies. Many ecologists propose that the *precautionary principle* is accepted as a means of dealing with ecological threats. The concept states that action on environmental issues should be taken even when scientifically there is uncertainty about whether such action is necessary.

It is not hard to argue that schools pay more attention to issues of environmental sustainability than do government departments. Environment projects led by young people are already on the go in most schools. What is lacking, however, is coherent and readily available programmes for young people to engage with local environment agencies on monitoring, research and development issues including the management of risk.

Democratic (third way) values

The values of third way politics bring together an overarching commitment to *equality* and the *protection of the vulnerable* with more recently articulated emphasis upon the autonomy of the individual. In this sense they combine elements of right and left thinking. These democratic values may be listed as follows:

- **Autonomy of action.** In the post-modern context freedom is defined as *autonomy of action* that has to be worked out and lived in the wider social community.
- **No rights without responsibilities.** Rights are no longer seen as unconditional claims – as some under post-war social democracy saw them – but rather as inalienably linked with responsibilities. For example, unemployment benefits now carry an obligation to seek work.

- **No authority without democracy.** In a society where custom is no longer king, democracy is the only way in which authority can be made legitimate. The emphasis on individualism does not necessarily erode authority, but it does require that it is actively recognized by those over whom it is exercised.
- **Cosmopolitan pluralism.** This welcomes and encourages cultural diversity in a single society, and requires that each culture respects and allows space for the others. Where there is a fundamental conflict of interest this has to be resolved through democratic processes and the law.
- **Philosophic conservatism.** This is essential in a world that is learning to live beyond tradition and custom. It advocates a pragmatic attitude towards change and a cautious approach to science and technology in view of the ambiguous consequences of so many discoveries and potential discoveries.

Two points are important here. First, these values belong to modern democracy and not exclusively to New Labour and third way politicians. They are fast becoming mainstream *democratic values*,[10] and will be referred to as such in what follows. The debate within the Conservative Party in the run-up to the Tory leadership election in 2001 made it clear that, though they differ from New Labour over the interpretation of the values (in policy terms), there is no fundamental disagreement between the parties about the values themselves. It was, in this context, no accident that the leadership contest raised issues about racism (rejection of racist attitudes among party members), equal opportunities (women candidates) and the link between authority and democracy (votes for all the membership).

Second, these values are of course directly and indirectly affirmed by the values and dispositions listed in the Crick Report,[11] which was in no sense a narrowly partisan document.

From this context and these values, Giddens sets out the guiding principles of a political agenda. Taken together these principles provide a framework for post-modern political debate. They also provide a useful checklist against which to review the progress of citizenship education both in schools and in society at large.

A political programme

From the point of view of introducing citizenship education in schools four elements of the new political programme are immediately relevant:

- **Positive welfare**
  The welfare state was, as we have argued, built around a set of negatives: want, disease, ignorance, squalor and idleness. The most recent political thinking offers a programme to promote *positive welfare* through supporting people's efforts to earn their living, stay healthy, manage their learning and achieve and enjoy decent surroundings. Welfare is not chiefly about money but about well-being. Therefore in place of the *welfare state* we need a society whose members enjoy *well-being* supported by a state that invests in human capital.
- **The social investment state**
  Policies should promote well-being in which citizens are active participants rather than passive recipients of various kinds of benefit. For example, unemployment and old age are examples of opportunities for people to seek government help in doing what they need to do to – including retraining, finding work and leading purposeful lives after the age of 65. Regular retraining and family-friendly employment policies can be more effective than unemployed people being bought off (cheaply at that). The notion of a pensioner was the product of insurance acts rather than a definition of what it is to be an older person. Older people in the prime of their lives will wish to remain active and should be expected to be so. Much older people who are also very frail will need significant support. Well-being policies should reflect these facts.

  As far as young people are concerned maybe the time has come to erode the equally artificial notion of youth, which is an administrative fiction arising not least from the need of youth services to define their remit! Young people are of course different from adults in some important ways: they can be more vulnerable and are usually less experienced. But there it ends. Young people tend to be better than adults at some things, particularly IT! They are often more physically adventurous and resilient and frequently have an intuition that is undimmed by the routines of experience. In the Middle Ages young people naturally helped out on the farm from an early age. In Victorian times they were sent up chimneys, and there lies the rub. The industrial exploitation of young people has rightly given rise to protective legislation. But there is no reason why teams of young people, appropriately supervised like the rest of us, should not be tackling tasks – some of them sophisticated – that need doing in society. At work, in community settings and around the school it should become a commonplace to see young people working and learning with adults on projects and meaningful activities.
- **The cosmopolitan nation**
  Nations bring people together around the idea of identity, mutual

obligation and a focus for self-determination. A balance is necessary between extreme libertarianism where no commonalities are expected or given and a rigid conformity to so-called mainstream culture. The balance is not easy, but it is one that all schools, and not only those working in multicultural settings, are challenged to achieve. There could be no more important focus for citizenship education. These challenges include:

- the relationship between politics and faith communities nationally and globally;
- distinguishing between mainstream religious values and extremist perversions of those values;
- loyalty to a country and loyalty to a faith community.

It is likely that these questions will become more rather than less pressing as we move into the new century.

It is an area of citizenship education where there are urgently needed opportunities for schools to share their successes and learn from the inevitable difficulties.

● **Cosmopolitan democracy**
Giddens points out that the cosmopolitan nation implies cosmopolitan democracy working on a global scale. International boundaries, as we have seen, have become fuzzy. We are now, in a way we were not 50 years ago, members of one another in the international community of nations. Some argue that the world is moving backwards towards anarchy and pervasive disorder, but the fact remains that, in a post-nuclear age, large-scale war is less likely than it was before the atomic bomb. Globalization will suffer military, economic and social setbacks; but the process is likely to continue. The major nations have too much invested in it to retreat at this stage. The issue of international terrorism has, in one sense, given added urgency to this development. Before the assault on the World Trade Centre in New York in 2001, it was possible to be complacent about the triumph of democracy as the world's number 1 choice of government. After 11 September it is clear that democracy still faces radical challenges, but in a very different form from those that shaped the old bipolar world of communism and capitalism.

We are, therefore, entering a period where democracy has consciously to re-establish its credentials on the world stage. In the long term this is almost certainly the biggest and most important challenge that faces citizenship education in democratic countries. In this context, therefore, citizenship education needs to be experienced as global as well as local. A growing number of schools, including those instanced in this book, have connections with young people overseas. Partnership in an electronic age is relatively easy to manage, and important to pursue. Even more important, however, is the emphasis in schools such as the Anglo-European School in Essex on creating a radical culture of world citizenship among young people. The danger, otherwise, is that the 'global dimension' of citizenship education will be treated as something that is bolted on to the mainstream business of schools, rather than central to its purpose.

These selected elements of the third way programme are, like all political ideas, open to debate and disagreement. They do, however, give those concerned with citizenship education a valuable set of criteria against which to examine the evolving purpose as well as the emerging outcomes of citizenship education. They help us keep our eyes on the big picture in a subject where it is all too easy to lose track of the overarching purpose of citizenship education.

The Citizenship Order does not, of course, formally require these principles. They are, however, consistent with the Order. They also provide a handy critique against which both political debate and citizenship education in schools can be discussed, developed and evaluated. Figure 10.1 expresses visually the framework of principles that is emerging from the new politics.

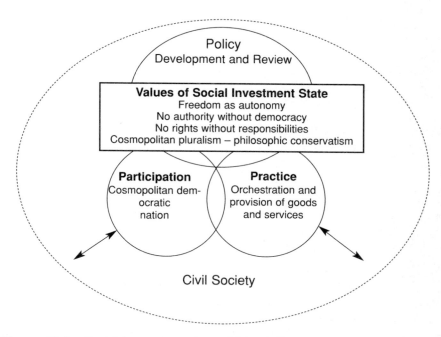

Figure 10.1   *Social investment state within civil society*

Notes

1. Sir William Beveridge (1942) *Social Insurance and Allied Services Report*, HMSO. If we include the summary copies, the sales of the Report exceeded an astonishing 600,000.
2. Will Hutton, Editor in Chief, *The Observer*. Quoted on the cover of Anthony Giddens (1998) *The Third Way*, Polity Press, London.
3. Giddens (1998) *The Third Way*.
4. Giddens (1998) *The Third Way*, pp 64–68.
5. The following analysis of third way politics is drawn from Giddens's book. The reader who is curious to know more should consult the original source, as much of the argument is necessarily omitted.
6. George Monbiot (2001) *Captive State: The corporate takeover of Britain*, Pan, London.
7. Enterprise or exploitation: can global business be a force for good? by Vernon Ellis, International Chairman, Accenture, in the New Statesman lecture, 11 July 2001, published by the *New Statesman* (see Chapter 16).
8. Ulrich Beck (1998) Cosmopolitan manifesto, *New Statesman*, 20 March.
9. Giddens (1998) *The Third Way*, p 37.
10. This point belongs to the present author. Giddens emphasizes the left-of-centre emphasis of third way values. It is worth pointing out that a comparable emphasis on equality of opportunity shaped the post-war welfare consensus, which was accepted by both centre left and centre right in Britain.
11. Crick Report, p 44.

11

A question of values

Values: Following on from the shifts in ideology we are faced with questions about values:

- How far do we share a set of common values?
- What values do we need to share?
- How do these values relate to schools?

Various attempts have been made in recent years to demonstrate that society in general and schools in particular are rooted in a set of shared values. These values are presented as the basis of moral and social education. Many argue that life is not so simple and that we need to be ready to cope with some tough and complex moral challenges including the need to identify the civic values required by a modern democracy.

Citizenship in action means taking real decisions that have actual consequences. The Crick Report talks about young people developing a 'proclivity to act responsibly: that is care for others and oneself; premeditation and calculation about the effect actions are likely to have on others; and acceptance of responsibility for unseen and unfortunate consequences.'[1] This is about developing a moral sense that informs and judges actions.

Those responsible for citizenship education need, therefore, to take *conscious* account of the ethical dimension of the work with young people. Every period of history has its distinctive moral challenges and arguments; the modern period is characterized by the debate between the relativists and absolutists, the modernists and traditionalists, alongside the gradual emergence of a set of *democratic values* (see Chapter 10).

Moral relativism

Moral relativists argue that in the post-modern world all values, including moral values, are relative and culturally determined. In art and architecture the point is clear for all to see. There is no single canon of accepted quality or taste. In matters of personal conduct the 'new morality', which swept through much of the Western world in the mid- to late 1960s, brushed aside many of the old rules, particularly those concerning sexual behaviour. People were increasingly encouraged to choose their own set of moral rules. Morality in this sense had become a consumer product – 'you pays your money and you takes your pick'. Many welcomed feminism, equal opportunities and the loss of defer- ence as a harbinger of freedom and fairness. Others, however, saw the new morality as licence not liberty, and with it they lamented the erosion of respect.

Relativism drew its philosophic justification from thinkers such as Jacques Derrida (b 1930) and Michel Foucault (1926–84). Derrida was angered by what to him were the arrogant and outrageous claims of 'reason'. He argued that reason was a human construct arising from our creation and use of language. The views that we hold about the world are our own and have no external validity. Everything, including the rule of reason itself, is relative. In his defence Derrida might point to the holocausts of mass extermination in Europe or the A-bomb in Hiroshima as examples of the bankrupt morality of Western reason. He did not argue that the language of morality was worthless, merely that it is rela- tive and rooted in the narrative of particular peoples at particular times.

The challenge of relativism to traditional morality is social as well as intellectual. Globalization questions the idea that in the United Kingdom we all share a single set of 'British' values. We do not share a single, monolithic culture, and never have done. We are a nation of immigrants and invaders. What has changed is the culture and colour of the most recent arrivals among our British population. In the past the majority of our newcomers were white and, nominally at least, Christian. We can no longer describe ourselves as a 'Christian nation'. We have no single, overarching system of religious or secular values. That is why ethical reflection has become a central element in citizenship education.

In the 1990s, therefore, the question was increasingly asked: can we reach agreement in an increasingly pluralist society on a core set of values that are acceptable to the bulk of the population? The question was especially important in schools, where teachers often felt uncertain of their role as moral mentors in a world of changing values.

In response to this concern the School Curriculum Assessment Authority (SCAA), the predecessor of QCA, convened the Values

Education Forum (VEF) in England.[2] The Forum developed its work around debates and consultations among educators and community representatives. These were followed up by a national survey. The resulting evidence suggested that there was indeed a clear consensus – 85 per cent of the general population, and 97 per cent of teachers – around a set of core values. These values were based on respect for oneself, for others, for society and for a sustainable environment. Each value was amplified by a simple set of statements that to a significant extent forms the backdrop of the values content of the Citizenship Order.

In summary, the core values were:

- **Valuing ourselves:** We value ourselves as unique human beings capable of spiritual, moral, intellectual and physical growth and development.
- **Valuing others:** We value others for themselves, not only for what they have or what they can do for us. We value relationships as fundamental to the development and fulfilment of others and ourselves and to the good of the community.
- **Valuing society:** We value truth, freedom, justice, human rights, the rule of law and collective effort for the common good. In particular, we value families as sources of love and support for all their members, and as the basis of a society in which people care for others.
- **Valuing the environment:** We value the environment, both natural and shaped by humanity, as the basis of life and a source of wonder and inspiration.

The broad conclusion was that teachers could be confident they had the support of society at large in teaching these moral values. The increasingly relativist culture of the 1960s and 1970s was, therefore, challenged on the basis of evidence of what people said they believed rather than on what moral philosophers or religious leaders claimed they should believe.

The irony of the situation, however, was not lost on some people. An attempt had been made to challenge relativism by taking a poll of what people believed about morality. But this process – the business of deciding morals by plebiscite – was itself a relativist project. Furthermore, the list of core values that emerged was based on respect rather than, say, obedience. Respect is built on relationships, and relationships are by definition relative. What, therefore, we have from the Forum is a simple – some would say simplistic – ethical framework around which we can debate moral issues. We do not have a template for moral decision making.

While this was going on in Britain, a US journalist and writer, Rushworth Kidder, became actively concerned about the erosion of moral values in and beyond the United States. Kidder, like the VEF, was in search of a set of shared values about which to promote a more consciously moral culture. He established the Institute for Global Ethics (1990) and through surveys, travelling and talking with individuals identified worldwide support for a set of shared values.[3] These values include compassion, truth, freedom, fairness, solidarity, tolerance, responsibility and respect for law. Put simply the Institute has distilled a set of five distinct core values that receive almost universal support:

- responsibility;
- compassion;
- honesty;
- fairness;
- respect.

It is not hard to see how the values charted by the Values Education Forum and the Institute for Global Ethics[4] elicited significant support. The lists, however, are not identical. The VEF values include tell-tale signs of third way thinking. Tucked among the traditional values are modern values that are unlikely to win universal acclaim particularly in cultures that derive their authority from tradition. For example, the recognition that love can be found 'in families of different kinds', that respect should be shown for religious and cultural diversity and that equal opportunities should be promoted among all people regardless of their sex, status and wealth are all secular democratic values.

Participative democratic practices are often the exception rather than the rule in communities rooted in custom and practice, and that includes many school communities! Furthermore, not all modern democracies formally and publicly subscribe to all the VEF values. For example, the environmental values listed by the Forum link with the recommendations of Agenda 21 and the 1992 Rio Summit for promoting a sustainable environment. Sustainability, though gaining ground, remains a hotly contested issue, particularly in the United States.

The core values listed by Kidder – responsibility, compassion, honesty, fairness and respect – are values held in common by many traditional and most modern societies. This is both their strength and their weakness. Their strength is that they provide a vital starting point for sharing mutual concerns. Their weakness is that they suggest a measure of agreement that may well be absent. Most cultures encourage responsible behaviour; but one person's responsible behaviour is another person's irresponsibility. For example, in a tradition-based school, many will consider it irresponsible to include students in staff selection. A school based on democratic values, however, may consider it irresponsible not to involve students in staff appointments. Responsibility means different things in different cultures.

Compassion may be interpreted as 'pity' in a custom-based culture, and as 'empathy' in a more egalitarian culture. The two responses can lead to very different consequences. Fairness is relative to the custom and practice of the community in which it is being exercised, and respect can be used to maintain or even foster inequalities of all kinds.

Thus our list of universal shared values provokes as many questions as it resolves. It cannot be used as a universal recipe for moral agreement.

Secular v traditional values

The differences between the traditional and secular views on values are fundamental. The two approaches are, as Janet Radcliffe Richards points out,[5] based on radically different worldviews. These views correspond to a large extent with secular and religious beliefs, and yield quite different approaches to problems of ethics.

Ordered universe

The traditional view is based on a belief in an *ordered universe*. This view has been at the heart of Western thinking, starting with Aristotle, and later adopted and modified by Islam and Christianity. The universe is perceived as naturally orderly and harmonious. All is well as long as everything keeps to its proper place. When things are out of kilter, there is turmoil and restlessness. Ethics, according to this view, is about our duty to understand our nature and to act appropriately. It is not our business to understand the whole: that is beyond us. God, or nature, has the whole under control, and will provide us with the guidance we need to act as we should.

Evolving universe

In contrast, the secular view is based on an *evolutionary approach to the universe*. The world is the result of the unplanned interactions of physical forces, and the appearance of order derives not, as traditionally believed, from design, but from Darwinian natural selection. 'There is', Richards argues:

no underpinning moral order, and there is no natural state of things according to which all will go well. Understanding the nature of things in this kind of world tells us nothing at all about the way they ought to be: it tells us only what raw materials we have to work with and, in doing so, what we are up against. If things are to be made *better*, that depends on *our working out criteria* for what would count as their being better, and getting enough of a grip on the world to remould it a little nearer to our hearts' desire.

The two views lead to different moral attitudes

Radcliffe Richards then shows how these two views lead to very different moral attitudes to advances in technology. 'Both groups want to achieve as much good as possible and to guard against danger, but they have very different views about how to set about this.' Those who hold the traditional view will be concerned 'with restoring things to the way they ought to be. We should try to heal the sick and save life; but we should not in any way play God and try to change the natural state of things'.

On the other hand the Darwinians will claim that 'there is no natural state, and if we are to achieve any kind of harmony, we must decide what sort and try to create it ourselves. There are natural constraints on what *can* be achieved, but not on which of the possibilities we should try to achieve'.

But which approach should we take?

The fundamental question is which of these approaches is right. Richards argues, 'If we have decided to accept one approach, we need to ensure that we are not distorting the way we think with assumptions inadvertently drawn from the other school of thought. Working on the old, "ordered universe" autopilot is quite unsuitable for the new, unplanned world'.

The teacher's question

This, however, fails to solve the teacher's question: how do I help an ethnically diverse bunch of young people from very different British cultures to work usefully together on citizen values? Three points are important as far as education for active citizenship is concerned:

- **Fully shared values are not possible:** Our society never has reached and never will reach complete agreement on shared values, traditional or secular.
- **The democratic values provide a useful basis** for our shared behaviour and relationships in society and, by the same token, in school.
  - These values are secular; they are not predicated on one or more religious views of the world. They have emerged from our evolving understanding of ourselves, and to that extent are open-ended.
  - They can tolerate difference within limits: they can allow groups of citizens – including teachers and pupils – to hold different views provided that those views do not threaten the rights of others. So, for example, a secular state can: 1) accept arranged marriages, freely entered into by both parties, but not forced marriages; 2) tolerate disagreement and freedom of speech among its citizens, but it cannot accept violence or incitement to violence against either a person or the state (terrorism); 3) democratically evolve guidance and legislation on issues arising, for example, from biological engineering. It can, at the same time, respect the freedom of individual citizens and medical staff to opt out of these decisions. For example, if certain types of cloning are allowed, citizens should remain free not to be involved with them. This should apply to medical staff as well as patients.
- **Morality is learnt through real-life experiences.** Active learning in the community offers students the chance to reflect and act upon moral issues. This approach is essential if young people are to learn how to handle questions of values in actual situations. Morality is – to adopt a phrase developed further in Chapter 14, under The curriculum: Creating learning experiences – not just a subject (ethics) but a practicum, something that we do together.

The educationist John Beck commenting on the same theme said, 'Such radical developments pose a whole array of educational challenges – and no panaceas exist. However, it seems clear that worthwhile forms of moral and social education [and citizenship] must respect cultural diversity, regard tolerance as more than a negative virtue, and employ methods of teaching and learning that involve dialogue while preserving a clear commitment to reason and evidential teaching.'

CSV has worked with the Institute for Global Ethics on aspects of ethical decision making and has included some useful exercises in *Active Citizenship: A teachers' toolkit* (2000).

Notes

1. Crick Report, p 44, col 2.
2. SCAA (1966) *Education for Adult Life: The spiritual and moral development of young people*, SCAA, London.
3. Rushworth Kidder (1994) *Shared Values in a Troubled World: Conversations with men and women of conscience*, Jossey Bass, San Francisco.
4. Ethics and Citizenship Tools for Moral Decision-Making will be published by the Institute and Hodder & Stoughton (London, 2002). Guidelines for moral decision-making based on the work of the IfGE also appear in CSV's Active Citizenship: A Teacher's Toolkit (CSV/Hodder & Stoughton, London, 2002).
5. Janet Radcliffe Richards (2000) *Human Nature after Darwin*, Routledge, London. This passage follows closely her argument in The wrong moral autopilot, *New Statesman* Essay, 20 November 2000.

12

The challenge to education

Aim: To show how the new politics requires educators to:

- support the introduction of citizenship education in schools;
- promote active citizenship in the community; and
- build both around a common set of values, aims and objectives.

As far as citizenship education is concerned the new politics offer a triple challenge to the education sector, that is, to those involved in developing, supporting and delivering education and education services. The challenges are to:

- support the introduction of citizenship education in schools;
- promote active citizenship in the community; and
- build both around a common purpose and shared action.

For the most part local authorities – through their education departments – have taken the first challenge seriously, but they are only now embarking on the other two challenges.

Challenge: supporting citizenship education in school

The first challenge is to 'deliver' citizenship against the stipulated outcomes of the programme of study. This in itself is challenging because citizenship is like no other subject. It has specific and far-reaching consequences not only for *what* is done in schools but for *how* it is done. This is the subject of Part III of the book and is clearly something that many local authorities and their teams of advisers are taking very seriously.

Challenge: promoting active citizenship in the community

The second challenge to education is that the sector should – in consort with government and in partnership with stakeholders in the community – act to forward the larger aim of the Citizenship Order, to create 'a change in the political culture of this country both nationally and locally: for people to think of themselves as active citizens, willing, able and equipped to have an influence in public life'.[1] This means promoting democratic participation and supporting appropriate social action.

Democracy and participation

Education authorities are well placed to support initiatives that will promote pupils' involvement in local decision making (see *Hear by Right*, Chapter 16). The initiative should not be left to schools on their own. Furthermore local and national government need to work together to ensure that the message is consistent. Some teachers fear they are being set up to take responsibility for the failures of others. The reasons for the decline in voting go deeper than apathy. People, particularly young people, often feel that their vote will not make any substantial difference. It is, therefore, quite possible – even likely – that the youth vote at the next general election will continue to decline, in spite of teachers' best effort. If this happens, who will be blamed?

A case in point

Take, for example, the current state of local democracy in London. The government made a considerable fuss over devolving power to a Mayor of London. It was to be a democratically elected post, and a first step in giving a face, and greater focus, to democracy in the capital. Ken Livingstone put up as a candidate. The New Labour Government had major reservations about his candidature, and so put up an alternative candidate. Livingstone left the Labour Party and campaigned as an independent. He focused on the need for a properly run tube and made his position clear to everyone. Londoners, desperate to enjoy effective public transport, gave him an overwhelming majority at the polls. The

New Labour Government still didn't like it, and was perceived by many – including thoughtful writers such as Simon Jenkins in the *Evening Standard* – as driving through a policy for the underground contrary to the wishes of London's elected representatives.

Imagine, if you would, the weekly editorial meeting of *Loose Cannon*, the student newspaper of a north London comprehensive. The features editor announces that she is to run a series of items on student attitudes to citizenship education.

'We could start with local democracy,' she says. 'I've done a piece headed "Democracy down the tubes". Cool or what! I propose we run a short, confidential questionnaire on the kids' views. Here are my questions:

Question 1: Was the Mayor's policy for the tube clear in his election campaign?　　　　　　　　　　　　　　　　　　　YES/NO
Question 2: Did any members of your family vote for the Mayor?　　　　　　　　　　　　　　　　　　　　　　　　YES/NO
Question 3: Is central government's behaviour on this issue:
　(a) democratic?　　　　　　　　　　　　　　　　　　　　YES/NO
　(b) hypocritical?　　　　　　　　　　　　　　　　　　　YES/NO
Question 4: Do you think voting in mayoral elections is a waste of time?　　　　　　　　　　　　　　　　　　　　　　YES/NO

'NB If your answer to (4) is NO, please write an article for *Loose Cannon*. We're short of positive copy on this one! Edwina Balls, Features.'

It would be funny, if it were not so serious.

Practice

Project opportunities

Education departments are also well placed to press for local government to work with school on community projects. In most, if not all, places local government is the biggest employer and already through its various departments is engaged directly or indirectly with thousands of project and placement opportunities. Local community development initiatives can offer ideal opportunities for student involvement.

Town and country – a possible nationwide initiative?

Some rural schools have partnerships with city schools, and the other way about. Such partnerships could do much to develop a purposeful debate about the relationship between town and country.

Multicultural education through partnership projects

After the terrorist assault on the World Trade Center in New York, citizenship education that promotes cross-cultural understanding is more important than ever. Some schools in largely monocultural communities are looking to forge partnerships with schools and other organizations in areas with diverse cultures drawing on a number of different faith communities.

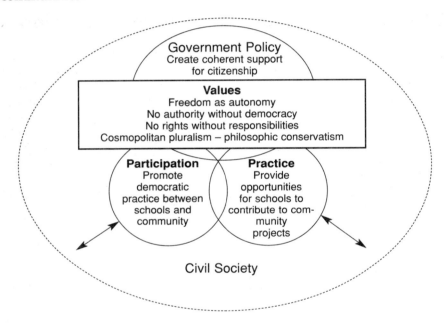

Figure 12.1 *Local government – supporting citizenship education*

A key role for the local authority

The relationship between the state and civil society was pictured graphically in Figure 10.1 in order to show complex ideas in a simple form. A similar diagram, Figure 12.1, serves helpfully to identify the relationship between local government and citizenship education. The local education authority may or may not act as the lead department in such initiatives, but it has a responsibility to explore with other local government departments the ways in which local government activities can foster democracy and social action. The Local Government Information Unit has identified a number of projects where the local authority has worked with schools to promote citizenship education.[2] These include major partnerships between Manchester City Council and school councils, and an innovative initiative in Cambridge whereby young people are 'juries' to quiz their local government members and officers about the provision of youth and other services. The Local Government Association/ National Youth Agency initiative on young people's democracy, Hear by Right, will also offer models of good practice through a series of pilot projects throughout the country (see Chapter 16).

Challenge: common purpose, shared action

Education for active citizenship also prompts a further challenge to the education sector. It invites the education sector to work with local government and community partners to promote active citizenship around a shared set of values. These values, as we have seen, include *freedom* seen as autonomy, *rights* being dependent on *responsibilities*, and *authority* being rooted in *democracy*. In addition there is a commitment to *valuing diversity* (cosmopolitan pluralism) and proper *caution* about undertaking change the consequences of which may be damaging (philosophic conservatism).

This challenge requires a response from schools, from local (and national) government and from their community partners.

Schools

The education sector has to be clear about its own purpose. This question can easily be lost among the many tasks of planning and offering an ever-changing curriculum. Professor Bart McGettrick raised the matter of the purpose of education in his address to a conference of citizenship educators.[3]

The curriculum is not the purpose of education

'The underlying purpose of education is to enable young people to grow up with a capacity to love, to show care and compassion, to recognize beauty and to serve one another. The *curriculum* is *not the purpose* of education; it is a tool to serve that larger purpose,' argued McGettrick. He then made the point that in order to fulfil this high purpose, we must not only combine learning with knowledge, skills and experience; we must also combine learning with the ability to develop positive and healthy relationships.

The capacity to love, show care and compassion and to recognize beauty demands every ounce of energy, knowledge and skill that we have. The curriculum exists to serve these values and not the other way about. It is important, therefore, for those directly involved in developing education for active citizenship to keep their eyes fixed on the wider purpose of education and to avoid becoming hung up on technicalities.

'Implementing' the curriculum or creating learning?

Teachers and policy makers talk about 'implementing' the curriculum. Educational terminology has changed in the years following the creation of the national curriculum. Educators use words like 'deliver' from the language of commerce, or 'implement' from the language of planning. The central purpose of education, however, is neither commercial nor bureaucratic. The purpose of education is to *create learning*.

We create learning when we bring content together with a love of the subject. We develop a love for a subject in much the same way that we develop a love for anything else. We come to feel that it belongs to us and matters to us. In other words the subject we love becomes part of us, and we part of the subject. This idea sounds fanciful, until we recognize and value the difference between teaching someone to 'know about something' and teaching him or her to become 'someone who is something'. A good history teacher enables his or her students to become historians. An English teacher helps children to become writers, readers and editors of their own and others' work.

The larger purpose of education in this context, of course, is to *produce good citizens*. Through citizenship the different disciplines within a school are consciously brought together, thus contributing to the school's capacity to fulfil its core purpose.

McGettrick reminds us that learning has five dimensions.[4] All learning involves:

- learning to repeat things;
- learning to learn;
- learning how to do;
- learning how to be;
- learning how to become 'something more'.

'Something more'

This applies as much to sculpture as to science, to music as to maths. It is this fifth dimension – learning to become 'something more' – that gives learning its special excitement and has a particular link with citizenship education. At one level it opens our awareness to the unknown territory around a domain of learning. Our understanding is experienced as a candle flame in the dark. It illuminates a small circle of the world about us, and at the same time exposes the darkness beyond, the extent of what we do not know and perhaps can never know. The 'something more' is also about our awareness of ourselves, the things that motivate and move us, the things we want to do, the relationships we wish to have. It touches our dreams about ourselves and the life we would love to lead. Finally, the 'something more' invites questions about our role and place in the world. Such questions as these are central, not marginal, to the aim of education. The pupil or teacher who has a good experience of learning will have been touched in some way or another by the 'something more' that has fallen like an unexpected shaft of sunlight upon the exigencies of the day. We have, for a moment, seen everything in a new and better light.

Education for active citizenship, arguably more than any other subject, brings together the five dimensions of learning. There are elements of information about society and the way it works that we need to be able to repeat. As citizens we need to learn to learn, to learn to do and to learn to be. But as citizens we need – perhaps more than anything else – the ability to become 'something more'. It is here that role models are needed to inspire and encourage this sense of the extra dimensions brought to citizenship by the salient leaders of our time. People of the calibre of Nelson Mandela have clearly had an impact that stretches far beyond their own countries. These leaders need not all be famous statesmen. Most cultures have their folk heroes, but it is also the case that most local communities have people – some of them young people – who inspire others to emulate them.

This theme is taken up in one of the exercises that CSV regularly uses in courses and training for citizenship education. The activity is called the Ideal Citizen. Students are invited to present as graphically as possible their insight into what constitutes the ideal citizen. There is, of course, no such person, but the discussion raises important questions of the qualities that we most value in ourselves and other people. It is this sense of 'something more', something that is compellingly attractive, or powerfully courageous and admirable, that gives these reflections their energy and focus.

Challenge: local government and community organizations

Citizenship education prompts local government, community organizations and schools to learn to work more closely together. Just as the purpose of education is to create learning, so the purpose of local government and community organizations is to create community. More exactly, the task is to offer an infrastructure of support and services that help people develop and sustain healthy communities around democratic values. The success of citizenship education will depend upon the extent to which the education sector can work with others to create shared agendas around shared values.

Many schools are setting up citizenship conferences with representatives from their local communities. These aim to identify shared concerns and joint activities. Citizenship education will, in the end, succeed or fail to the extent that it is encouraged and supported by institutions and individuals who are prepared to work on a shared vision and a common purpose in settings where neither can be taken for granted.

The challenge to education

The protagonists in the education sector, therefore, face a threefold challenge:

1. to provide appropriate professional support – training (initial teacher training and continuing professional development), consultancy and access to local resources – for teachers who are tackling the challenge of creating learning around citizenship education;
2. to work with other (local) government departments and agencies to achieve joined-up strategies for fostering active citizenship that take democratic involvement seriously locally, regionally and nationally;
3. to work with local government and community partners on a shared vision and a common purpose in settings where neither can be taken for granted.

Notes

1. Crick Report, para 1.5.
2. Local Government Information Unit (2000) *Citizenship: Challenges for councils*, LGIU/Institute for Citizenship, London.
3. This section draws upon an address by Professor Bart McGettrick of Glasgow University to the Four Nations Conference on citizenship education held in Glasgow, 27–29 September 2001. The conference was organized by the Institute for Global Ethics with support from the Gordon Cook Foundation.
4. McGettrick, address to the Four Nations Conference.

PART III:

HOW – How schools are meeting the challenge

- **Chapter 13: A whole-school strategy for education for active citizenship**
  Here we explore the importance of a whole-school strategy that will both meet the requirements of the Citizenship Order and bring wider benefits to the school and its wider communities.
- **Chapter 14: The six challenges**
  We identify a sequence of six challenges that face schools and their communities as they plan, implement and develop citizenship education. These challenges include:
  - leadership;
  - curriculum development;
  - professional development;
  - management, structures and inspection;
  - context: governance, finance, buildings and partnerships;
  - inspection.

Notes on the case studies and commentaries

1. **Examples in main text:** The main body text is illustrated with appropriate *brief* examples of education for active citizenship.
2. **Boxed case studies:** These brief studies have been chosen because they show some of the imaginative and encouraging ways in which schools have tackled the challenges of citizenship education. In most cases we offer a CSV commentary on these case studies that links them to the themes in the main text. The studies include: The Deanes School, Colne Community College, Deptford Green School, The Anglo-European School, Lipson Community College, and Marshfields Special School.
3. **School commentaries:** We offer a running commentary from three schools on the ways in which they are handling key issues raised in the areas touched on in our sequence of six challenges:

St Peter's Collegiate School
Compton Park
Wolverhampton
W Midlands WV3 9DU
School: Secondary voluntary aided. Mixed. Roll – 1,057
Head: Huw Bishop
Citizenship Education Coordinator: Julie Lawton (Deputy Head), Head of Pastoral and PSHE / Citizenship
CSV contact: Cicely Thomas, Head of Careers and History

The Nobel School
Mobbsbury Way
Stevenage
Herts SG2 0HS
School: Secondary comprehensive. Roll – 900
Head: Robert Whatmough
Citizenship education: Liz Byrne, Head of RE (from September 2001)

Tanfield School
Good St
Stanley
Co Durham DH9 8AY
School: Secondary comprehensive. Roll – 636. A CSV Lighthouse School
Head: Archie Howatt
Coordinator Active Citizenship and CSV contact: Ann Nelson

13

A whole-school strategy for education for active citizenship

The need for a whole-school strategy

We recognise that citizenship education can be enhanced by and can make significant contributions to – as well as draw upon – other subjects and aspects of the curriculum. We stress, however, that citizenship education is education for citizenship, behaving and acting as a citizen, therefore it is not just knowledge of citizenship and civic society; it also implies developing values, skills and understanding.

(Crick Report, para 3.1)

Aim: Here we:
- list the requirements of the Order;
- show the wider benefits of education for active citizenship;
- identify the impact of active citizenship on local communities;
- provide a framework for the development of a whole-school strategy.

Citizenship education demands a whole-school approach, because education for active citizenship impacts not only on everyone in the school, but also upon the school's work with the communities that it serves (see Chapters 15 and 16).

The challenge of citizenship education is to create a citizenship curriculum for the whole school that: a) meets the requirements of the Order; b) supports the vision and mission of the school; and c) contributes to the school's wider communities (see Figure 13.1). CSV's experience through working directly and indirectly with over 1,000 schools is encouraging. Many schools are well on the way to meeting the requirements of the Order and are already benefiting from promoting learning through student participation in their schools and wider communities.

We shall take each issue in turn and then – on the basis of our experience – offer d) a *framework* around which heads, their senior managers, staff, pupils and other stakeholders can audit, plan, develop and review an effective curriculum for citizenship education. This framework will provide the context for the challenges discussed in Chapter 14.

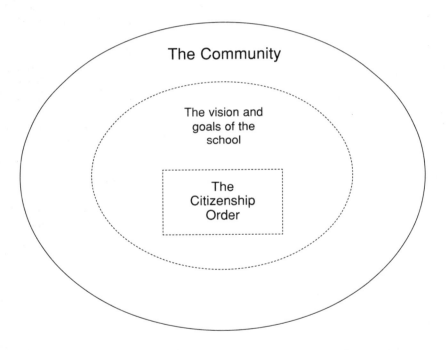

Figure 13.1   *The challenge of creating a citizenship curriculum*

The requirements of the Order

Citizenship education is a unique and complex subject

Citizenship education is different from every other subject in that it combines a whole school and community dimension with a new and complex foundation subject that will be assessed and accredited. Furthermore, citizenship education is an entitlement for *every pupil* in key stages 3 and 4. Citizenship education, therefore, brings with it a distinctive set of challenges that go beyond its role as a foundation subject. The challenge of creating a citizenship curriculum for the whole school is the single most complex and demanding element of what is required by the Order.

The wider purpose of citizenship education, as we have seen in previous chapters, goes beyond the learning outcomes; it aims 'at no less than a change in the political culture of this country both nationally and locally: for people to think of themselves as active citizens, willing, able and equipped to have an influence in public life'.[1] This poses a challenge to the whole school in relation to its wider impact on the communities it serves.

Citizenship education involves everyone

Citizenship education concerns the life of the whole school; it involves everyone in the school. Every pupil, member of staff and governor should be aware of the part that he or she can play; and, where appropriate, other stakeholders – parents, local government, business and people from voluntary organizations – should be involved at some level in the work of citizenship education.

Democracy in action

Citizenship education is also about democracy in action. Students and pupils have a significant part to play through participating in the life of the school. They can and often do take part in making decisions that affect their own lives and learning in school (referred to below). For example, students often support younger peers through tutoring, mentoring, and mediation programmes. Students are increasingly involved in school, year and class councils. Increasingly they have links with the local town or city council. In Manchester, for example, the City

Council has developed a partnership with a network of school councils. In some schools, students take an active and democratic part in reviewing the learning and teaching within the school. Pupils and students are increasingly involved with governors' meetings or the appointment of new staff. Student engagement goes beyond discussion and debate and extends to a whole variety of activities beyond the school (see Chapter 14, under The curriculum, pages 205–18).

Community partnerships

Citizenship education also requires pupils to learn through taking positive action in their local and wider communities. In the chapters that follow we shall note how a variety of schools in different parts of the country and serving very different communities have tackled the challenge of building local partnerships that can offer pupils the chance to engage with active learning in the community.

Values-centred

Citizenship education is values-centred and, as we have seen in Chapter 11, the values and dispositions described in the Crick Report sit easily under the five values headings of the new politics.

Critical success factors

If citizenship education is to achieve its ambitious aims, four critical conditions will be met from the start:

1. Nothing substantial can or will be achieved without the active *support of the head* and the senior managers. 'If the head isn't behind citizenship, you can forget it,' said one citizenship coordinator with his usual directness. 'Fortunately,' he added, 'our head is fully committed.'
2. There must be *a clear vision for citizenship education* that relates the purpose of the whole school to the larger goal of the Citizenship Order.
3. Staff, students and parents must be helped to understand *the importance of the big picture* of citizenship education and be clear about the ways in which they can contribute to its success.
4. Citizenship education must be *well managed* and take imaginative account of what else is going on in the school. As we have seen from

teachers' initial reactions to the Order (Chapter 4) their overwhelming anxiety concerned fitting citizenship into an already
packed timetable. The most effective citizenship programmes are
those that draw their energy from the wider purpose of the school
and contribute to the success of every dimension of school life.

> We believe that we can make a quantum leap in achievement if, in addition to
> academic skills, we develop in our pupils a better sense of themselves as
> agents of change – in their school, in their community, in the wider society and
> in the world. Through citizenship education we see exciting opportunities to
> build links between developing pupils as active and informed citizens, shaping
> their attitude to learning and opening up for them new horizons for what the
> future might bring.
>
> (The senior staff at Deptford Green School in South London)

It can happen

The Deanes School in Benfleet, Essex, illustrates vividly the ways in
which one school has embarked upon a whole-school strategy for citizenship education. Much of the work predates the Citizenship Order
and inevitably there will be more to do to cover all aspects of the Order.

Case study 1: CSV commentary on the Deanes School

The Deanes School offers a strong example of the imaginative way in which a
comprehensive (specialist) school is meeting the challenge of citizenship education. The case study illustrates clearly how citizenship education serves the larger
purposes of the school and its communities locally and abroad. In other words the
vision of the school embraces but is larger than the programme of study.

CSV has enjoyed a significant association with the school through the Barclays
New Futures programme.

Vision

The school has developed education for active citizenship around the clearly
stated vision of the Headteacher, Paul Beashel. He describes his vision for the
school in these words:

> We believe that the key to success in the future lies in our students developing high
> standards of basic skills together with an ongoing desire for learning and a real zest for

life. Academic achievement alone is not enough, however. We expect students to be self-motivated, confident and able to take on the challenges which lie ahead. We also expect them to be aware of the world around them and the needs of others. These attitudes and values are developed through the ethos of the school as a caring community.

Breadth and variety

The breadth and variety of the school's citizenship education illustrates one way in which the taught and whole curriculum can be enriched by Active Learning in the Community (ALC). It is important to remember that building up a range of such opportunities takes time, and needs the active commitment of staff. Members of staff generally support initiatives of this sort when they can identify clearly: 1) the benefits to the students; 2) the benefits to their own work; 3) the support and recognition that they will be given if they take part.

Entitlement

Jim Mulligan from CSV knows the school well. 'We are very aware that schools such as the Deanes School have been working for years to build up their citizenship profile. Schools that are only starting their journey should not be discouraged – the longest journey starts with the first step.'

He goes on:

The Deanes School is a long way down the road of introducing every student to the experiences described here. But in common with most other schools that are making strong progress on citizenship education, they are not quite there yet – as they would be the first to admit. There are still young people, usually the disaffected, shy or those with low self-esteem who are not yet fully included. Strategies for involving such groups might include:

- mentoring/peer support;
- developing their own interests in the context of citizenship;
- active involvement in a subject such as drama, music or sports coaching;
- links to work experience or vocational studies.

All schools need systematically to review how far they are able to include every young person and enable them to work on projects that will interest them.

A whole-school strategy

The Deanes Foundation School was opened in Benfleet, Essex in 1971. It is a modern, purpose-built comprehensive catering for just over 1,000 students of all abilities. In 1998 it was designated a DfEE sports college. The school is situated in a semi-rural setting with extensive grounds including 19 acres of playing fields and four extensive hard play areas. There is a nursery on site and the school is a centre for adult education.

Student participation

Citizenship through the school council

The Deanes School has year councils with a boy and girl from each tutor group elected to meet during lunchtimes every other week. The school council consists of two male and two female students elected from each year council. The aim of the councils is to empower students to take an active role in the school.

Education for citizenship through the Mock Trial Competition

In recent years the Deanes School has entered teams for the regional Mock Trial Competition.* Teams of 14 Year 8 and Year 9 students play the roles of magistrates, defence and prosecution lawyers, court clerk, usher and witnesses. Recent scenarios have included a nightclub assault case and a case of vandalism. In 1999 the team won the regional competition and went to the national finals.

Citizenship through projects

The school supports a range of projects including:

- **The Roache Valley Way**, a 23-mile-long footpath that has been restored by the Deanes School and Essex County Council. It now appears on Ordnance Survey maps and is recognised by the Long Distance Walkers Association. The school has written and published a guidebook.
- **The school environment,** including a memorial garden and refurbished cycle shed, a project for which students and parents worked together to raise funds.
- **Work with older people.** For the past 20 years the Deanes School students have supported two local residential homes for the elderly. The students provide regular entertainment and concerts and help with serving lunch.
- **Nature trail.** The Deanes School won a Barclays New Futures award to develop a nature trail with Little Haven Hospice for sick children, which is near the Deanes School.
- **Citizenship through the Changemakers Project** in Year 8. All Year 8 students are involved in projects of their choosing. Projects have included: analysis of students' and teachers' journeys to school; reform of the canteen queuing system; making a rocking horse worth £1,000, which was raffled for the children's hospice.

* Organized by the Citizenship Foundation

- **Partnerships.** The Deanes School does not attempt to develop everything from within its own resources, particularly in the area of education for active citizenship. The staff and pupils work closely with partners from the wider community, including CSV/Barclays New Futures, the Duke of Edinburgh Award Scheme, Changemakers and the Trident Gold Award Scheme.
- **International projects.** The Deanes School runs an exciting range of international links and partnerships including work with Germany, Japan, France and Kenya. These are described in more detail in Chapter 16.

— The benefits of a whole-school strategy —

Effective citizenship education clearly demands significant investment in terms of leadership, curriculum development, management and staff support across the school. An investment on this scale must be justified in terms of the rewards that it brings to the school in terms of learning, behaviour, relationships and benefits to the community. We have noted that the Deanes School was already well on the way to meeting the requirements for citizenship education before the Order was even passed. The reason for this is, of course, that the leadership of the school believed that education for active citizenship brings educational benefits that go beyond the confines of the Citizenship Order and its programme of study.

CSV has undertaken two significant investigations into the value of education for active citizenship: 1) the CSV Lighthouse Schools; and 2) a piece of research into the impact of student participation upon standards.

CSV Lighthouse Schools

CSV worked closely with a group of CSV Lighthouse Schools in the late 1990s to explore in more depth the benefits that education for active citizenship can and does bring to students, schools and their communities. The results were encouraging and give us grounds to be confident about the value of citizenship education. It is demonstrably a powerful stimulus to personal development and lifelong learning as well as the occasion of civic understanding and engagement.

Active learning in the community

During the 1990s CSV developed work on 'service learning' – the phrase 'active learning in the community' is often preferred in the UK, a methodology that links learning with service to other people. In what follows we shall simply refer to 'active learning in the community' (ALC) for the sake of consistency and clarity. ALC offered an ideal approach for education for active citizenship. CSV enjoyed help from colleagues in the United States who had over a number of years refined the techniques into an established methodology. By 1997 CSV had developed and tested programmes for paired reading and active citizenship through community involvement. It had by that time become evident that citizenship education was about to be given a new priority in the national curriculum.

Testing the approach

CSV seized the moment to develop partnerships with a group of interested schools across the country. The aim was to explore, test and evaluate ALC strategies not only in individual classes or year groups but across the whole school. An initial network of nine CSV Lighthouse Schools was augmented by a further 20 Associate Schools across the UK. The Esmee Fairbairn Charitable Trust supported the initiative and an evaluation was organized through Lynne Gerlach of the International School Effectiveness and Improvement Centre (ISEIC) at the London Institute of Education.

This book draws extensively on the work of the CSV Lighthouse Schools[2] and the following pages are amply illustrated with examples from these pioneering institutions. The ALC methodology is explored in depth in Chapter 14, under The curriculum.

The CSV Lighthouse Schools developed and tested a number of approaches in the taught and whole curriculum. This included formal lessons, projects and initiatives in school democracy. Colne Community School in Brightlingsea, Essex worked closely with CSV and achieved an ambitious range of projects and activities across the life of the school (see Case study 2 below).

Evaluation findings – 'ALC adds substantial value to students' education'

'CSV and the Lighthouse Schools are well placed to make a significant contribution to the delivery of the citizenship curriculum,' commented project manager Peter Hayes[3] on the findings of the independent report on the work of the CSV Lighthouse Schools. 'Their commitment and expertise will, on the evidence of the evaluation exercise, enable them to offer exemplars of successful strategies to help other schools develop their programmes of citizenship and PSHE in the context of lifelong learning.'

The evaluator[4] concluded that ALC enables schools to 'add substantial value to students' education' through programmes of active citizenship. She set out the main findings of the evaluation of education for active citizenship in the CSV Lighthouse Schools as follows:

- **Added value:** The Lighthouse Schools are adding substantial value to students' education through planning, supporting, endorsing and promoting approaches to community-based learning and the creation of opportunities for active citizenship.
- **Developed key skills:** The Lighthouse Schools have improved standards of personal, social and citizenship development and have contributed substantially to the development of key skills.
- **Improved learning:** The experience of active citizenship enhances learning and improves personal and social development. The students increase in maturity, gain self-esteem and confidence, develop their sense of moral and social responsibility and demonstrate an increased willingness to contribute productively to their school and wider communities. Students are better able to sustain productive relationships, manage change more optimistically and with increased confidence, and are more accepting of diversity.
- **Developed experiential/reflective practice:** The emphasis on active experiential and reflective practice within schools committed to developing ALC or active community-based citizenship education is a significant contributory factor in improving progress in students' learning and attainment.
- **Supported participation in a learning community:** Active community-based educational opportunities have a positive influence on students' level of involvement in school life and contribute to the creation of a sense of the schools as 'learning communities'.
- **Value of development plans:** School development plans where they target active learning or related activities do have a positive impact on the status, quality and range of provision. They can be further enhanced by focusing more closely on the impact of activities on students' learning.
- **Membership of the Lighthouse Schools Project:** This does endorse, support and raise the status of citizenship education and its positive impact on students' learning. The project could further develop its role to improve the impact of active learning on staff and students' learning.

Case study 2: whole-school approach – Colne Community School, a CSV Lighthouse School

Colne Community School is a mixed school with approximately 1,300 pupils in Brightlingsea, Essex. As a CSV Lighthouse School, Colne took a leading part in the CSV-initiated US exchange with Valdosta City School in Georgia. Terry Creissen is the Principal and Candy Garbett (at the time of this report) was the Link Coordinator.

Commitment to ALC

The school has been committed to ALC for many years, and worked closely in the mid-1990s with CSV and CSV's US partners to develop a whole-school strategy for ALC. Community involvement is now embedded in the ethos of the school and radiates out from both form and year groups that seek to engender a sense of self, belonging and relationships. In Years 7 and 8 circle time is seen as important in order to give students the chance to reflect together on their experiences at school and to offer appropriate feedback to staff.

Innovative projects

- **School council:** A boy and girl from each form are elected to be year council reps. Students negotiate and contribute to making policy. A recent example involved the use of mobile phones by students in school. Emphasis is often on charitable work and fund-raising. Senior school representatives from each Year 11 form elect to receive training as mentors or volunteer to take on other responsibilities. It was a Colne idea to try out different voting systems within different year groups!
- **Governors' committees:** Students are represented on governors' committees and are involved in interviews and staff recruitment.
- **Sense of community:** Year-group, key stage and whole-school assemblies reinforce the sense of community, responsibility and reward and are frequently used to recognize and celebrate achievements.
- **Changemakers – student-led projects:** All students participate in a Changemakers project in Year 7 and are encouraged to continue with their involvement beyond the first year.
- **Citizenship projects:**
  - international ALC exchange (CSV Lighthouse Schools);
  - World Challenge 2002;
  - literacy project (Year 9 supports Year 7);
  - drugs education peer group project (Year 11 work with Year 8);
  - peer-led sex education (Year 12 work with Years 9 and 10);

- PACE programme for personal and social development;
- student links with primary schools;
- project liaison with Brightlingsea Town Council (Year 9 students and local skate park);
- community coordinators' meeting involving crime prevention panel, youth service, police, school nurse, Town and District Council reps.

Dissemination is through review and celebration, the termly magazine, *Colne Courier*, form reps and tutorial. Each faculty has a commitment to provide a community dimension to the curriculum area.

The school has received the Sportsmark Award and has been involved in fund-raising activities for the Kosovo Appeal and replacement of school equipment. Pupils promoted World Book Day by participating in events such as book-cover design and quizzes, and the school ran a numeracy day for prospective students. A student involved in the school council stated: 'We feel responsible to our fellow students and want to do whatever we can to help them.'

The contribution of citizenship education to standards

CSV's second investigation was into the impact of student participation upon standards.

The majority of education reforms since the mid-1980s have addressed the issue of measurable academic standards. The concern with standards was generally welcomed but in recent years there has been a growing concern that the standards agenda – with its emphasis on measurement and testing – is in conflict with the wider purpose of education.

The revised national curriculum

The introduction to the revised national curriculum states clearly:

The school curriculum should aim to provide opportunities for all pupils to learn and to achieve. It should develop pupils' enjoyment of, and commitment to, learning to encourage and stimulate the best possible progress and the highest attainment for all pupils. It should build on pupils' strengths, interests and experiences and develop their confidence in their capacity to learn and work independently and collaboratively. It should equip pupils with the essential learning skills of literacy, numeracy, and information technology capability, and promote an enquiring mind and the capacity to think rationally.[5]

Alongside this agenda sits the broader government commitment to deliver a social agenda, an education that will equip young people to cope effectively with the challenges and rewards of modern life. These sentiments were expressed in the foreword to the curriculum materials:

> The school curriculum should aim to prepare all pupils for the opportunities, responsibilities and experiences of life.
>
> It should pass on the enduring values of society, develop pupils' integrity and autonomy and help them to be responsible and caring citizens capable of contributing to the development of a just society. It should promote equal opportunities and enable pupils to challenge discrimination and stereotyping. It should promote pupils' spiritual, moral, social and cultural development and develop their knowledge and understanding of different beliefs and cultures, including an appreciation of their diversity, and of their influence on individuals and on societies. It should develop their awareness, understanding, and respect for the environments in which they live, and secure their commitment to sustainable development at a personal, local, national and global level.
>
> The school curriculum should promote pupils' self-esteem and emotional well-being and help them to form and maintain worthwhile and satisfying relationships based on respect for themselves and for others at home, at school, at work and in the community. It should develop their ability to relate to others and work for the common good. It should enable pupils to respond positively to opportunities, challenges and responsibilities and to cope with change and adversity.

The writer then makes the connection with a new education agenda, the commitment to *lifelong learning*.

The national curriculum 'should prepare pupils for the next steps in their learning, training and employment and equip them to make informed choices at school and throughout their lives, enabling them to appreciate the relevance of their achievements to life and society outside school, including leisure, community engagement and employment'.

Teachers ask how these two agendas fit together. The answer is, on the face of it, quite clear: '*these two aims reinforce each other* [my italics]. The personal and social development of pupils plays a significant part in their ability to learn and to achieve. Development in both areas is essential to raising standards of attainment for all pupils.'

A damaging and unnecessary tension

Values and standards are united in theory, but in practice they are encouraged to compete. Standards are promoted and publicized through league tables. This significantly affects, for good or ill, the public standing of the school. The consequence can be a tension between standards-based education – where the league tables reign supreme – and values-centred education as defined, for example, by McGettrick (see Chapter 12).

The CSV inquiry into the impact of citizenship on standards

During the period of preparation for citizenship education it became clear, not least from the remarks of David Blunkett himself, that the DfEE and its senior advisers were actively interested in making a more positive link between citizenship education, active learning and standards. The Department invited CSV to work with the education consultant, Derry Hannam, on an investigation of the links between student participation and standards of achievement.[6]

Positive findings

The evidence from the CSV Hannam Report, which was based on a small sample of 12 schools chosen for their high levels of student participation, showed that, in terms of low exclusions, good attendance, staff and student assessment and exam results, these schools performed *better* than might have been expected.

As far as exam results were concerned the evidence was encouraging. In participative schools the indicator of five (or more) GCSEs at grades A*-G was significantly higher than in comparable non-participative schools. When we take five A*-C grades, the difference is present but less marked.

In other words student participation in well-run schools is associated with better-than-average performance and outcomes.[7] It is also clear that citizenship education can – for the very reasons set out in the Hannam Report – be used to support educational reform, school improvement and lifelong learning.

If citizenship education is to play a central role in the development of education during the early years of the 21st century, the connection between citizenship education, school improvement and lifelong learning needs to be made more explicit at every level. One commentator has aptly said, 'The successful introduction of active citizenship education is unlikely unless pupils value their education as a lifelong process – an education they are increasingly involved in managing for themselves.'[8]

Uniting the twin aims of education

At present there is a real danger that the big picture of citizenship will be lost somewhere in the interstices of a curriculum that is packed with detail but short on deliberate strategies *to unite the twin aims of education*. The experience of other countries such as Norway, where education for democracy is relatively advanced, is that only a minority of schools take student participation seriously. The approach is taken up quickly by those schools with headteachers and a nucleus of staff who are already disposed to work democratically. Hannam comments that these teachers 'speak of feeling legitimised by the Reform in the same way that a few English teachers speak of the Citizenship Order. *Bringing about change beyond the 25% has proved to be a very slow process however.'* [9]

Community involvement

Citizenship education – under various names – has already shown that it can make a significant contribution to the quality of life in local communities. Students are involved in everything from environmental projects to community festivals, from personal support for people with special needs to running IT courses for parents and other adults. A whole school approach to community involvement greatly strengthens the value and impact of citizenship education on local communities.

Communities benefit from education for active citizenship in three ways:

1. The good service provided by the young people's events, personal support, coaching for games, newsletters, tutoring, environmental improvements, etc.
2. The positive relationships built up between the young people and sometimes-suspicious local people. Intergenerational projects can be particularly valuable in this respect.
3. The stronger relationship between the school and community organizations, a form of social capital upon which further initiatives or developments can be built.

In Chapter 14, under The curriculum: Involving students, we give a wide range of project outlines depicting the range of activities in which students are involved. Here are just three further examples to give a taste of the ways in which schools can through their students make an important contribution to the quality of life in their local communities:

- **Water-based physical education:** Senior students are working on a range of accredited water-based physical education activities with severely disabled young people from local special schools.

  Student involvement: 10 in S5 and 2 in S6, Whitehill Secondary School, Glasgow

  (Source: Barclays New Futures)
- **Intergenerational – oral history:** This is an oral history project involving pupils from Years 8 and 9 and the residents of a local home for elderly Asian women, culminating in the production of a booklet for distribution to local feeder primary schools and within the local community.

  Little Ilford School, London E12

  (Source: Barclays New Futures)
- **Community health – health café enterprise:** A French-style café is being developed at the college in order to entertain and provide a stimulating learning environment for the residents of a local home for the blind and senior citizens in the community. The students will organize a weekly event, prepare and serve refreshments and develop a range of learning resources.

  Student involvement: 9 in Year 12 and 9 in Year 13, Eccles College, Manchester

  (Source: Barclays New Futures)

– A framework for a whole-school strategy –

Peter Mitchell is the former Director of Education for Camden. His experience includes being a secondary headteacher in inner London; Chief Adviser for Leicestershire; and Senior Tutor at the Institute of Education, London, with responsibility for initial teacher training. CSV is grateful for his contributing the following framework for developing a whole-school strategy. The text that follows and parts of the forthcoming chapters draw on his CSV book on promoting citizenship education through active learning in the community.[10]

CSV has consistently advocated a systematic approach to planning the citizenship curriculum across the life and learning of the whole school. This approach includes involving pupils in each stage of the planning and review process. The sequence of six challenges and accompanying case studies are designed to illustrate this central principle.

Frameworks for participation

Frameworks or strategic plans are familiar to schools. They can be outlined in such detail that they leave little scope for initiative by teachers and pupils. A framework designed to support education for active citizenship must aim to secure the status of this work alongside a revised national curriculum, and remain committed to the involvement of *pupils in the planning* of their learning.

The framework outlined here should be used in the context of the revised national curriculum and the Order for Citizenship Education. It will also need to be seen in the context of parallel curriculum initiatives such as careers education, the healthy schools standard and education for a sustainable environment. All these aspects of the curriculum require a coherent whole-school approach to planning.

Education for active citizenship grows from a curriculum that offers young people the chance to develop their knowledge, skills and understanding through ALC. The thinking and experience behind this approach are further developed in Chapter 14, under The curriculum.

A vision statement for education for active citizenship

CSV's vision statement for education for active citizenship offers a clear description of the nature and purpose of active learning in the community. It provides the starting point: 'Active learning in the community gives every child and young person an opportunity to understand the nature and practice of being a citizen. Students and pupils will learn through experiencing real life responsibilities that help to improve the lives of others. These experiences will be their introduction to active citizenship.' [11]

The school curriculum will take account of national policy and priorities. It will also respond to the needs of pupils and the community. The DfES/QCA has in the revised national curriculum published learning outcomes for each of the three strands of effective citizenship (social behaviour, community involvement and political literacy). The aims give direction to the work of the school and expression to what the school values. Broad statements covering such aspects of school life as social behaviour, community links and types of learning will indicate the level of support there is for ALC and citizenship education.

The school's organization for managing the implementation will outline senior teacher responsibilities, identify curriculum planning to be undertaken, including assessment and evaluation, and identify teachers' in-service training needs.

The school's community context

Schools vary in the significance of the local community to the life of a school. A school's understanding of where their pupils live in terms of social and economic activity will be increasingly important if active learning in the community is to be a significant part of the curriculum.

Schools working in partnership with local business, voluntary groups and the local authority will open up opportunities that enhance not only active learning in the community but also employability and lifelong learning. Schools can foster networking between community organizations and contribute to raising the quality of life in communities. The local authority is in a strong position to promote networks at a local level, thus supporting the work of schools.

Parents are key partners with schools in raising standards and levels of achievement. In addition to supporting basic skills development and homework they can work with young people in identifying service learning projects. They can act as advisers or mentors for young people working in the community.

The relationship between a school and its communities is explored further in Chapter 14, under Context.

Curriculum planning

The sections on curriculum planning and development are based on the Kolb Cycle,[12] which is commonly used in planning experiential learning (see Figure 13.2). We move in a continuous spiral from our present experience, through reflecting on that experience, to learning from the experience and applying it in new or similar situations. The cycle is driven by the vision and aims of the learning organization – in this case the school. The leadership provides these aims and the means to support them, which is where we shall begin.

Framework of challenges

Our framework for developing a whole-school strategy is set out under six challenges and these provide the heading and contents of Chapter 14:

1. **Leadership**
   The leadership offered by the head and the leadership style encouraged throughout the school, including among the students, is critical to successful education for active citizenship.

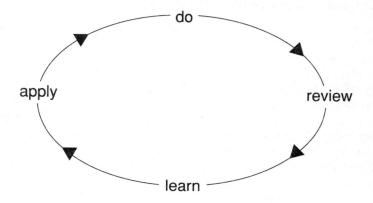

Figure 13.2   *The Kolb Cycle*

2. **The curriculum**
   Curriculum development is by far the most complex and demanding aspect of creating effective education for citizenship. The elements of the process are broken down into six steps:
   – aims and objectives;
   – audit;
   – learning experiences;
   – the global dimension;
   – student participation;
   – assessment, evaluation and research.
3. **Professional development**
   Work on curriculum development will bring to light issues for continuing professional development.
4. **Management**
   The task of management is to ensure that the aims and objectives of the citizenship curriculum are realized in ways that are clear, transparent and accounted for.
5. **Context**
   An exploration is needed of the ways in which governance, finance and the school's community partnerships support education for active citizenship in and beyond the classroom.
6. **Inspection**
   Citizenship education will be inspected and this can be a source of encouragement to schools with a well-developed citizenship curriculum.

Whole-school approach

A coherent whole-school approach to the planning of learning is essential if the status and importance of this work are to be acknowledged.

In future, the teaching of all themes outside the national curriculum should consider the contribution of learning outcomes to improving pupils' motivation, to raising standards of achievement and to school improvement.

In opening up opportunities for work and study outside school, active learning in the community is contributing to the debate on the changing nature of education and schooling in the 21st century.

Summary

- **The task of citizenship education** is to create a citizenship curriculum for the whole school that:
  - meets the requirements of the Order;
  - supports the vision and mission of the school;
  - contributes to the school's wider communities.
  CSV's experience through working directly and indirectly with over 1,000 schools is encouraging. Many schools are well on the way to meeting the requirements of the Order and are already benefiting from promoting learning through student participation in their schools and wider communities.
- **A sequence of six citizenship challenges** provides a useful framework in which to plan and implement citizenship education through active learning in the community:
  - leadership;
  - curriculum planning (aims and objectives; audit; learning experiences; the global dimension; student participation; assessment, evaluation and research);
  - professional development;
  - management;
  - context (including community partnerships);
  - inspection.

Notes

1. Crick Report, para 1.5.
2. The CSV Lighthouse Schools included Tanfield School (commentary throughout Part III) and Marshfields School (see Chapter 14, under Context). The Deanes School (see above), St James C of E Middle School (see Chapter 14, under Inspection) and Plantsbrook School (see Chapter 14) became Associate CSV Lighthouse Schools and are referred to extensively in these pages.
3. Subsequently Acting Director of CSV Education for Citizenship.
4. Evaluation of Lighthouse Schools carried out by Lynne Gerlach, CSV/ISEIC, July 1999.
5. The review of the national curriculum in England – consultation materials (1999).
6. Derry Hannam/CSV (2001) A pilot study to evaluate the impact of the student participation aspects of the Citizenship Order on standards of education in secondary schools, Report to the DfEE (Hannam Report).
7. See Chapter 14, under The curriculum.
8. Peter Mitchell, previously CEO of the London Borough of Camden.
9. Hannam Report.
10. Peter Mitchell (1999) *A Curriculum Framework for Citizenship and Social Education*, CSV.
11. Peter Mitchell (1999) *A Curriculum Framework for Citizenship and Social Education*, in consultation with CSV staff.
12. D A Kolb (1984) Do, *Review, Learn, Apply: A simple guide to experiential learning*, Blackwell, Oxford.

The six challenges

Leadership

There can be no effective whole-school strategy for citizenship education without the full support of the head and the senior management team (SMT). The unique task of the headteacher is to foster a culture of mission-centred leadership among senior staff.

The role of leadership in citizenship education is to offer the vision, the *motivation* and the *means* to enable members of the school to work together to create, provide and review the learning experiences that meet the requirements of the national (citizenship) curriculum in the context of the declared aims of the school.

This is a complex, creative and challenging task.

The context of leadership

Figure 14.1 offers just one way of viewing the task of the head and SMT in promoting leadership for citizenship education across five dimensions of school life:

1. **Values and vision**
   The central concern of the head and SMT is the well-being and achievements of the students, and in the case of citizenship education their legal entitlement to experience and respond to a wide range of learning experiences. The values and vision of the school community are therefore crucial to this task.
2. **Curriculum development**
   Secondly, effective leadership demonstrates a clear understanding of how the taught and whole curriculum can and should be developed around the vision and values of the school. This involves the seven-

step process that will be developed later in the chapter: a) setting aims and objectives; b) audit; c) mapping and planning; d) creating learning experiences (pedagogy); e) embedding a global dimension; f) student participation; and g) assessment, evaluation and research.

3. **Motivation**

Thirdly, the head and leadership team will have the insight and skill to motivate staff, students and stakeholders around the vision and values of the school and of the school's commitment to citizenship education.

4. **Quality management**

Fourthly, good leadership will foster quality management that will make it all happen in practice. Management involves the allocation of responsibilities and resources to achieve, monitor and evaluate the vision, aims, objectives and targets of citizenship education across the life of the school.

5. **Boundary management**

Finally, effective leadership will enable the school to relate to the needs, challenges and opportunities presented by the school's local and wider communities. We shall refer to this as 'boundary management'.

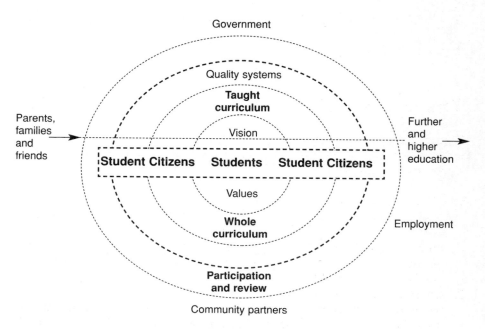

Figure 14.1 *The context in which leadership is exercised*

Leaders and leadership

Democratic leadership is particularly important in relation to citizenship education, which specifically encourages democratic participation across the school. Students, when in school, are both learners and members (citizens) of the school community. In both roles they need to develop the experience and skills of leadership. The nature and quality of the leadership that is modelled by the headteacher and staff will significantly affect the way in which students understand and develop their own contributions to the life of the school.

Bringing it together

The critical issue, of course, is for the head and the leadership team to bring these five dimensions together into a coherent and dynamic whole. Citizenship education, because it directly impinges on every aspect of school life, offers a distinctive challenge to everyone with leadership responsibility in the school, and that includes students and non-teaching staff as well as the head and senior managers. These five dimensions of school life in which leadership is both exercised and fostered can be represented even more simply, as in Figure 14.2. Some readers may find it a useful context against which to map the challenges that will be addressed in the following chapters.

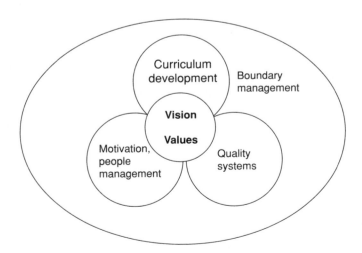

Figure 14.2 *The five dimensions of leadership for citizenship education*

Dimension 1: Vision

It is the unique responsibility of the head to nourish the vision around which the school develops its life and celebrates its achievements. A good head will draw others, including students, into refining and developing the vision, but there can be no escape from the fact that the head is responsible for holding the vision.

What is learnt in class and through the wider life of the school is directly relevant to citizenship education. It follows that the vision and values that inform the taught curriculum need to be consistent with the vision and values that underpin the wider life of the school community. It is the task of the head and those who share in the leadership of the school to ensure that this is the case. It is already clear that the schools where citizenship education is being promoted most strongly and effectively are schools with a clear and vigorous sense of the values and vision that sustain their work.

The effectiveness of education for active citizenship will stem directly from the way it is shaped and supported by the values and vision shared by the school community. Citizenship education is likely to be most powerful, imaginative and effective in those institutions where it is given a clear purpose linked to the wider mission of the school in its communities.

Vision and values

A vision[1] (see Figure 14.3) will directly or indirectly include statements about values. We have already seen (Chapter 10) that the key values of our time are increasingly focused on:

- freedom as autonomy;
- no authority without democracy; and
- no rights without responsibilities.

These values now influence the behaviour and attitudes in schools. They underpin the emphasis on:

- **lifelong learning** where learners choose and take responsibility for their own learning (freedom as autonomy);
- **student democratic participation** in the way the school is run and even developed (no authority without democracy);
- **formal agreements** between students, their parents and the school defining mutual obligations and expectations (no rights without responsibilities).

Vision and Values

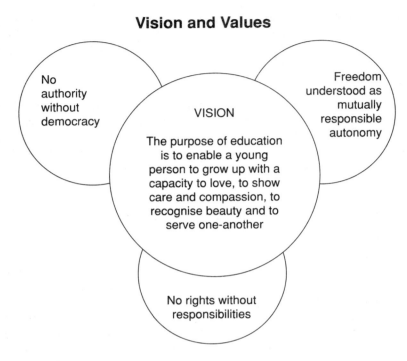

No authority without democracy

Freedom understood as mutually responsible autonomy

VISION

The purpose of education is to enable a young person to grow up with a capacity to love, to show care and compassion, to recognise beauty and to serve one-another

No rights without responsibilities

Figure 14.3   *Vision and values*

A good vision statement will also provide a platform on which all five dimensions of leadership can be developed. Tanfield School has this community mission statement:

> Tanfield School believes that community is the essence of democracy and is central to personal development and lifelong learning. We encourage our students to play an active part in the wider community in order to provide for and learn from society.

This vision is based on a clear set of values, linked with the curriculum and offers a strong basis around which to develop work with students, staff and the local community. It also says enough to suggest appropriate indicators for quality assurance.

The vision statement for Plantsbrook School is equally clear and to the point:

> At Plantsbrook School we aim to be a learning, caring, successful school serving the community and preparing our students for the opportunities of

adult life in the 21st century. We will work together in a spirit of mutual respect and co-operation serving the local community and utilising it to enrich our learning. We will prepare students to become responsible citizens, able to take advantage of the opportunities of adult life and be respectful of the values and cultures of others.

It is clear that the schools that link citizenship education to the main thrust of their vision are those that appear most excited about the prospect of education for active citizenship and most effective in its implementation. The case studies that intersperse this chapter all illustrate and confirm this point.

Leadership – the Nobel School

Robert Whatmough, Headteacher

1. **Developing the vision, 2001**
   The Nobel School is a vigorous and humane learning community in which high achievement *and creativity* are the expectation and the norm.

2. **Creating the curriculum**
   The vision in brief: a curriculum closer to what pupils and their parents want and we believe in (and which is less and less the outcome of external regulation); school organization that serves learning (and not a factory model that parcels out learning in hour-long chunks, day in and day out).

3. **Involving partners: parents, local organizations**
   A learning community where the core purpose of pupil learning is enhanced by the learning of parents, staff and governors.
   The Nobel School is designated as one of 82 training schools in the country, linked with the University of Hertfordshire and with the School Improvement and Advisory Service.
   In 2004 [we will be] a place where learning takes place for *all* with all that that implies... a community dimension offered to different sectors from pre-school to adult education.

4. **Supporting staff**
   Support for staff teaching citizenship is given by Robert Whatmough; Keith Weekes, Deputy Headteacher; and Liz Byrne, Head of RE (from September 2001).

5. **Reviewing progress**
   Currently an audit is being undertaken of citizenship across the school.

The strategy for the coming year is set out by the Headteacher in his vision statement, *The Year Ahead, Realising the Vision*.

Vision and citizenship

Deptford Green is a successful inner-city school in New Cross, South London. It has a roll of 672 boys and girls and has recently been given an achievement award. The school has a strong history of community involvement and is now campaigning to be recognized as a 'specialist school in citizenship'. The Headteacher, Keith Ajegbo, and senior managers have set out a vision for the school's development over the next few years. He is clear that citizenship education is central to this vision. 'Citizenship will take different forms in different schools but it requires schools which see it as a central part of their vision to lead the way. We wish to be one of those schools.' Members of staff are equally clear about their shared vision. 'The school should be a centre of learning for the whole community. We aim to enable our pupils to take an active part in the regeneration of the local community and we will encourage the community to take an active part in our school.'

Leadership and vision

Deptford Green: a vision for a citizenship school

'At Deptford Green citizenship is a way of learning and a way of life.'

Deptford Green is a successful inner-city school in New Cross, South London. The local area has a classic inner-city profile. The most recent figures show that 58 per cent of pupils are eligible for free school meals, 55 per cent have English as an additional language and 4 per cent have statements. The school has over the years built up strong and effective relationships with a number of local organizations and has been closely involved in the regeneration of the area.

Citizenship education is central to the purpose of the school

> We aim, therefore, to enable our pupils to take an active part in the regeneration of the local community and we will encourage the community to take an active part in our school. Citizenship will take different forms in different schools but it requires schools which see it as a central part of their vision to lead the way. We wish to be one of those schools.
>
> (Keith Ajegbo, Headteacher)

The school has made a practical case to the DfES to be given specialist status as a citizenship school and would welcome other schools joining the campaign.

Student participation

'Participation is the most fundamental right of citizenship; it builds motivation and motivation breeds achievement. We aim to embed student participation in the structure, strategy and culture of our school.'

The school has strong links with Childeric Primary School and Year 8 pupils have hosted Year 6 children from Childeric to support them in their transition to secondary school. The Year 8s have also run assemblies and classes on citizenship themes. 'We are building similar links with other primary schools.'

Community partnerships

- **City Challenge initiative:** The school has been involved in the City Challenge initiative since the early 1990s.
- **Deptford Community Forum:** Senior teachers are involved and have worked with the Forum to secure two local Single Regeneration Budget grants for community outreach. The school is a key member of the local Get Set for Citizenship Project, which includes businesses and local primary schools.
- **Education Action Zone:** The school is part of a mini Education Action Zone (EAZ) along with six local primary schools. The EAZ's citizenship aims have been written to tie in with the school's own development plan.
- **ICT for school and community:** The school has set up a new community ICT room and aims to provide e-learning facilities for parents, carers and members of the local community as well as school students.
- **Lead citizenship practitioner in the borough (Lewisham):** The school is a source of ideas and information for developing citizenship work right across the borough. 'We are taking a leading role in organising a Borough-wide citizenship conference in the autumn.'
- **Consultations:** Pupils, as well as staff, have taken a leading part in promoting citizenship education beyond the school. Students have taken part in a number of consultations and have sat on interview panels with agencies outside the school, including consultation on the DfES's new citizenship Web site, and consultation at a number of King's Fund events, along with interviews with the Children's Society and the National Children's Bureau.
- **Global citizenship:** Overseas links include prospective partnerships with schools in Africa and Asia in order to encourage global awareness and exchange among pupils. A small group of students visited Ghana to explore issues around child labour.

Dimension 2: Curriculum development

Curriculum development is, of course, more than curriculum planning and timetabling. Many schools give the task of curriculum management to a deputy. The challenge of curriculum development is wider than this. It involves the nature, purpose, style and sequencing of learning experiences across the life of the whole school and beyond. It links with out-of-school learning, the role of students in and beyond the classroom, and the attitudes of parents. It concerns the 'hidden' as well as the taught curriculum.

Citizenship and lifelong learning

Citizenship education takes place in the context of lifelong learning. This is for two reasons.

The first is that the purpose of citizenship education is to influence young people's behaviour and attitudes long after they have left school. The Order aims to educate young people to grow up as a generation who 'think of themselves as active citizens, willing, able and equipped to have an influence in public life and with the critical capacities to weigh evidence before speaking and acting'.

Secondly, citizenship education aims to help young people take responsibility for their own lives and this includes responsibility for their own present and future learning. A growing number of schools regard their students as the front-line commentators on the quality of the teaching and learning that is on offer. In commenting critically but constructively on how learning in a school can be improved, students are combining their role as citizens (members of the school community) with their role as learners (pupils). At Lipson College in Plymouth the College Principal, Steve Baker, stresses that his school is above all else 'a learning organization where everyone is searching for continuous improvement'. It is no accident that Steve Baker refers to himself as the 'head learner' and his students are encouraged to work with staff on seeking continuous improvement in learning.

The curriculum shapes the learning environment

Education for active citizenship is uniquely challenging in relation to curriculum development because it touches on every aspect of the life and work of the school. It is as much to do with process as content, relationships as performance. Curriculum development, therefore, is about shaping the whole learning environment around the vision and values of the school. It is a matter that requires the active experience and commitment of the head; however, much may then be delegated to others.

Leadership – St Peter's Collegiate School

1. **Developing and sharing the vision**
   The vision comes from the head, Huw Bishop. Citizenship education is supported by the senior management team and developed through a small PSHE/citizenship team led by Deputy Head, Julie Lawton.
   - Teachers: The programme has been commended and explained to all teaching staff, particularly through a high-profile INSET day on citizenship in spring 2001. The policy is to list the relevant committed and experienced staff and work with them to spread the possibilities among other staff.
   - Pupils: the teachers will further explain the initiative to the pupils (2001–02).
   - Parents: There is general support from parents. Parents will hear about the programme through the school newsletter (twice a term) and general addresses (2001–02). One reason for starting citizenship education early is to create opportunities for all stakeholders, including parents, to be informed, aware and where appropriate involved before the formal start of citizenship education in September 2002.

2. **Creating the curriculum**
   Citizenship education is commended not only for itself but on the grounds that it makes learning more *relevant to students/pupils*. Citizenship education can *improve students' motivation to learn*. Staff are encouraged to makes links between their existing work – it doesn't all have to be new – and the citizenship curriculum.
   The school has a highly developed planning process. It is a Beacon School, specializes in IT and has the Investors in People award. These planning processes form the backdrop for the development, implementation and review of citizenship education.

3. **Supporting staff**
   The citizenship education team supports staff members. This is done through personal support (see below, Management) and through INSET days. The school's commitment to its Investors in People award offers a range of support strategies for staff development.

Dimension 3: Motivation

Leaders motivate those around them, particularly those directly responsible to them. The capacity to motivate is allied to the capacity to support and encourage individuals. The head and the leadership team need to 'walk the talk' and act as role models for the values and mission of the school. This is particularly the case with education for active citizenship. The schools that most strongly encourage young people to become active citizens are schools where the head and staff are experienced as active citizens within the school.

The morale of the teaching profession is low although there are signs that it is improving (Chapter 4). Many older and more experienced teachers are taking early retirement, younger teachers are moving out in large numbers and those who are left are – all too often – feeling undervalued and overstretched. Citizenship education is only possible through a well-motivated and enthusiastic group of teachers. Education for active citizenship is all about changing our political and social culture, and that can only be achieved through motivating people with the will to do it. Citizenship education, although demanding, does provide schools with the opportunity to develop activities and learning styles that are richly rewarding for both staff and students.

Schools are about people

Extract from The Little Red Book *from Lipson Community College*

Schools are about people. We believe in encouraging and supporting people so that they are able to have joy in teaching and learning. Our central tenet is that staff and students want to do their best, and if they are unable to, then our job is to find out why and to change the things which vitiate their efforts. We are looking to analyse the systemic causes of problems and to apply quality tools in order to rectify them, rather than to apportion blame, or look for individual failure.

We are thus attempting to institute systems whereby feedback in the form of performance data and that derived in softer form from our internal and external customers is used to solve problems and to drive development. We therefore value and encourage involvement in the decision making process at every level. The College Year Councils have an important role to play in this.

In short, our belief is that the key to good teaching and learning is intrinsic motivation and that that only comes through ownership of, and personal involvement in, the learning process. Our purpose, therefore, is to enable the people we work for at every level to find intrinsic motivation.

High expectations

Motivating people around a vision often requires challenging staff and students with high, even tough, expectations. This can demand courage and a readiness to take risks. A new head had been appointed to turn round Pendre High School, a failing school on a large, deprived housing estate in Merthyr Tydfil, South Wales.[2] The academic performance of the school was poor. The staff – for all their disappointment – comforted themselves with the thought that with such poor material to work with they were unlikely to do better. The issue of standards came up at a staff meeting, and the usual excuse for poor results was given. The head was furious. In the words of one teacher, 'He tore into us and pointed out in no uncertain terms that we were letting the kids, the school and ourselves down. If we expect nothing, we shall get nothing.' By the end of the following year the results were dramatically better. Morale had improved, new and more flexible learning projects were in place and staff and students had begun to feel good about themselves and each other. The head had taken a lead. He had risked a showdown with his staff on a matter of principle and the risk was rewarded with success and mutual appreciation. He had shown how it is necessary to 'walk the talk'. Leadership of this kind is about citizenship and it is infectious. It spreads to other people.

Dimension 4: Good management

Good management is essential if an organization is to achieve its vision, aims and objectives. This is particularly the case with citizenship education because of the scale of the logistical challenge. Here again the early evidence suggests that the schools that are proving most effective in pioneering citizenship education are those that have developed quality-management systems. Quality management involves allocating responsibilities and resources against objectives, supporting and monitoring performance and reviewing achievement with a view to ensuring continuous improvement.

Good management requires the headteacher to have a firm grasp of the principles of curriculum development. Nowhere is this more important than in education for active citizenship, the subject that potentially affects every aspect of the ethos and work of the school.

Dimension 5: Boundary management

Boundary management (below, Context) is all about responding to and influencing the expectations and demands of the external world, which includes government, parents, employers, the media and a host of other organizations. There is evidence from the schools sampled in this book that strong local community partnerships lead to quality community involvement among the students. There was a time when most schools saw themselves as quite distinct from their local communities. Even parents were required to keep outside the yellow line that was drawn about the school. 'Fortress schools' still exist, but they are becoming fewer and in no case are they able effectively to provide real-life experiences of community involvement beyond the classroom.

Engaging with local communities

In many places the external environment will be supportive and responsive to the ideas and needs of the school. This, however, is not always the case, and some schools feel that they are creating and nourishing a culture that is radically different from that beyond their gates. Education for active citizenship requires the leadership of the school to address opportunities for students to engage constructively with their local communities. The quality of citizenship education, therefore, will depend in significant part on the richness and variety of the school's relationships with people and organizations in the external world. There is an increasing trend for school boundaries to become more and more permeable. Schools are welcoming a greater range of visitors from outside, mentors, business and community organizations and a growing number of volunteers who bring their special experience to share with staff and students. As lifelong learning becomes a reality, it is likely that schools will more and more become centres of learning for the whole community and not simply for children and young people.

Promoting the school as part of the community

Under boundary management can be placed the whole business of promoting the school among its local and wider communities. Some schools are developing their brochures and publicity in the form of a manifesto that sets the vision and objectives of the school in the form of commitments to what young people will be offered in each year group as they progress through the school. This approach has the dual benefit of clarifying the purpose of citizenship education while spelling out clearly and in stages the entitlements that it will bring.

Challenge 2: Leadership – Tanfield School

1. **Developing and sharing the vision**
   The school has a long tradition of community involvement. The head's vision of creating a caring ethos within the school is gradually being realized.
2. **Creating the curriculum**
   It is intended that citizenship will be taught within existing subjects in the curriculum and through whole-school events. The approach so far has been incremental in that new developments have been implemented gradually, one at a time.
3. **Involving partners: parents, local organizations**
   Many opportunities arise for parents, the business community and other elements of the local and wider community to support the work of the school (eg mentoring of KS4 pupils by the local business community, link courses with local colleges, work experience, etc).
4. **Supporting staff**
   Staff are made aware of developments in citizenship. Information on good practice is shared at staff meetings, briefings, in school bulletins, in the newsletter *Tanfield Matters* and at governors' meetings. The coordinator supports the citizenship work of subject teachers and learning coordinators and disseminates information about the development of citizenship education across the school.
5. **Reviewing progress**
   The work is reviewed and monitored within the school's established reviewing and monitoring procedure.

Summary – leadership

The head and the SMT will foster leadership for citizenship education across five dimensions of the school's life and learning. This will include:

1. **Values and vision**
   The head and SMT will relate citizenship education to the vision and values of the school. This might helpfully include a consideration of the three democratic values of our time:
   - freedom as autonomy;
   - no authority without democracy; and
   - no rights without responsibilities.

2. **Curriculum development**
   The effective leadership will ensure that the taught and whole curriculum is developed to achieve the vision and objectives of the school with due regard to the requirements of the national curriculum (Challenge 2).
3. **Motivation**
   The head and leadership team will have the insight and skill to motivate staff, students and stakeholders around the vision and values of the school (Challenges 3 and 4).
4. **Quality management**
   The good leader will know the importance of quality management (Challenge 4).
5. **Boundary management**
   The effective leadership will enable the school to respond to the needs, challenges and opportunities presented by the school's local and wider communities (Challenge 5).

The curriculum

Aims and objectives

The aims and objectives of the citizenship curriculum are developed within the community of the school and its partners. In this context every school comprises three communities rolled into one. It is: 1) a **community of learners** (pupils, teachers and others); 2) a **community of fellow citizens** (pupils, teachers and others, including non-teaching staff); and 3) a **community of stakeholders** – people with a stake in the school's relationship with its local communities (parents, local organizations and groups, local government and business).

These three communities are borne in mind at each stage in the creation of a whole-school policy for citizenship education.

Figure 14.4 brings together the elements that have already been explored in the previous chapters. It includes: 1) **policy**, as expressed through the taught and whole curriculum, which will be centred in values and committed to quality; 2) **participation** – the manner and extent to which members of the school participate in democratic decision making; 3) **practice** – the management, provision and experience of learning. These three aspects of school life are grouped around the values that underpin the vision and mission of the school.

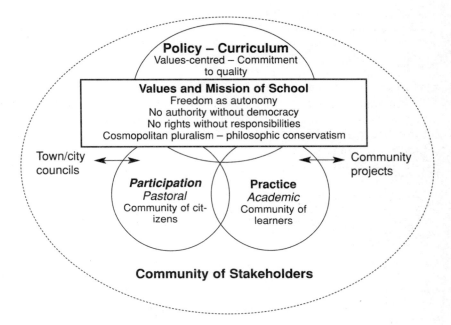

Figure 14.4 *Citizen education – elements of the whole-school challenge*

Curriculum – Tanfield School

Whole-school approaches

It is accepted that citizenship is a whole-school issue. A whole-school approach was essential to create the required ethos. Citizenship is almost a way of life, not simply a subject. The programmes of study can be covered within the established whole curriculum. It is felt that citizenship is too important to be taught in small pockets within the school. It is taught holistically within the subject knowledge of each department including PSHE. Active learning is already an established teaching and learning style in all areas of the curriculum. Active learning in community projects is a strength of the school. Every opportunity is taken to encourage active participation by the pupils in almost all areas of the curriculum.

Pulling the three strands together

School/class council involves political literacy, social responsibility and active learning in the community. World issues, and social and moral issues also provide the opportunities for all three strands of the Order to be approached in a holistic manner.

A question of values

The work increases the pupils' knowledge and understanding, and also develops skills, value and personal qualities.

Student participation in and beyond the classroom

Pupils are required to contribute towards the school community in a wide range of activities. Every pupil in Year 9 carries out reception duties, thereby contributing to the smooth running of the school. All Year 10 pupils are trained to act as mentors to pupils in Year 7. These examples of active participation within the school community are part of the citizenship entitlement for every pupil.

Doing politics

Political awareness and democracy is generally covered in PSHE. School council work, starting with class councils through year councils and finally to the school council, is an active learning method of understanding the dimensions of political power and decision making.

Define the objectives and outcomes

The **objectives** of citizenship education will be derived from the school aims and will be linked with the programme of study. They will set out what should be achieved by pupils at each key stage. They will be expressed in terms of knowledge, concepts, skills and attitudes.

The **outcomes** should be discussed with parents and pupils. There is a distinction between the first and second languages of citizenship.[3] The first is the public language of shared civic, moral and religious education. The second language is cultivated in the context of families and communities, which are intermediaries between the individual and the state. Discussing the outcomes of citizenship education with young people and their parents aims to create harmony between the development of these two languages.[4]

Theory is happily borne out by practice. In CSV's experience the schools that have most effectively developed a framework and curriculum for education for active citizenship have all set out their citizenship objectives clearly within the framework of their vision and mission for the school as a whole. Here are some examples:

- **The Deanes School** – love of learning and a zest for life
'We believe that the key to success in the future lies in our students developing high standards of basic skills together with an ongoing desire for learning and a real zest for life. Academic achievement alone is not enough, however. We expect students to be self-motivated, confident and able to take on the challenges which lie ahead. We also expect them to be aware of the world around them and the needs of others. These attitudes and values are developed through the ethos of the school as a caring community.' From this vision statement it is readily possible to identify specific learning objectives, such as:
  - personal confidence and motivation;
  - a desire for quality learning;
  - commitment to a caring community.
These objectives in turn break down into specific learning outcomes linked to the citizenship and wider curriculum.
- **Deptford Green School** – specializing in citizenship education
Central to Deptford Green School's commitment to becoming a 'citizenship school' is a belief in the central importance of student participation. 'Participation is the most fundamental right of citizenship. Participation builds motivation and motivation breeds achievement. We aim to embed student participation in the structure, strategy and culture of our school.' Once again such clear objectives can be identified through clear behavioural and learning outcomes. It is worth noting that these outcomes will be shown through all three roles – learner, citizen and stakeholder – that students play in the life of the school and community.
- **Marshfields** – 'at the heart of community'
The mission statement of Marshfields Special School has clearly stated for the last seven years that 'we strive to be at the heart of the community'. This commitment is worked through in the leadership, curriculum, management and daily life of the school community.
- **The Anglo-European School** – global citizenship
The Anglo-European School puts education for global citizenship at the heart of its work. 'The world for which we are preparing our children is an increasingly small and interdependent one. Students will need to be flexible, tolerant and cosmopolitan. They will need a clear understanding of their roots but also to be able to move confidently between cultures.' The school believes that the ability to grasp and use a foreign language should not and cannot be separated from understanding the history and culture of those for whom that language is their native tongue. 'Language and cultural under-

standing, therefore, are part of something wider – the experience and challenge of being a world citizen.'

Citizenship education and the school's wider objectives support each other

In planning the citizenship curriculum, therefore, it is essential to be clear about the educational objectives of the school as a whole and how these relate to and support the specific objective of citizenship education.

In CSV's experience the schools that show evidence of making the most vigorous and effective progress with education for active citizenship are those that make the link between the three communities of the life of the school.

Learning: the school as a community of learners

The learning styles that foster citizenship education best are those that focus on enabling students to take responsibility for reviewing and enriching their own learning. There are schools where the teachers model what it is to be both a learner and a teacher, and where students are encouraged not only to learn but also to help each other learn.

Owning our work

At Lipson College in Plymouth students and staff have, for example, an interesting perspective on homework:

> For us, the justification for homework is as a preparation for lifelong learning for which we all have to develop the skills of learning on our own. To this end, we have renamed homework as own work and encouraged students to look upon the time they spend and the work they do as their own. The *student planners* are an essential part of the learning process. They are a 'quality tool'. They not only act as recording and communication devices, but also as planners and sources of guidance and information.

Many schools link the use of organizers with recording achievement through the TREE programme (see below, Assessment). This is an ideal way for students to record their active learning in the community as well as all other aspects of their work.

Our work can benefit others

Citizenship education prompts the question: how can the work that I have learnt to own be turned into work that also benefits other people?

The growing emphasis upon mutual mentoring and tutoring makes this connection. Many schools such as Plantsbrook School in Sutton Coldfield build tutoring into the life of the school and its partner primary schools.

Plantsbrook School, Sutton Coldfield – primary partnership initiative

A wide range of inter-phase curricular projects takes place. Primary children come to Plantsbrook School to use the facilities and Plantsbrook School staff and pupils go to the primary schools to teach the children and train primary colleagues. One of the most obvious benefits of the project is the growth in confidence of the Plantsbrook School students as they work with younger children. For two years now Year 10 students have gone to the nearest primary school over lunchtimes to work as classroom assistants or to help with reading. In many cases this has been used as part of their Duke of Edinburgh award scheme.

Behaviour: the school as a community of citizens

The democratic ethos and practice of the school is fundamental to effective education for active citizenship. Dave Marsh, who is responsible for citizenship education at Littlehampton Community School in West Sussex, comments: 'We are looking at citizenship education as one way of improving student behaviour. Students discover real commitment and motivation through active citizenship.'

A growing number of schools are using citizenship education to engage disaffected students in taking responsibility not only for their own behaviour but also for supporting the good behaviour of other pupils. The work done with CSV at Battersea Technology College was designed to improve both student learning and behaviour. The effect was that the programme, pioneered in a single class, was transferred to three whole year groups because it had proved so positive. Behaviour not only improved in citizenship lessons, but there was a positive knock-on effect in other classes. There is also anecdotal rather than researched evidence that paired reading schemes, such as CSV Reading Together, stimulate responsible and caring behaviour not least among the less able and often disaffected older students.

Peer education and anti-bullying programmes offer opportunities for schools to link student learning with projects that contribute positively to the ethos of the school (see below, The global dimension, for further examples).

Dr Challoner's High School – health: peer support (whole school)

The project aims to extend a current pilot project of internal and external counselling and support groups for pupils. The objective is to develop coping skills, especially in relation to managing stress at examination time, which can lead to low self-esteem and sometimes to problems such as eating disorders.

Student involvement: 150 in Year 8, 150 in Year 9, 30 in Year 10 and 30 in Year 11

Civic engagement: the school as a community among other communities

All the schools in our sample of pioneers in citizenship education take their relationships with the wider communities seriously. It takes time to build good relationships with local (and international) partners. Schools that are relatively new to this need to pace themselves and not expect to achieve in a year what it has taken some people many years to achieve. The important thing is to start small and to build strongly (see above: Colne Community School and the Deanes School).

Citizenship manifesto

The curriculum citizenship objectives, once established, can become the basis for a citizenship manifesto that sets out clearly for everyone involved what the school means by saying that it provides citizenship education as an entitlement to all pupils in KS3 and 4. This manifesto can be built up gradually as the citizenship curriculum is augmented and reviewed.

Curriculum – St Peter's Collegiate School

Citizenship education is part of a whole-school approach to the taught and hidden curriculum. It is managed and developed through: 1) the weekly PSHE/citizenship lesson; and 2) links with other subjects developed through a whole-school audit linked to INSET training (see below).

The citizenship/PSHE programme is made up of three-week blocks of 50-minute PSHE/citizenship blocked themes including: personal skills; health and sex education; study skills; drugs education; careers; environment; religious education; citizenship.

Subjects by year groups are:

- Year 7: rules and responsibilities, rights and possible activities, linking to references in the programme of study;
- Year 8: tolerance of others, racism, sexism, awareness disability, mutual respect, local communities, country;
- Year 9: local and national systems of government, young people's rights and responsibilities under the law;
- Year 10: crime and law, magistrates;
- Year 11: economy, EU, consumers;
- Year 12: national, international and local – Oxfam, Amnesty, Christian Aid, research and report on community-based voluntary groups;
- Year 13:
  - question time with MP/MEP, deputy editor of newspaper, local councillor (first week – prepare; second week – question time; third week – press release, thank-you letters, etc);
  - democratic activity, free press, UK/EU.

In KS3 there is a review of learning outcomes, some of which are thought to be too advanced. Knowledge about political systems will be emphasized in KS4 and KS5 (sixth form), ie nearer the time when young people need it. Additional citizenship education activities are based on a growing interest in encouraging students to do politics as well as learn about politics:

- **Youth parliament in general studies:** The school has entered twice.
- **Law and rights, mock trials, visits, etc:** Magistrates have, for example, offered opportunities for students to visit the courts during the period following exams. The programme includes a three-week theme on crime, where the students prepare a PowerPoint presentation on an issue that particularly interests them. (The school specializes in IT.) The school has a developed booklet/questionnaire that can be used for three consecutive weeks (one-hour lessons): 1) basic information about courts and sentencing; 2) case studies, which can include magistrates' visit and role-play; 3) follow-up.
- **Work placements:** There are work placements in solicitors' offices and the courts, and with the police. Individually the young people share their learning with one another.
  Note: Peer education and dissemination – there are opportunities for young people to disseminate their learning to others through group work.
- **School council:** There is growing recognition of the importance of the school council, with possible opportunities for students to research school issues. The chaplain runs the school council.

Curriculum audit

Carry out a simple audit across the whole curriculum of activities and learning that contribute to education for citizenship. This information will assist in the development of new opportunities for citizenship education including ALC. The audit will also inform planning for in-service training.

Reflect the priorities of the school's mission and citizenship objectives

The questions in a citizenship audit need to reflect the priorities of the school's mission and citizenship objectives.

An audit of citizenship education therefore applies – potentially at least – to every aspect of school life. For that reason it must relate directly to the strategic management of the school and the curriculum, not simply to the taught or specialist subject curriculum. Most schools already address aspects of citizenship education. An audit is a good starting point for developing the citizenship curriculum. It is important to know what you are already doing.

The audit (in one way or another) should include the three overlapping communities of the school: 1) learners; 2) citizens; and 3) stakeholders. Responsibility for auditing citizenship work of these different communities might be allocated to different groups of people. For example:

- **learning:** staff audit (consulting students at appropriate points);
- **citizenship activity:** student research project (consulting teaching and other staff);
- **stakeholders:** governors' survey and comments, possibly assisted by teams of student researchers where appropriate.

Audit active citizenship

In order to ensure that education for active citizenship includes a strong component of ALC, it is important to enquire where in the school young people are learning through activities that contribute in one way or another to the school and its wider communities (see below, Involving students).

Sources: A very full audit form is available from the Institute for Citizenship and NfER on http://www.citizen.org.uk/auditsks.htm.

There are further audit formats in the QCA draft scheme of work for citizenship in KS3 (pages 22–23).

Avoiding the tick-box mentality

The value of an audit by a questionnaire set against the programme of study is that it gives quick and clear evidence of where the school is in relation to the listed learning outcomes, particularly the knowledge outcomes. Some kind of audit of this sort is clearly necessary. However, audit sheets can easily foster the tick-box mentality in which we lose the big idea behind citizenship education. They can also reinforce past practice rather than open up new possibilities.

One school avoided much of the detailed audit work and instead asked each department to come up with an idea linked with two sample lesson plans detailing what they thought they could do that was new and innovative. Anthony Gell School in Derbyshire used an INSET to invite each department to come up with one or more contributions. Another school, St Peter's Collegiate School (above), linked the audit with an INSET day in which staff offered citizenship workshops to colleagues on innovative practice. The audit can be a useful instrument, but it needs to be implemented in ways that foster motivation and lateral thinking. A simple tick box, though useful for making a quick review of what is happening, tends to encourage convergent thinking. Hence derives the value of inviting staff and students to speculate about possibilities.

Auditing for democratic participation and ALC

The emphasis throughout this book is on developing education for active citizenship. A whole-school audit necessarily must address knowledge and skills, but – as QCA staff have consistently stressed – this knowledge and these skills need to be learnt through participation and responsible action. An audit should refer consistently and throughout to this connection. The audit should therefore include questions about – and reflection on – the extent to which what is already provided stimulates:

- democratic involvement;
- learning through experience and action; and
- partnerships for active citizenship in and beyond the school.

Three approaches to audit

The QCA have suggested three different approaches to an audit.[5] They can be used separately or in combination. Once again it is important to look out for ALC that contributes to the learning outcomes.

Programme of study approach

List the outcomes against key stages and ask departments to tick, and where relevant comment on, what they are already doing:

- Knowledge?
- Understanding?
- Skills? Concepts? (Compare with programme of study.)

The audit can lead to a useful INSET day for everyone. It can be useful to add a further question or two to encourage lateral and creative thinking. Audit forms tend otherwise to encourage convergent/tick-box attitudes. The questions might be: 1) suggest a learning activity that benefits the community that your department could undertake; or 2) submit a couple of lesson plans around good new ideas.

The strands approach

1) Where are students gaining experience of the three strands – social and moral responsibility, community involvement and political literacy – and how? In school and in the local and global community? 2) Does the school have a distinctive contribution to offer to citizenship education?
   This could be a student research project.

The concept map approach

In this approach we use the citizenship concepts to judge the effectiveness of citizenship education in the school.
   The concepts are:

- democracy and autocracy;
- cooperation and conflict;
- equality and diversity;
- fairness;
- justice and the rule of law;
- rules;
- the law and human rights;
- freedom and order;

- individual and community;
- power and authority;
- rights and responsibilities.

Concept: democracy and autocracy

Where in the life of the school are the pupils experiencing democracy in action?

- In the school/class council?
- In the conduct of the school?
- In the conduct of parents' evenings?
- In shaping class/school values statements?
- In helping shape the school environment?

A survey such as this could be researched by the school council.

Curriculum mapping and planning

Planning the curriculum for education for active citizenship typically involves addressing the traditional questions of what, who, where, when and how. In this section we focus on the first four questions in the context of what students do in the learning process. If outcomes are to be achieved, what types of learning experience are most appropriate and what content (knowledge and concepts) should be studied and skills applied?

Active learning in the community involves active learning through the study at first hand of concrete issues or problems. The systematic organization of an enquiry or a project activity will involve the acquisition and employment of increasingly higher-order skills as pupils pass through the key stages. The content chosen will also become more demanding as pupils become more sophisticated in their identification of issues to address.

The pupil's experience of citizenship education should provide a balance between learning in and out of school. Some outcomes, particularly elements of the knowledge outcomes, will be most appropriately met by classroom discussion stimulated by second-hand resource materials. Even here, however, the learning experiences should invite the students to reflect on the implications for themselves of the knowledge that they are acquiring. The knowledge outcomes must be justified by their relevance to the students.

What?

The outcomes of the audit will prompt staff to consider:

- what the school is and is not doing;
- what needs to be done (against a manageable timetable);
- what links can and should be made between citizenship education and the aims and objectives of the school.

Before planning the learning experiences that promote active citizenship, we need to be aware of the wide range of potential activities and experiences that are already available in school.

Categories of ALC

We can categorize ALC under approach, type and content. We can, at the same time, note the aspects of school life to which these approaches can contribute: 1) learning; 2) behaviour/relationships; and 3) civic engagement.

Approach

- **Peer support:** Peer education, learning and mentoring – literacy, numeracy, other subjects, sport, health education, mediation/anti-bullying etc, sympathetic listening.
- **Research:** Pupils enquire into views and attitudes of peers or members of the public on issues around which democratic opinion is sought. This can include developing class and school codes of ethics.
- **Service:** Pupils meet real community needs through project activity.

Type

- **Direct:** Face-to-face involvement with service recipient(s).
- **Education and learning:** This could involve peer education or peer tutoring.
- **Environment and sustainability:** Landscaping or special garden creation, nature trails, contribution towards external initiatives (eg redevelopment schemes).
- **Citizenship and democracy:** Campaigns, registration drives, etc.
- **Personal, social and community needs:** Intergenerational work, personal and community services and projects.

- **Indirect:** Activities that support but do not involve face-to-face meeting with service recipients – recruiting, collecting, designing or preparing materials, for example.
- **Advocacy:** Researching, presenting and campaigning on behalf of a particular need or group of people.

Content

There is a huge range of different activities:

- research teams;
- decision making;
- intergenerational projects;
- peer education;
- buddying (HIV/AIDS);
- training workshops;
- environmental projects;
- handling moral and social dilemmas;
- information and advice;
- school and local councils;
- transition teams/preparing for change;
- sculpture, theatre;
- designing and making;
- tools for living;
- newsletters;
- pollution control;
- nature trail;
- enquiry into health provision.

Who?

- **Who is involved?** Leadership, classroom teachers, specialist contribution from staff/outsiders, parents, volunteers, student council, etc.
- **Leadership:** How does the leadership actually support the management and the coordination of education for active citizenship? Liz Byrne at the Nobel School in Stevenage stresses the link between citizenship education and the vision and mission of the school. 'Our vision in brief is a curriculum closer to what pupils and their parents want and we believe in and which is less and less the outcome of external regulation.' She then adds that the school aims at 'a school organization that serves learning and not a factory model that parcels out learning in hour-long chunks, day in and day out'.
- **Members of staff:** Are members of staff aware of the nature and

purpose of the initiative? How far are the subject specialists able to contribute to a particular theme, project or set of learning outcomes?

- **Other people:** Do the students and their parents understand the nature and purpose of citizenship education? How far do the governors understand the need for the school to build community partnerships around citizenship education? Are the non-teaching staff aware of the aims and possibilities of citizenship education? How far would it be appropriate to involve them?

Later in the chapter we shall explore specific questions concerning the management of education for active citizenship.

Where? Curriculum location

Education for active citizenship can be located across the entire taught and whole curriculum. It can be helpful to list the various areas in school where citizenship education is (from the audit) and could be taking place. The schools illustrated in this book for the most part emphasize that it is good to mix discrete citizenship provision with elements of citizenship offered through subjects and the wider life of the school within and beyond the school gates. Areas are:

- In school – formal and taught curriculum:
  - discrete citizenship provision;
  - links with subject areas;
  - links with themes: PSHE, careers, Healthy Schools Initiative; sustainable environment (Agenda 21), international/global dimension and exchange programmes;
  - tutorials: how are they conducted?
- In school – whole curriculum:
  - school, year and class councils;
  - codes of ethics;
  - circle time;
  - peer learning, peer mentoring and support programmes;
  - assembly/school newspaper, radio, etc;
  - non-curricular activity;
  - out-of-school activity and learning.
- Outside school:
  - placements (including work placements);
  - projects: environment, science, design technology, IT, arts, drama and humanities projects;
  - global links.

When?

This relates closely to curriculum location. It includes:

- **Class time:**
  - citizenship time;
  - subject time;
  - tutor time;
  - suspended timetable.
- **Own time:**
  - at school;
  - out of school.

Remember: pupils spend much more time out of school than in! There are a number of ways in which pupils might choose to have their out-of-school activities recorded as contributing to citizenship education.

Putting it together

We now have the ingredients for a citizenship curriculum linked with schemes of work and lesson plans. The emphasis throughout this book is upon active citizenship developed through ALC.

The QCA have, with help from practising teachers, devised some flexible schemes of work in KS3 to help teachers develop their own curriculum around their citizenship objective (see Figure 14.5 on page 150). These are illustrative, not mandatory, and are intended to stimulate thinking and action rather than slavish replication.

Curriculum: project case study – community care at Yardleys School

CSV introduction

This report on a community care project is a synopsis from a fuller study for CSV by Connie Prever, project coordinator, written in March 1994. It provides a valuable example of curriculum planning for active learning in the community. It is also significant to the extent that it predates the most recent developments in citizenship education. It is important to remember that the school enjoyed financial help from Birmingham City Council. This made it possible for a teacher to give significant time to the project. Such productive partnerships are worth pursuing. The project also received advice and support from CSV.

QCA scheme of work for citizenship

Contents
The scheme of work comprises:
- Teacher's guide
- Booklet of ideas for pupil participation
- Range of units

Teacher's guide
- Materials to support whole-school approach
- Examples of how to use PoS flexibly
- Teaching and learning approaches
- Initial guidance on assessment
- Links with KS3 strategy

Contacts, resources and Web site

Subject leaflets
- Map citizenship against subject PoS
- Identify some opportunities for delivering citizenship through the subject
- Identify compatible units in subject scheme of work
  NB Schools need to decide which opportunities to exploit and which to leave as implicit support for citizenship

Key stage 3 units
- Starter unit for Y7 building on KS2 and introducing main themes of citizenship
- Examples of units suitable for discrete provision
- Examples of units suitable for delivery through subjects
- Units describing whole-school or off-timetable activities

Review and assessment unit for end of KS3

Key stage 4

Scheme of work for citizenship at key stage 4
- Supplement to KS3 teacher's guide
- Citizenship units that link provision with other statutory requirements such as careers, ICT, PE, RE
- Booklet to support increased opportunities for pupil participation and responsible action
- Enable pupils to identify contribution of other GCSEs

NB Different pupils may have different provision

Key stage 4 units
- Introductory unit
- Units linking with careers, ICT, PE
- Specific units to enable pupils to investigate, discuss and take action on issues relating to sustainable development, ethical consumerism, human rights, science
- Young people and local, national and European government, the economy, the law

Looking forward to post-16

Key stages 1 and 2
Integral part of whole PSHE and citizenship non-statutory framework
- Guidance to build on foundation stage
- Unit to support secondary transfer
- Ideas to link citizenship and other subjects
- Ways to develop citizenship through the wider curriculum and participation in school and community

See: www.standards.dfes.gov.uk

Other initiatives
Guidance for pupils with learning difficulties published – including PSHE and citizenship
To be developed:
  Exemplification Web sites
- 'Respect for all'
- Creativity
- 'Gifted and talented'

Figure 14.5   *QCA scheme of work for citizenship*

Yardleys School

Yardleys School is a multicultural, mixed comprehensive school of approximately 890 pupils from the ages of 11 to 16, drawn from a wide area and coming from approximately 20 partnership primary schools. It is situated on two sites in the Tyseley district of Birmingham. The school takes its name from the amalgamation of Yardley Grammar School and Leys Secondary School in 1975.

The project

Care in the community has become, for a lot of elderly and disabled people, a very important part of their lives. In Birmingham alone, 10,000 people care seven days a week for their elderly dependants. It was decided that if the number of volunteers working out in the community were increased then this would alleviate the whole burden being placed on the carers of these elderly people. This project, set up and run during the period when citizenship was only a cross-curricular theme, offers a practical insight into curriculum planning and project management. It still offers a valuable model for education for active citizenship. Birmingham City Council social services invested some money in providing for a project support worker.

Initial contact was made in November 1993 and the school began to plan this project around the following aims:

- to develop pupil awareness of the needs of elderly people in the school community;
- to provide additional carers working out in the community to help both the carers and those who are being cared for;
- to develop closer links with the organizations involved in the care of the elderly, that is, the Neighbourhood Office;
- to encourage pupils to use their initiative, in taking responsibility for events happening on each visit made to the elderly person in their home;
- to recruit adult volunteers to become involved in the project and assist pupils in the tasks undertaken, eg gardening;
- to encourage pupils to be of value to others – community work will allow pupils to give as well as to receive (CSV booklet 1981);
- to enhance pupils' self-esteem by giving them the opportunity to gain a sense of achievement from the tasks undertaken in the elderly person's home.

Yardleys was asked to find 25 pupils to undertake a minimum of 10 hours' community service. Pupils chosen would also receive a certificate for their record of achievement.

Pupil's diary extract

Sarah enjoys reading, watching TV and writing/receiving letters. She thinks that her health is slowly improving, even though she suffers from white blindness. She got this condition from working in a laundry all her life and the only laundry she worked on was white, so now she can't look at white buildings or snow. Sarah is 90 years old and she really is a friendly nice lady and likes everyone. She can't get around without her Zimmer frame to balance her and she needs help because she can't move her left side. She seems grateful for the life she has led and she is not afraid to face death. She said she was very grateful for my company because she said I was someone new to gossip to. She has taught me not to be afraid of getting old, because she is 90 years old and can hardly do anything, yet she is still happy.

Setting up the project

Pupils' involvement in community work has been well established. The philosophy behind this involvement is twofold: 1) there are needs to be met within the community; and 2) pupils are the resource to be used to meet these needs. Young people participating in such projects will gain more of an insight into society and its problems, and be in a position to do something about them. They will be dealing with 'real' situations.

Teachers wishing to set up a community project must be aware of the need for thorough planning and organization if the project is to be successful for all involved. This includes agreeing:

1. **Target audience:** It needs to be decided whom the pupils will be making contact with during their community project. At Yardleys identifying elderly people as a target audience was not a problem, as the school had a list of 85 people in the area to whom it delivered Christmas hampers. This gave a starting point for the project.
2. **Finance:** Yardleys was given funding to set up the project and this made it easier, with the extra money paying for cover staff, paying for transport costs and providing money for all project materials that were required.
3. **Time available for project:** Time is required in two ways:
   - time available for the teacher(s) involved to set up the pupil placements and visiting programme;

  – lesson time available for pupils to carry out the visiting
   programme.
At Yardleys there were about 10 weeks to plan, set up and run the
project. Time for the teacher(s) off normal timetable commitments
must be given, if the project is to run effectively. Time is needed for
administration, liaison outside school (both visiting the elderly and
liaising with other organizations), setting up pupils' projects and
monitoring the work undertaken by pupils. Without this time, minor
problems can get out of hand, because there may not be the opportunity to deal with them straight away. At Yardleys all the work for the
project was run through lesson times, giving 1 hour 10 minutes per
week. Pupils had nine lessons to carry out their community project
work.
4. **A first step:** At Yardleys this project is viewed as a first step, in
   the hope that it will open up a whole range of possibilities and potential for a continuing community involvement in the school. Any
   school thinking about setting up a project needs to be prepared to
   give it timetabling space if the programme is to run smoothly and
   effectively.

Practicalities

Contact with agencies helping the elderly in the community

Contact with organizations is essential if the project is to be set up well.
For example, local community centres may have coffee mornings for the
elderly where it is possible to meet elderly people and the person in
charge.

   Across the road from Yardleys school buildings there is a church and a
Hindu temple, so contacts were also made there. Other organizations are
available to help and these could be contacted to become involved in the
project, particularly if it is going to be over a much longer period of time.

Insurance

It is important for the teacher arranging any type of community placements for pupils to check out the insurance coverage of the school. The
key words are 'approved out-of-school activities'. Some insurance policies cover pupils out on their placements, while others do not and an
additional premium will need to be paid by the school for each pupil
involved.

Identification cards

For the visiting programme undertaken at Yardleys every pupil and teacher had an identification card. Identification cards were also developed for adult volunteers who joined the project later on.

Pupil's diary extract

Arrived. Two friendly faces who were polite to us. They were friendly but presumed we were here to work, work, work! They had lived in their house for fifty years. Next week we will start the real work and we'll also try to get to know them better.

We bought all the equipment needed and we started as quickly as possible. We had a 'litter maker' (to burn the bush litter into decomposable litter), a hedge cutter and the safety equipment of goggles and gloves. We took turns in cutting (one cut, the other picked up the cuttings and put them in a pile). It was hard work. It was the first time we had done this and we were very pleased. But there's so much work to do in such little time.

Teacher activities

Visiting the elderly/setting up pupil placements

It is very important for the teacher(s) involved to spend time meeting the elderly in the community. This is time-consuming and can sometimes be quite a difficult task, as many elderly people are reluctant to let strangers into their homes. On the visits made around Yardleys an identification card was carried and shown to the elderly. The project was then explained fully and the elderly people gave information about themselves, which proved useful in the allocation of pupils later on.

Signed agreements

The elderly people on agreement were then 'signed up' and information about the visiting programme given to them. This is essential, as contact can be made directly to school should the elderly person have a query of some kind or if a visit is not possible on a particular day.

Pupil's diary extract

She is 95 years old. She is partially blind in one eye and needs a Zimmer frame to get around. She loves the outdoors and misses going out now. She also talks a lot about her sister whom she hasn't seen for ages. Maybe I could arrange a visit or something.

> Today was the last visit. I made her a family picture frame. I gave it to her today and she loved it. She is really jolly. I think after today I may even miss her a bit because I really got to know her. I think she also felt a bit sad. I think she gets a bit lonely at times.

Recruiting adult volunteers

It is important to recruit adult volunteers to become involved in the project, as it will enhance the scope of tasks pupils may be able to undertake. One important thing to stress is that adult volunteers are there to help and assist the pupil – not to take over the project themselves. At Yardleys School, governors and the school caretaker acted as our source of adult volunteers.

Informing parents about the project

It is important to inform parents about the care in the community project for several reasons:

- Parental consent is needed if a child is leaving the school premises to undertake curriculum work elsewhere. At Yardleys a letter was sent out with a brief outline of the project and a consent form for parents to complete and return to school.
- Parents may offer to become adult volunteers or support the project in some other way.
- If parents are aware from the beginning that their child is undertaking community service work and what exactly they are doing, it clears up any misunderstandings as the project progresses.

Informing other staff about the project

It is important to keep other staff informed about what the project is about, how if at all it might affect them and the dates of all visits. Staff need to have this information and are far more likely to be understanding and helpful if they are kept informed about the project, rather than left in the dark.

Identification of pupils and preparatory programme

For this type of project it is advisable to work with Year 10 or Year 11 students. If pupils are going to gain the most out of their placements they need a certain amount of maturity to be able fully to understand the aims of the project. At Yardleys two groups were chosen to work with: 1) Year 11 City and Guilds group; and 2) Year 10 catering group.

City and Guilds group

The City and Guilds group were the main visiting group. The catering group's main function was to plan, prepare, cook and serve a three-course luncheon for the elderly people on the visiting programme.

Links to City and Guilds assessment: diploma of vocational education

Ideally community projects should draw on volunteer students who would like to take part in a visiting scheme. At Yardleys, there was not the necessary time or timetable space for this to be achieved so it was decided that the Year 11 City and Guilds group were in the most appropriate position to take part in the visiting programme. This was for two main reasons: 1) pupils in this group had begun work with the teacher within a health and social care context; 2) pupils would not lose out on any assessment towards their final qualifications because case studies could be written around the care in the community project.

The diploma of vocational education at Yardleys involves pupils having one City and Guilds lesson a week. Pupils are required to complete case studies made up of a number of completed tasks. For each task there is an assessment focus and pupils are generally assessed on one or two skills per task, for example skill area 10 – able to use a computer. Teachers record whether pupils have achieved the skill on an A–D scale and this is also seen in terms of distinction, credit, pass and fail. Assessment is recorded by staff, and a pupil profile is built up. Pupils are finally awarded the diploma of vocational education on leaving Yardleys.

Pupil activities

One of the most valuable activities pupils undertook was to get to know the elderly person or elderly couple they had been placed with. It was important for them to establish good relationships so that stereotypical barriers could be broken down. On their first few visits, some pupils would come back saying they had just chatted to the elderly person. They almost felt guilty and yet their diary entries illustrated that they had been able to find out a lot about the elderly person concerned. The other activities taking place included gardening, a family tree project, cleaning tasks, DIY jobs, shopping and a competition to design the front of the publication about their project.

Care in the community luncheon

This was the main task of the GCSE catering group. Initial planning began in January and by mid-February pupils had decided on the menu, the type of food service, additional entertainment for the elderly after lunch and the invitation design. Invitations were hand-delivered by pupils shortly after half-term. Pupils then began to allocate different tasks amongst themselves, for example napkin folding, table laying and preparation of drinks for guests upon arrival.

On the morning of the luncheon, pupils had to be taken off timetable to prepare all the food and the function room. Pupils served all the food and made sure guests were all catered for. Musical entertainment followed and involved some Year 7 pupils directed by the head of music in the school.

Activities with the older people at the school

It is important for any teacher wishing to set up a community programme to prepare additional tasks that pupils can undertake back at school should there be some insurmountable problem with the normal visit.

Finally, if pupils continue a visiting programme on a formal basis the scope of the jobs they undertake will increase. For example, at one placement where two pupils had been cleaning and shopping, the elderly person said that she would like to have her garden sorted out. Once links have been established successfully, the school should endeavour to continue with them.

Monitoring and evaluation

There are two opposing arguments as to whether community involvement work at schools should be formally assessed. At Yardleys a case study was developed around the project, so pupils would still receive their City and Guilds assessments. It was then important to distinguish between assessment of individual pupils and assessment of the care in the community project as a whole.

The global dimension

There is always the danger that the global dimension of citizenship education is bolted on to the curriculum as an afterthought. The wording of the Order, however, makes it clear that global citizenship is integral to citizenship education. The programme of study for KS3 requires pupils to acquire knowledge and understanding about 'the world as a global community, and the political, economic, environmental and social implications of this, and the role of the European Union, the Commonwealth and the United Nations'. Multicultural schools in our largest cities are, of course, permanently and powerfully aware that we are a society of citizens from the world over. Global citizenship, however, means more than this. It refers to the fact that our nation is permanently and in almost every particular influenced by world events. In the light of the terrorist attack on New York on 11 September 2001, we no longer need reminding of the urgency of this. The following examples show how a number of schools have started to introduce a global dimension into their schemes of work.

A variety of practice

Most of the schools depicted in our examples are explicit about the global dimension of their citizenship programmes. Some have developed ambitious exchange programmes with other countries. At Marshfields Special School we find older pupils working with the community in Colorado in the United States and others planning trips to Kenya. Staff at Deptford Green have set up links with twin schools in Europe, Vietnam and South Africa and are developing ongoing communication and mutual support with these schools. In Chapter 7 we have seen the refugee club at work in Forest Gate Community School. Opportunities for schools to develop and maintain regular links with young people around the world become easier as electronic communications become ever faster and more accessible. It is not essential to involve students in overseas visits to create a genuinely global curriculum. Indeed the critical dimension of global citizenship is that which explores and addresses global and multicultural issues in our own British communities.

The Deanes School

Young people at the Deanes School have opportunities to connect with several countries overseas:

- **Japan:** For the past three years the school has been host for one day to teachers and students from Oita High School. Mr Yasunao Koyoma, from Oita, comments that 'the visit of our students to the Deanes School is the high spot of our tour'. Many of the Deanes School students keep in contact with their Japanese friends by letter and e-mail.
- **France:** For 25 years students from the school have exchanged visits with students from the lycée in the French town of Artix. The students learn about their partners' cultural differences by living at

home with their hosts. There are usually civic receptions, participation in lessons and visits to the mountains and the coast.

- **Germany:** A similar exchange has been going on for 20 years with students from the Gymnasium at Weingarten.
- **Kenya:** All Year 8 students took part in a study of world sports and contributed to the Game with Two Halves Project to provide sports equipment for schools in Kenya. The whole of the school was involved in raising £6,000 to send six Year 10 students to some of the poorer areas of Kenya to coach students in football skills as part of their sports leadership qualification. Senior teacher Peter Marrett said, 'These students spent time in coaching as part of a health awareness project. I believe this was a life-transforming experience for them. They came back somewhat sober after seeing shanty towns and playing on dirt pitches with kids who had played barefoot. They gave some wonderful assemblies and communicated on a personal level with their friends.'

CSV comment: selecting students for overseas visits

A number of schools offer a wide variety of opportunities for students to develop work on projects with young people from around the world. In most schools foreign trips are usually seen as interesting (but sometimes expensive) perks, and it is important to ensure pupils enjoy equal opportunities to take part in such expeditions. Jim Mulligan was the CSV manager responsible for developing the service learning partnerships between the CSV Lighthouse Schools and Fort Collins Schools in Colorado. He explains how the selection process worked:

In order to avoid elitism and to make sure nobody is excluded from prestigious projects we at CSV Education encourage schools to have interviews following applications based on clear criteria:

- responsible behaviour;
- good attendance;
- a record of some community or public service;
- parental support (and the readiness to be away from home for the fortnight in question);
- a pledge to help raise money for the project whether or not the application is successful.

The interview panel should include students, teachers, governors, community members, etc. The whole process should be open to all and transparent.

Case study on global citizenship: the Anglo-European School

The Anglo-European School in Essex is making a distinguished contribution not only to language education but also to global citizenship. Its work offers an exciting and instructive case study.

The Anglo-European School in the small town of Ingatestone near Chelmsford in Essex is distinctive in that it offers its students and European partners a radically global approach to learning and personal and social development. It provides an education in world citizenship, and so actively encourages young people to develop the multiple identities that are the mark of modern and future citizens.

CSV commentary

The Anglo-European School is included here for four reasons:

1. **Radical commitment to global citizenship:** The Anglo-European School offers an important example of global citizenship linked with the specialist focus of the whole school. Citizenship stems from the heart of the school's work over the past 30 years.
2. **School transformation:** In the 1960s Ingatestone Secondary Modern was a failing school threatened with closure. Local people campaigned to keep it open. In 1971 the Chief Education Officer for Essex, Jack Springett, agreed that the school should stay open and develop an international approach – along the lines of a US Magnet School. It should develop a European ethos across the whole and taught curriculum. Under the leadership of headteacher Norman Pitt, the school set about transforming itself into the Anglo-European School of today and embarked on an extensive programme of new developments across and beyond the curriculum.
3. **Language and culture:** The curriculum makes a clear link between learning a language (with a specific but not exclusive emphasis on European languages) and understanding the culture of a people. The principle might usefully be radically extended to other schools, and not only those specializing in languages.
4. **Staff commitment:** Over 30 years the school has developed a culture of commitment among staff where everyone is expected to play an active part in the wider activities of the school. This culture is explicit and widely respected among members of staff who are properly proud of their achievements.

Educating the global citizen

The world for which we are preparing our children is an increasingly small and interdependent one. Students will need to be flexible, tolerant and cosmopolitan. They will need a clear understanding of their roots but also to be able to move confidently between cultures... The European and international dimension is not a slot in the curriculum in which the students are taught about Europe and the wider world. In this school opportunities are taken to create an atmosphere in which European and international awareness is at the very heart of education in its widest sense.

The aims of the Anglo-European School

Our aims are:

- To provide the highest quality of education that is enriched by a strong European and international dimension.
- To respect individuals and their culture whilst developing an understanding of and a respect for the culture of others.
- To give students the academic and social skills which enable them to move freely and productively beyond the boundaries of their own community.

The five strands of the European dimension

A truly cross-curricular approach to the European and international dimension involves every subject area of the school. The objectives of this curriculum are to promote:

1. Knowledge and understanding of Europe, its peoples and its place in the world.
2. Positive but critical attitudes towards other peoples and cultures, respect for different ways of life, beliefs, opinions and ideas.
3. Enhanced language capability to facilitate communication and cooperation.
4. Preparation for economic life.
5. The development of an internationalist perspective.

Specialist school in languages

The additional resources and money designated for specific language work within departments also develops cultural and international understanding around the learning of languages. For example, in addition to the European projects there is a wider international dimension, which focuses on other cultures. Recently students tackled a history of blues in black America. 'The school believes that the ability to grasp and use a foreign language should not and cannot be separated from understanding the history and culture of those for whom that language is their native tongue. Language and cultural understanding, therefore, are part of something wider – the experience and challenge of being a world citizen.'

A visits programme for the whole school

International understanding is best developed when students have the opportunity to make personal contacts and to experience the culture of others directly.

The visits and exchanges programme involves about 600 students each year to 15 destinations in 24 separate groups. Each year a number of extra opportunities arise out of the school's activities:

- The programme begins in Year 7 with a visit to the Chateau of Wegimont in Southern Belgium.
- In Year 8 students exchange with French schools in five locations.
- In Year 9 the destinations are four schools in Germany. In Year 10 students choose between France, Germany and Spain with six partner schools.
- Some Year 10 students are invited to participate in longer exchanges – four weeks in France or eight weeks in Germany; these students attend school with their partners.
- The sixth form has exchanges to France, Germany, Spain, a Business Studies visit to the Czech Republic and Art visits to Paris or Amsterdam. In recent years sixth form students have taken part in international conferences in Belgium, Ireland and Denmark, and the school orchestra has toured in France and Spain.

An international approach to KS3 and 4

Induction

Every department contributes to the European dimension of the syllabus and takes part in offering new students a 14-day induction programme. Thereafter each department offers its students the opportunity to develop a particular international strand through its work, for example the art department takes students to Amsterdam or Paris to explore the history and practice of art.

The European citizenship award

The European citizenship award is the Anglo-European School's own means of recognizing each student's participation in the European dimension of school life and studies. Other schools in the United Kingdom and elsewhere in the European Union have taken up the scheme, which has the support of the European Commission.

The award aims to develop:

- knowledge and understanding of Europe, its peoples and its place in the world;
- positive but critical attitudes towards other peoples and cultures;
- respect for different ways of life, beliefs, opinions and ideas;
- language capability to facilitate communication and cooperation;
- skills for economic life.

Science across the world

The science department participates in a worldwide sharing of astronomy observations on the Internet and data sharing on energy and drinking water topics. Its partner schools include one in Greece and one in Austria.

Students are encouraged to participate in student conferences with an international dimension.

An international approach to post-16 education

The International Baccalaureate (IB) was introduced and is now taken by a third of the Year 12 students. A further third of the sixth formers take A level, while the remaining students take a mixture of the two. Since 2001 the school has also built in AVCE to enrich further what is offered:

- **Creativity, action and service:** All students in the sixth form partici-pate in the IB creativity, action and service (CAS) programme The CAS courses include a significant element of citizenship education or projects that link well with citizenship education.
- **International study and visits programme:** All sixth form students and staff are involved in the international study and visits programme.
- **Citizenship projects:** Special events and projects include: charity week; model United Nations; and Cosmos and Worldwatch.

Further details are on the school Web site, www.angloeuropean. essex.sch.uk.

Curriculum guidelines on global citizenship

The DfES, in their guidelines on global citizenship, point out that the revised national curriculum offers more opportunities than ever before for a global dimension to be incorporated into the life and work of schools.[6] It includes, for the first time, a detailed overarching statement about the values, aims and purposes of the curriculum. The statement of values and aims relating to a global dimension is:

> Education is... a route to equality of opportunity for all, a healthy and just democracy, a productive economy, and sustainable development. Education should reflect the enduring values that contribute to these ends. These include valuing... the wider groups to which we belong, the diversity in our society and the environment in which we live... The school curriculum... should secure commitment to sustainable development at a personal, national and global level.

The statement of values, aims and purposes also reflects the growing need for young people to be educated to live in a world characterized by rapidly increasing communications:

> education must enable us to respond positively to the opportunities and challenges of the rapidly changing world in which we live and work... we need to be prepared to engage as individuals, parents, workers and citizens with economic, social and cultural change, including the continued globalization of the economy and society, with new work and leisure patterns and with the rapid expansion of communication technologies.

Some programmes of study, such as geography, history, art and design and music, ensure that a global dimension is included. For other subjects, it is the individual school curriculum, developed around the framework of the national curriculum, that offers opportunities for including a global dimension. 'The school curriculum should contribute to the development of pupils' sense of identity through knowledge and understanding of the spiritual, moral, social and cultural heritages of Britain's diverse society and of the local, national, European, Commonwealth and global dimensions of their lives.'

Key stages 3 and 4

At key stages 3 and 4 pupils develop their understanding of their role as global citizens and extend their knowledge of the wider world. Their understanding of issues such as poverty, social justice and sustainable development increases and they realize the importance of taking action to improve the world for future generations. They critically assess information available to them and challenge cases of discrimination and injustice.

Within this progression, certain key concepts form the core of learning about global issues:

- citizenship;
- sustainable development;
- social justice;
- values and perceptions;
- diversity;
- interdependence;
- conflict resolution;
- human rights.

Further useful advice and guidance is available from organizations such as the Development Education Association and Oxfam.[7]

Global curriculum – the Nobel School

Students visit the Somme and Auschwitz with the history department and France and Germany with modern foreign languages. In the past they visited Russia and raised over £1,000 for victims of Chernobyl.

Students have the opportunity to correspond with students in Kadoma, Zimbabwe as part of the Stevenage–Kadoma link (the school participated in a BBC World Service programme on town twinning). The Amnesty International group writes urgent action letters all over the world on behalf of prisoners of conscience. Students in Years 10 and 11 have been in touch with Vanunu's support group in Israel. The in-depth study morning involved all sixth formers with staff from the United Nations Commission for Refugees and Amnesty International as well as visiting students, some of whom were asylum seekers, from a school in Luton. Students in Year 8 RE have corresponded with Cadbury's about slave labour in cocoa plantations.

Many links in the community are formed through work experience placements.

Politics made simple*

Cristin was 17 years old and studying at school for a GNVQ in business when she applied for her CSV Millennium Award. She was a senior prefect, a peer educator and youth leader in her local youth club. Cristin was a very active young woman. She wished to empower a group of young people in Northern Ireland to take part in the political process, train them as peer educators and encourage them to produce an information pack for other groups of young people.

Political engagement in Northern Ireland

During the last 30 years of conflict, political engagement in Northern Ireland had been difficult for the ordinary person let alone young people. Now that Northern Ireland had its own political assembly, people were beginning to engage in local politics. However, many young people did not have the skills or motivation to do so.

Link with Europe

Cristin hoped that a simple information pack would help to make politics accessible. Her project team was recruited from both the Catholic and Protestant sides of the community. They visited and developed links with the political systems in Northern Ireland, Great Britain, the Republic of Ireland and Europe. They were trained as peer educators and they also helped to compile the information pack. The project team were exposed to differing political ideologies that they had to interpret in a meaningful way for other young people. In doing so they all gained a valuable insight into political processes. When the packs were completed they were circulated to youth groups, schools and libraries in the local area.

The real Latin America

Laura Baéz was a highly motivated, energetic young woman who was totally committed to her CSV Millennium Award project that aimed to promote Latin American culture in Northern Ireland. Both she and Andrea Bapitía came from Colombia and were temporary residents in Northern Ireland. Andrea was quieter, more reflective and acted as the strategist for the project.

The cultures of Latin America were not promoted even within the ethnic community groups in Northern Ireland. The two young women believed that a common understanding and tolerance of different cultures, religions and ways of life were becoming more important as the global community

was getting smaller. They thought that this objective had a particular significance in the Northern Ireland context. The Award winners recruited their
project team from the local further education college. The team was a
mixed ethnic group who wanted to improve their English.

The two Award winners used their CSV Millennium Award grant to
promote Latin American culture by creating and designing posters, calen-
dars, postcards and leaflets. The Multi-Cultural Resource Centre, which was
always willing to promote minority cultures, distributed the resources.
Laura and Andrea visited schools and libraries with their material when
they were tackling cultural diversity issues. They also organized and hosted
a cultural event to promote their materials. Latin Americans living in
Northern Ireland attended the event and valued the fact that their culture
was so positively presented.

* These two examples are from CSV's Millennium Awards programme,
whereby young people bid for a grant to undertake a volunteer project
linking school with community.

Creating learning experiences

Active learning in the community is essential to citizenship education

An effective curriculum for active citizenship requires that pupils are
given appropriate, imaginative and challenging learning experiences
through real-life situations on which they reflect. A pedagogy for citizenship education concerns how these learning experiences are structured, offered and evaluated.

Citizenship is a practicum

It makes no sense to teach football, the violin or motor racing only from
books. No more can it make sense to teach active citizenship only from
books. Citizenship is a 'practicum', in the same way that engineering,
doctoring, soldiering or keeping a shop is a practicum. It is an activity
that combines knowledge with experience, and experience with skills
and attitudes. A practicum is usually based on a code of practice and is
built round a discipline of subject knowledge that comprises facts linked
together by concepts. Universities and institutions of higher education
have traditionally assumed the role of guardians and developers of the
disciplines that underpin established and respected practica: engineering, medicine, military science and business studies.

Too often there has grown a gap between the discipline and the practicum. Donald Schon compares those academics who live on the high ground of intellectual rigour with the practitioners (planners, architects, designers... and teachers?) who live down below in the swamp of everyday life.[8]

The fact, of course, is that a practicum is *more* not less than a discipline. To be a footballer you need to know the offside rule; but knowledge of the rule doesn't make you a good footballer. No more does a knowledge of biology make you a good doctor. No more, of course, does knowledge of parliamentary procedure in itself make you an effective citizen.

Schon and his university colleagues in Boston argued that the right way – indeed the only effective way – of teaching town planning was to set up a studio and expose planning students to the *real challenges* of the job but in semi-protected circumstances. This approach to professional development is increasingly becoming standard practice in relation to many jobs. Where matters of life, death and personal safety are at stake the point is well taken. If someone is accepted for training as a psychotherapist, or a train driver or a brain surgeon, that person receives on-the-job training as well as the necessary theoretical instruction. The more complex and varied the challenges faced, the more important it is to learn strategies to cope with new and sometimes unexpected situations. It is called professionalism.

The aim of the Citizenship Order is to create a generation of young people who:

> will think of themselves as active citizens, willing, able and equipped to have an influence in public life and with the critical capacities to weigh evidence before speaking and acting; to build on and to extend radically to young people the best in existing traditions of community involvement and public service, and to make them individually confident in finding new forms of involvement and action among themselves.

This is a description of a practicum, not simply a discipline. If citizenship education is to achieve its goal it is not merely desirable but necessary that it is taught as a practice, not simply as a body of knowledge and ideas.

Citizenship can only be learnt through reflecting on real experience

Citizenship, therefore, can only be taught through engaging students in the practical business of reflecting on their involvement with the school and its wider communities. The three strands of citizenship education – social and moral responsibility, community involvement and political literacy – combine to form a single rope. Each element is necessary to the whole. There has to be real responsibility, real participation and genuine political reflection across the whole range of experiences that make up the programme of study.

This point is not new. In the mid-1980s HMI published a document that stated:[9]

> Active learning, and a sense of purpose and success, enhance pupils' enjoyment, interest, confidence and sense of personal worth; passive learning and inappropriate teaching styles can lead to frustration and failure. In particular, it is necessary to ensure that pupils are given sufficient first hand experience, accompanied by discussion, upon which to base abstract ideas and generalizations.
>
> Teaching and learning might, for example, extend to using the local environment, undertaking community service and establishing contact with commerce and industry.
>
> The national primary survey found that the work children were given to do was better matched to their abilities when teachers employed a combination of didactic and exploratory approaches.
>
> The national secondary survey points to the care needed to avoid teaching styles developing within subjects and across the curriculum as a whole which overemphasise:
>
> - the abstract and theoretical at the expense of the experimental and the practical;
> - writing at the expense of talking;
> - factual knowledge at the expense of skills and understanding; and
> - narrowly prescribed work at the expense of that in which pupils might use their own initiative.

'Making the known more knowable'

Peter Mitchell comments: 'This wise advocacy of a balanced approach to curriculum and learning gives support to the importance of active learning.'[10] Eric Midwinter (1971) in addressing the issue of underachievement in inner-city communities advocated more emphasis in the curriculum on studying in the local community:[11]

> Only on a thorough grounding in and understanding of their situation can one hope to develop the abilities to perceive exactly what is amiss and how it might be righted. It is not so much moving from the known to the unknown as making the known more knowable... By stretching the children, intellectually and creatively, on the social issues that confront them, one hopes to produce adults provoked and challenged into a positive and constructive response.

Active learning, including in its community context, is not something that belongs exclusively to those concerned with citizenship, PSHE and the performance subjects. It is a pedagogy that relates to *all* curriculum areas.

Active learning requires a positive ethos in the classroom, trust and respect between student and teacher, and a range of teaching methods that meet the different learning styles of individual pupils. In schools such as Lipson Community College commitment to quality learning is at the heart of the life of the school. Quality learning involves students taking responsibility for their own transferable learning in a context where the effectiveness of learning is monitored and reviewed by students and staff. This commitment to quality learning requires a social as well as an intellectual stimulus. It is rooted in citizen values – freedom as autonomy, no authority without democracy and no rights without responsibilities – and unites the roles of students and staff as learners and citizens around a common purpose.

Recent research

A recent research report on current learning theory was directly and indirectly supportive of experiential learning such as is encouraged by citizenship education.[12] In other words, what is good for teaching citizenship is good for all teaching and learning.

Three of the report's conclusions are particularly relevant here. They concern: 1) the way children learn; 2) the importance of transferable knowledge; and 3) the value of learning in a variety of contexts including the community. The conclusions are summarized, and interested readers should turn to the original text for fuller information.

The way children learn

- Young children actively engage in making sense of the world, but some domains – language, number, and biological and physical causality – they seem predisposed to learn.
- Children are ignorant but not stupid and can reason well with the knowledge they do understand.
- Children are natural problem solvers. They are also persistent because success and understanding are motivating.
- Children develop knowledge of their own learning capacities.
- Children's natural capabilities require assistance for learning. They depend upon adults and others as catalysts and mediators of learning.
- Neuro-cognitive research findings suggest that the brain is a dynamic organ, shaped to a great extent by experience and by what a living being does. That is, active learning can actually *improve* brain capacity.

The message for citizenship education as for other subjects is simple, but sometimes forgotten. People in general and children in particular are programmed to learn, to make sense of their world and to solve problems. They need mentors and tutors. Peer mentoring and adult volunteer mentors can make an important contribution (see box below, CSV Reading Together). Children can also improve their brain capacity through active learning. The findings of Hannam and Gerlach (see Chapter 13) underline this point. ALC can, therefore, promote quality learning across the curriculum.

Transfer of learning

Memorizing facts in itself does not make for fruitful learning. In a world dominated by change, we need to develop the capacity to apply old learning to new situations. We need, that is, to develop a strong grasp of underlying principles and the appropriate factual background. Teaching styles vary considerably in their ability to create learning environments where students develop transfer learning. It is of course obvious that education for active citizenship requires students to transfer their learning from one context to another and has little use for a person's ability to memorize chunks of information without context.

Learning in a community context

Learning environments are important to learning. Collaborative learning between teachers and other adults can significantly improve learning, as can interaction with members of the local community. 'Opportunities to use knowledge to create products and benefits for others are particularly motivating for students.'[13] In other words a book concerned with quality learning recommends service learning as an effective methodology.

CSV Reading Together

CSV has developed a paired reading package, Reading Together. Young people are trained to support each other in learning to read and to understand the written and spoken word.

Once again this is a five-step tutoring programme. Young tutors are taught:

- to determine the pupil's reading level;
- to identify suitable books;
- to read aloud clearly and accurately;
- to convey enthusiasm by using expression;

- to develop the pupil's vocabulary and understanding through open-ended questions – this can usefully be linked to the language hierarchy described below.

CSV also developed, in partnership with the Ibis Trust, a peer education development programme designed to support young people in tackling the scourge of HIV/AIDS (see below, Involving students)

Lipson Community College: notes on teaching and learning

Teaching is a complex and difficult art to master. An effective teacher is one who is able to convince not half or three quarters but all her/his students to do quality work.

Lipson students tell me a good teacher is deeply interested in them and the material being taught. They also say that such a teacher frequently conducts class discussions and does not lecture very much. Almost all of them say that a good teacher relates to them on their level; the teacher does not place himself/herself above them, and they are comfortable talking with him/her.

Lipson students also tell me that a good teacher rarely threatens or punishes and that they have little respect for teachers who do. Students say that they appreciate teachers who make an effort to be entertaining. To maintain student interest month after month in potentially difficult courses, good teachers try to inject humour, variety and drama into their lessons. Boredom is the enemy of quality.

Besides the immediate caring that gets the job done, the Lipson teacher slowly helps the student at the start to gain at least a little short-term satisfaction. Once the students gain confidence in the teacher's ability to provide the leadership necessary for their long-term satisfaction, they become more and more willing to put up with short-term pain and frustration.

Effective teachers at Lipson place emphasis on hard work and getting the mood right. The atmosphere is one of enjoyment. As long as we have to work let's have some fun along the way. The more effective teachers also search out feedback. These teachers spend a small part of almost every lesson asking students for their input on how more can be learned, or what can be done to make the class more enjoyable.

If you ask turned-off students why they are not working, they will say it is boring, they don't need it – that no one cares. When we do quality work we carefully evaluate what we are doing and come to the conclusion that it is worth the effort. You must teach quality before you teach anything else to your students.

(Steve Baker, Head Learner, Extract from the Lipson *Little Red Book*)

Three approaches to active learning

The spectrum of active learning

ALC is an important element on the whole spectrum of active learning techniques. There is not precise universal agreement about the use of terms in association with active and experiential learning. For the purposes of this book the terms are used as follows (see Figure 14.6):

- **Active learning:** The distinguishing mark of active learning, as its name suggests, is inter*action* and engagement with other people. As we move from the left to the right of the spectrum these activities engage increasingly with the wider community. On the right of the spectrum learning experiences are based on activities that meet real needs of people in or beyond the classroom. Active learning, as used here, applies to the whole range of teaching and learning strategies that deliberately and systematically engage young people in learning through interacting with others.

  We shall explore below how young people can be active in developing the skills of description, reflection, speculation, discussion and decision making. These simple skills build frameworks for transferable learning and are as relevant in academic subjects as they are necessary to education for active citizenship.
- **Experiential learning:** By this we mean learning that comes from experiencing a situation – either directly in real life, eg playing an instrument or measuring the pollution in river water, or indirectly, through role-play and simulations. Experiential learning is contrasted with the straight teaching of facts and concepts (eg the theory of violin technique or the chemistry of water pollution).

Active Learning

Description, reflection, speculation, discussion and deciding
+ Experiential Learning + ALC

$\longrightarrow$

Experiential Learning

$\longrightarrow$

rehearsal, role play, mock events + ALC

Active learning in the community

$\longrightarrow$

Active learning in the community (ALC)

Figure 14.6 *Active and experiential learning*

● **Active learning in the community** (ALC), as we have noted earlier, is referred to as *service learning* in the United States, where it has been most systematically developed as a methodology. ALC refers to learning strategies based on active service to the school and its wider communities.

Description, reflection, speculation, discussion and deciding (active learning)

This exercises comes from the Lipson College *Little Red Book*. It begins with an experience, preferably a shared, real experience as far as citizenship education is concerned. It could, however, be based on a piece of speaking or writing (newspaper cutting, book, video) or a role-play.

The language hierarchy goes from **description** at the simplest level, through **reflection**, which girls are good at, to **speculation**, which is what boys are good at. Building in opportunities for students to progress through all three will ensure that they all develop good learning and excellent literacy skills. Active learning of this kind can be built into citizenship education in subject areas as well as into discrete citizenship lessons:

● Step one: Talk with the person next to you/give five quick responses.
● Step two: Note-making task in previous pairings/descriptive base and quick feedback.
● Step three: Reflective decision-making task in previous pairings.
● Step four: Join up pairs into groups of four and structured brainstorm.
● Step five: Speculative differentiated tasks to feed back in x minutes' time:
   – low attainers task;
   – average attainers task;
   – high attainers task.

Interactive learning of this kind: 1) gives young people a firm grasp of transferable principles; 2) can be applied to a wide range of subjects and settings; and 3) offers a crucial citizen skill – reflection and speculation built upon initial understanding. At the same time it can help bridge the divide between intellectual knowledge and the understanding gained in interactive learning. CSV's paired reading programme, CSV Reading Together, can be used to promote pupils' capacity to describe, reflect and speculate. The five-step sequence of the language hierarchy is a useful tool for reflection. It can be used in a variety of settings in citizenship education, including peer education and community projects.

Snapshot: student reflection on a mentoring project

Sidney Stringer Community Technology College, Coventry
This is a student mentoring project (Year 12 with Year 8) managed by Sheila Chennells (PE, Deputy Head of sixth form and link teacher). Twenty students sat in a circle and the CSV adviser used the Barclays New Futures career skills questionnaire as a basis for the discussion. The following points and ideas emerged:

● Students are paired with a Year 8 mentee in class time in particular subjects but they also pursue a more informal (buddying) relationship as well.
● They have to negotiate with the subject teacher as to the kind of support required. One girl had asked that her mentee be taken out of one class so that they could do additional work together.
● One boy had had problems striking up any kind of relationship with a pupil deemed to be 'difficult' in school. Suggestions were made by the group for strategies to improve this situation.
● Most students testified to improvements in key skills and some (boys!) had improved their timekeeping in order not to let their partner down!
● The group comprised mainly Asian students (the majority, girls) but one of the boys was a refugee from Bosnia.
● Records are kept by teacher and students and recognition is achieved via the ASDAN award scheme.

Rehearsal, role-play, mock events (experiential learning)

Citizenship education regularly draws on simulations, games, mock events, debates and elections. The more realistic these are the better. History students can debate real past events, drawing on documentary and other evidence. Current events are likely to be even more fruitful as sources of genuine topics that demand thought and attention. The 'war' on terrorism has produced a large crop of real, urgent and very challenging issues.

The more contentious the issue, the greater the care that needs to be taken in managing the discussion, reflection and subsequent action (if any.) Newcomers to such exercises are recommended to consult with those experienced in the field.

Some schools, such as for example St Peter's Collegiate School, have links with their local magistrates' courts and can combine real experiences with mock trials and debates.

If a school runs a mock election in parallel with the general election, every student will have the opportunity to take part in at least one such event while at secondary school.

Active learning in the community

Many teachers treat learning through community involvement as opportunistic, that is something you only do if the opportunity comes your way. They may be strongly in favour of experiential learning, regularly encourage mock elections and debates, but fail to see that it is possible to *plan* for learning that tackles real-life issues.

It is true that the particular projects you will choose will depend on your circumstances, but that does not mean that these projects are not planned, monitored and evaluated like any other sequence of learning experiences. ALC is not opportunistic; it is a methodology that can be planned into the curriculum. This is fully explored below.

ALC should not be confused with community service

A simple example makes the distinction clear. Young people engaged in a clean-up campaign in their neighbourhood will do useful service, but they may learn little or nothing from it. Students in a south coast community college linked its litter campaign with a piece of real learning. They undertook simple research, made videos and presented their case to their peers and to the local authority. In doing this they tackled the problem at its roots. They also added significantly to their knowledge and ability to make good things happen.

By linking learning with service and service with learning, schools, colleges and universities can devote serious energy and resources to activities that have real learning outcomes.

ALC is a strategy that can make a significant contribution to achieving the goals of lifelong learning and education for active citizenship.

Active learning in the community – a methodology

Background and definitions

In the United States there have since the late 1980s been many established active learning in the community (service learning) programmes in schools. These have been encouraged by federal initiatives to promote community service activities in and beyond education. These programmes, however, have their own intellectual and pedagogical provenance. They draw significantly upon the work of the philosopher and educator John Dewey. The principles of ALC are clear and well established. They constitute a methodology of teaching and learning that can be grasped and practised by educators in almost any setting.

A methodology for education for active citizenship

ALC is a methodology that is perfectly suited to education for active citizenship. It links values, knowledge and skills around a core of activities that meet real needs in the school or its wider communities. ALC is an education method that links meaningful student community service with academic learning, personal growth and civic responsibility.

ALC: defining characteristics

Active learning in the community:

- **offers concrete opportunities** for young people to learn new skills, think critically and test new roles in an environment that encourages risk taking and rewards competence;
- **is incremental**, and progresses from one year to the next;
- **is appropriate** for use with all students and in all curricular areas;
- **is integral** to the taught and whole curriculum (and not a bolt-on activity);
- **provides structured time** for the students or participants to **reflect** on what they have learnt from the experience;
- **is accredited and celebrated**;
- **responds** to a wide range of needs in the school and wider community.

Learning activities

There can be as many ALC activities as there are needs in the community and opportunities in the school, college and university. Typically – as we have seen – projects involve peer learning, community service and work on the environment, intergenerational projects and initiatives to develop communities through the arts, sciences and sport.

An effective ALC strategy

ALC is ideally suited to education for active citizenship because it:

- provides a range of activities linked with clear learning outcomes;
- develops whole-institution strategies;
- combines:
  - action with learning;
  - learning with the community;
  - community with citizenship.

The active learning process

Learning through community service usually involves a four-step process:

1. **Preparation**
   This consists of learning activities that take place prior to the service itself. Students must understand the purpose of the project and what is expected of them as well as what they can expect to gain from the work. This includes:
   - identifying and analysing the challenge;
   - selecting and planning the project;
   - training and orientation.
2. **Action**
   The project itself must:
   - provide for student ownership;
   - be developmentally appropriate;
   - be meaningful;
   - have academic integrity;
   - be supervised well.
3. **Reflection**
   Reflection enables the students to think critically about their service experience. They can reflect on their experiences through: writing, reading, discussion, developing critical thinking and problem-solving skills, developing a portfolio.
4. **Celebration**
   This is an occasion to recognize what the students have achieved. It may include media coverage, a special event, the award of certificates or other ways of marking the end of the project.

Quality practice

The following checklist has been distilled from experience in the United States and the UK.

Service learning: a quality checklist

Does your service learning programme:

1. strengthen service and academic learning through integrating the work within the mainstream taught and whole curriculum? (Service learning cannot usually be delivered as a bolt-on to existing activities.)
2. feature in your development plan and publicity?
3. provide concrete opportunities for young people to increase their knowledge, learn new skills, think critically and test new roles in an environment that encourages risk taking and rewards competence?
4. involve students in planning the project?
5. involve students in preparation and reflection?
6. offer students skilled adult guidance and support?
7. recognize the students' achievements?
8. offer a meaningful contribution to the community?
9. develop purposeful partnerships with the community and others involved in the project?
10. provide staff and tutors with the appropriate training and professional development to promote effective service learning activities?

Benefits to students

ALC offers students the opportunity to develop intellectually, emotionally, socially and politically. The methodology supports assessment through discernment and through measurement against external criteria (see below, Assessment). Most important of all, the approach enables students to reflect on, record and take responsibility for their own learning. Table 14.1 can be used for any of these purposes.

Teaching the skills and dispositions of active citizenship

CSV has initiated an ALC training and development programme around the theme of active citizenship. In this we have been pleased to work with US colleagues from the Institute of Service Learning and, more

Table 14.1 *The benefits of active learning in the community*

Intellectual growth	– acquire new knowledge and concepts – apply knowledge critically
Personal growth	– self-confidence and self-esteem – self-understanding – a sense of identity – independence and autonomy – openness to new experiences and roles
Social and personal development	– communication skills – leadership skills – ability to work with others – acceptance and awareness of others from different cultures and backgrounds – a sense of caring for others – a sense of belonging – peer group affiliation
Citizenship (this involves developing an understanding of the responsibilities and rights of citizens through meeting real needs in the community)	– learning how decisions are made – analysing community needs – taking positive action – developing political literacy – ability to take risks and accept challenges – a sense of useful purpose – positive personal values and beliefs – responsibility for one's self and one's actions
Preparation for work (ALC complements work experience)	– realistic ideas about work – key skills – leadership and the ability to follow directions from others – teamwork – responsibility, reliability – the ability to see a task through – contacts and references for future job opportunities
Benefits to schools, colleges and universities	– positive partnerships with the local community, including employers and the local authority – democratic participation – a reflective approach to learning rooted in real experiences/projects (see Donald Schon's practicum, described above)

recently, a team of educators working on a project headed up by staff from Clemson University in South Carolina. This international partnership has enormously strengthened our work and itself reflects a commitment to global citizenship.

The active citizenship 'toolkit' for teachers

CSV has in association with US colleagues[14] developed a teacher's toolkit for 'active citizenship'.[15] These classroom materials provide teachers and students with a framework for a citizen curriculum in key stages 3 and 4. Through the five competencies listed below all students develop the skills necessary to become productive working citizens, caring members of their neighbourhood and contributors to the improvement of their school and community.

The five competencies that guide students on a journey towards a lifetime of good citizenship are:

1. the ability to work effectively in a variety of group settings;
2. the ability to identify and evaluate the values and ethics of themselves and others in the community;
3. recognizing, appreciating and supporting vital elements of the local community and encouraging community involvement;
4. gathering and evaluating data necessary to effect positive change;
5. implementing effective decision making and problem-solving strategies.

CSV developed demonstration projects in London. The intention was: 1) to apply the model in inner-city schools; 2) to test the methodology across a range of subjects; and 3) to encourage whole-staff involvement. The outcomes from London projects were greatly encouraging and are described in Table 14.2 (page 184).

Pedagogy – Tanfield School

The teacher as a leading learner

A wide range of teaching and learning styles includes the opportunity for teachers to learn alongside pupils, for example while carrying out research using the Internet or during a visit by a guest speaker or a specialist teacher (eg an artist specializing in mime).

Facilitation

The problem-solving approach in a wide range of activities provides opportunities for the teachers to act as facilitators. The Year 10 Changemakers project requires the teacher to facilitate the work of the pupils, but all the work must be peer-led.

Reflection

All teachers and pupils include reflection as part of their approach to teaching and learning, especially as they set personal targets at the end of each unit of work, termly and annually.

Assessment

Assessment in all subjects is continuous, and takes the form of self-assessment, teacher assessment and peer assessment. Portfolios of evidence of activities in citizenship in all areas of study will be kept to support end of key stage 3 statements and also citizenship studies GCSE. The pupils keep their record of progress and reflections on their achievement in their organizers. These are linked with the TREE project (see below, Assessment).

The Nobel School

Leading learner

The Nobel School is a learning community where the core purpose of pupil learning is enhanced by the learning of parents, staff and governors.

Facilitation

In circle time (recently introduced) the teacher has the role of facilitator.

Reflection

The bedrock of the Nobel School is individual reflection and school self-evaluation that rest on confidence and self-belief.

Assessment

Students regularly assess their own work and that of other students; they have evaluated the reward and behaviour policies, and sixth form teaching styles and will be increasingly involved as evaluators.

St Peter's Collegiate School

There is a strong emphasis throughout the school on developing quality teaching and learning styles and methods:

- There has been a stress on differentiation in all departments.
- There has been a general move towards more interactive and experiential teaching and learning, for example group work, research assignments, class portfolios and personal portfolios. National Record of Achievement (NRA) is used throughout Year 7 to Year 13. In INSET and departmental training, attention is paid to key skills, differentiation and learning styles.
- Learning is experienced through both subject-specific lessons and pastoral work.
- There is a strong emphasis on IT – St Peter's is an IT school.
- Students, through the Duke of Edinburgh scheme, are trained in mountain leadership, and Year 9 are sent on outward-bound-style activity weeks.

Developing political literacy

In the context of active learning, teaching political literacy gains a broader and richer meaning than that which is often given to it. It can also be wrapped into a circle (see Figure 14.7), starting with the processes of literacy, communication and decision making and progressing through to action in the real world that meets real needs.

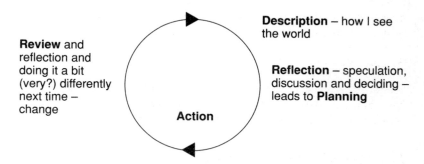

Active Learning

Description, reflection, speculation, discussion and deciding/rehearsal, role-play, mock events/**ALC**

Description – how I see the world

Reflection – speculation, discussion and deciding – leads to **Planning**

Action

Review and reflection and doing it a bit (very?) differently next time – change

Figure 14.7   *ALC and the teaching of political literacy*

Table 14.2 *CSV active citizenship: outcomes from pilot projects in London* (*see page 181*)

Participants	Wandsworth Battersea Technology College
Students Year 7 (11–12 years)	23
Boys	18
Girls	5
Ethnicity	
Afro-Caribbean	85%
Asian/Caucasian	15%
Percentage of children in care	60%
Community participants	4 Peabody volunteers
Wandsworth residents	20
Outcomes **Direct impact of project**	
Behavioural improvement	80% of pupils
Attendance improvement	35/50% to 89/90%
Exclusions	reduced from 11 to 2
Improvement in verbal and written skills, documented by English teacher	66% of pupils
Indirect impact	
Direct participants have mobilized whole of Year 7, 8, 9 students	230
Indirectly impacted on the whole school	450 – improving general attitude to the environment
Significant contribution to development of international materials for citizenship education	– interest from USA partners – interest from Government, DfES and Qualifications and Curriculum Authority
Impact beyond the school	– national press and TV coverage – support of Wandsworth Borough Council

Customarily teaching political literacy has generally been equated with teaching about politics, and more narrowly with lessons about government and constitutional matters. The political learning outcomes in the programme of study – in spite of reassurances elsewhere in the text – are largely about political institutions. Now political institutions, parliaments, parties and pressure groups are important features of the political landscape. There are already quality materials, activities and courses dealing with voting, debating and the whole business of democratic institutions. But politics is about more than these institutions and formal processes. It is about how power is distributed, used and developed between groups in society. Politics is about how the school is run; about how the school bus service operates; and about how seriously young people are treated when it comes to their opinions.

In this broader context political literacy means more than knowing about politics. It is about how I see the world in terms of relationships, rights, responsibilities and duties. Politics begins with my capacity to describe, reflect on, speculate about and discuss – and finally decide on actions that affect others. Any piece of learning that has to do with these things directly or indirectly impinges on my political literacy. For this reason CSV stresses the double benefit of promoting paired reading initiatives. There is the intrinsic importance of reading as a window on the world, and the additional benefit of learning through providing a service to others.

Some may argue that it is all very well for subjects like history, English, geography and RE – to name a few obvious choices – to lay claim to work on political literacy; but maths, physics and biology are a different matter. But wait, the biology teachers will say, their subject is producing more contentious moral issues (spare-part surgery, cloning, euthanasia) than almost any other field. And much the same goes for other parts of science and IT. Maths is interesting. It is morally and politically neutral, some will say. Others will reply that it is as morally neutral as a piece of lead piping that can be used as a murder weapon by Colonel Mustard in the ballroom. Maths may be neutral, but the uses to which it is put have powerful moral connotations.

The biggest political event of the last century was made of numbers

Donald Schon when describing the complaints from students about their subject areas talked of how initially his department had judged statistics to be a necessary core course for all planning students. The students, however, felt otherwise, not because they were shy of figures, but because they were suspicious of the way in which statistics were being used in developing social policy. So numbers matter morally as well as mathematically. The hydrogen bomb was built from a profound under-standing of numbers. The biggest political event of the last century was therefore made of numbers.

At the heart of political literacy is ordinary literacy – the ability to understand, empathize with (or attack) other people's worlds. There is a debate among philosophers about which comes first, the concept or the word for the concept. Do I understand my world because of language, or do I communicate my instinctive understanding with hard-won words? Wherever we may stand on the spectrum of the way language mediates our understanding of the world, there can be no doubt that language is inseparably bound to the way we relate to people and events. The case study above of the Anglo-European School made it clear how language is seen in that school as an introduction to diverse cultures (p 161). Language is at the heart of global citizenship.

So politics begin at the extreme left of our line. As we come to the centre – experiential learning through debates, roles-plays and simu-lated events – it is easy to see the connection. One school, Colne Community School and College in Brightlingsea, cleverly built different electoral systems into the voting procedures for the school council. Each year group had a different voting system. These were not mock elec-tions. It was a real council and made real decisions. Thus we move from simulation to real action.

Working with local councils

An increasing number of schools engage with their local council on a number of issues, particularly environmental issues. In Plymouth there is a city council of students. In most European countries there is a national student council body. In the UK we have a long way to go, but we are now making a start. The recent Hear by Right programme from the Local Government Association is promoting democratic involve-ment of young people through local government (see Chapter 16).

If we bend our active learning line into a circle (Figure 14.8) it becomes a Kolb Cycle where experience, reflection and learning form a spiral. This is how it needs to be in schools.

Learners and citizens

If we return for a moment to our diagrammatic way of looking at schools in their communities (Figure 14.9), we can see how young people apply their learning to their lives and their lives to their learning by recog-nizing that they have *multiple identities*. They are learners, and citizens in school and beyond. As citizens they will be engaged with their commu-

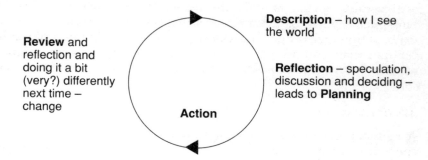

Figure 14.8   *Active learning as a Kolb Cycle*

nities and hopefully helping influence and shape those communities according to democratic values. As learners they will be taking in their experiences, reflecting on them, sharing their reflections and deciding on better ways of learning, being and doing in the future. In other words at the point where citizenship and learning overlap – the point at which

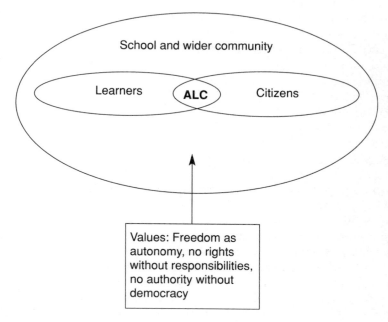

Figure 14.9   *Young people as learners and citizens*

pedagogy is most creative or deadly – we find students and teachers consciously wrestling with issues of values and politics as we make sense of the world about us. It is at this overlapping point of the Venn diagram that we find Schon's practicum, his living studio where real issues are tackled under supervision and with support in the context of both *learning* and *citizenship*.

Assessment: introduction

'How will citizenship be assessed?' the teachers asked when they first heard that citizenship education was to be a foundation subject. 'Will children and young people be put in a position where they fail citizenship? If they were, the whole endeavour will become counter-productive. We'll simply alienate young people still further from school and from society.'

The Angie test!

This same question had similarly exercised the minds of the policy makers and teachers who had been responsible for shaping the final texts of the Order. The case of a Yorkshire teenager, 'Angie', was cited. Angie was a lively 15-year-old with a penchant for getting into trouble. She would regularly appear on detention for one reason or another. Her written work was poor, as was her academic work generally. Angie, however, did have the 'gift of the gab'. She had – in the language of competency assessment – highly developed oral communication skills. She could persuade almost anybody to do almost anything. She was a natural leader with imagination, good will and the power to influence her teachers as well as her peers. If Angie felt that something needed doing, she would organize a bunch of people to do it. There was one memorable occasion when Angie, finding herself once more in detention for some misdemeanour, said to the teacher, 'What shall I do, Miss?' The teacher grinned and replied, 'Why don't you finish the posters for your community project? We all need to know about it.'

Thus it was that a serious-minded group of educators in an airless hotel conference room in London applied the 'Angie test' to accrediting citizenship education. If the 'system' put Angie in a position where she would fail citizenship, there was something wrong with the 'system'; and it was the system not Angie that needed to be put right. The point was taken. A clear distinction was subsequently made between 'citizenship studies', an optional but formal qualification, and 'citizenship education', which is an entitlement for everyone. Angie might show little interest in citizenship studies and elect not to take it, but she was clearly a star performer when it came to political literacy, community involvement and social responsibility. There should be *no question* of Angie failing citizenship.

Assessment should recognize achievement of all pupils

Matters of assessment and accreditation raised questions that go beyond the 'Angie test'. Teachers wanted to know precisely how citizenship education was to be inspected. So much else hung on the answer to that question. Representatives from the QCA told the teachers at the regional conference/workshops that 'assessment should be active and involve pupils in the process; it should recognize the achievement of *all* pupils, and that it should reflect the full range of knowledge, skills and understanding in the programmes of study'.[16] The QCA officer then added, 'The challenge is to measure what we value rather than valuing only that which is easy to measure.' This aphorism touches on what some believe to be a fundamental problem with outcome assessment.

In what follows we shall explore the various options open to us, but it is good to begin with some definitions and distinctions.

Definitions

- **Assessment:** Judgement on the quality of the achievement – agree the criteria for these judgements in advance. Encourage students to contribute to these criteria.
- **Recognition:** Formal comment or record of individual and class achievement. Again, recognition can come from the student, the class or team, and the client group or partners. Recognition can be an element in circle time, and certainly should be part of project reflection where the students review:
  - how the project is doing;
  - what they are learning from the work;
  - the implications for what they are going to do next.
- **Celebration:** One of the golden rules of active learning in the community (service learning) is that student achievements should be celebrated. This can include project celebrations such as the opening of exhibitions (in or outside school), the unveiling of arts or environmental projects, publications of books (oral history), assemblies, drama and sports events. Have the students invite their community partners wherever possible. Involve the community partners in eval-

uating the projects and the contribution of the students. Ensure that the students take some or all of the responsibility for collecting this valuable feedback.

- **Monitoring:** An opportunity to ask and reflect on the questions: Is it working as it should? Are we doing what we said we would do?
- **Evaluation:** This is an opportunity to ask the question: What is the value of the activity/product/experience? We may be doing what we said we would do, but it may not be the best thing to do.

Evaluation: a cautionary tale

As part of their citizenship work, a group of Year 8 pupils decide to arrange a lunch club for housebound older people. They organize everything well. The old people are duly collected and brought to the school. The meal is ready on time, and the food well cooked (albeit rather mountainous). The disco music can be heard throughout the hall, and after lunch there is a vigorous game of bingo. The older people are grateful and duly thank the students for their kindness. In terms of assessment, the indicators all look good and each young person has recorded measurable achievement against the knowledge, skills and understanding that they have gained from the project.

Weeks later Jenny, one of the project leaders, talks to her gran about the project and suggests that they repeat the experience next term. The old lady looks doubtful, but is clearly anxious not to hurt Jenny's feelings.

'Didn't you enjoy it, then, Nan?'

'It was very good. You all took such trouble...'

'What then?'

'It was partly the music, and that hall. It's very noisy. I don't hear well at the best of times, especially in public places like that...'

To cut a long conversation short, Jenny came to realize that they had not consulted the older people sufficiently about what they wanted. Not all of them liked bingo. Most of them disliked loud music, and the acoustics of the hall, which the children were quite used to, were hard and even gave some of them a headache. She was even told that Mrs Franwell didn't like being called an old person. 'I'm older than most, but that doesn't make me old. "Old" sounds like "useless" to me,' she had said.

Jenny talked to her friends on the committee about it and they agreed two things: 1) in future they would consult more closely with the older people before planning the event, including the menu and the music; and 2) they would have more optional activities. They would find out things that the older people might like to contribute or do. It turned out that one was an accomplished singer who could accompany herself on the piano.

Following Jenny's comments the class agreed to meet and re-evaluate their work. They concluded that next time they would do things very differently. They had set themselves the wrong task. They had decided on what *they* thought the older people liked. They had not worked *with* the older people to find out what *they* would most like. It was, they reflected, a bit like the time last year when their teachers wouldn't let them discuss teaching and learning in school council. The teachers had just served up the lessons they thought would be good for them! Now, since the new principal had arrived, they had a regular opportunity to discuss the way things are done, and to suggest improvements.

This tale is drawn from a variety of experiences rather than a single specific study.

The value and dangers of assessment

Assessment in citizenship education has from the start proved a controversial issue. Dave Brockington has been invited to explore in this chapter some of the controversial aspects of assessing citizenship education from his perspective as a trustee of ASDAN, a national organization for the development and recognition of personal, social, health and citizenship education. Many of the schools in our case studies have used the ASDAN awards as a way of measuring, valuing and accrediting the achievement of their pupils. David is a member of the Government's national PSHE Advisory Group, and was a member of the DfES/QCA citizenship education sub-group on assessment. He picks up the theme of linking the aims and methods of assessment with the larger purpose – the 'big picture' – behind citizenship education.

You don't get anything to grow faster, or stronger – or was it higher? – by simply measuring it.

Whoever it was that first came out with this comment, did so in the context of the English obsession with assessment. I subscribe to the view that there is such an obsession, that it is also linked to an ungenerous and limited perception of what it is to be intelligent and able, and I believe these assumptions and perceptions of ourselves and others to be unhelpful and unhealthy.

It isn't by chance that newspaper headlines increasingly focus on our exam-dominated culture and on the fact that our children are the most assessed in the whole of Europe. Yet there is an important sense in which assessment, which is after all just one part of the learning cycle, could, if we let it, help the process of learning and the growth of understanding.

It can do this if it is used as a specific tool with a specific purpose in mind to enhance the development of the learner.

The trouble is that we have a tendency not to use assessment so much in this developmental sort of way. Our assessment systems, certainly those used for terminal examination, are based more on making a judgement at the end of a process of learning, often with huge life consequences, which can be dramatically and profoundly negative on the morale of the learner.

This emphasis on terminal examination as an accurate guide to person development or to intelligence, or to knowledge, or to skills acquired, seems to me to be the least sophisticated of the ways in which we could productively use the process of assessment.

If we assess as we go, in small steps, sharing our perceptions as teachers of the progress of the learner, seeking the learner's own view of progress at each stage, we use the assessment process itself as a way of *encouraging* learning. The learner is helped to understand where he or she is and what is to be done next in an active planning and developmental process. That is precisely the sense in which assessment can play a hugely significant part in the development of learning.

The difference is, of course, between seeing and using assessment as a process (which itself contributes to the learning cycle), and seeing and using it more as a means of a one-off end-of-process judgement.

The importance of this distinction is especially relevant to the arena of citizenship and personal, social and health education within the curriculum.

Pre-16: citizenship and PSHE in the national curriculum

In 1998 the Personal, Social and Health Education (PSHE) Advisory Group was set up by the Labour Government under the dual chairing of Estelle Morris, then Minister of State for Education, and Tessa Jowell, then Minister of State in the Department of Health, as a joint initiative between the two ministries. Their joint plan was to establish a framework for the delivery of PSHE within the national curriculum.

At the same time as the establishment of the PSHE Advisory Group at the then DfEE, Bernard Crick was making great headway in promoting the cause of citizenship as a subject area distinct in itself within the national curriculum. In this context PSHE was seen as a necessary, but not sufficient, contributory component of citizenship. I think it is fair to say that the PSHE Group, for its part, saw citizenship as a necessary but not sufficient condition of PSHE.

The separate PSHE and citizenship groups worked in parallel but with connecting points represented by individual members and civil servants common to each.

Throughout its deliberations, the PSHE Advisory Group maintained a light touch (even, one might say, a hands-off) approach to the topic of assessment for the areas of personal, social and health education it was concerned to develop. The consensus view seemed to be that the significance of this area of learning and development was not so much to be located in its susceptibility to yielding outputs subsequently to be measured, but more by establishing inputs to be accepted and implemented as *important curriculum entitlements*. That was certainly my own view, and I suspect it was shared by others.

Wide spectrum

The debate in both groups spanned a complete spectrum of views. On the one hand there were those who believed that status in the curriculum could only be achieved for the subject area by ascribing external assessment (of equal weight to that of other curriculum subjects). On the other hand many took the view that it was neither desirable nor possible to measure personal development and values in individuals. The latter view emphasized the need to focus on seeing that there were opportunities to learn, to explore, to develop one's skills and intellectual and emotional understanding.

In the final report of the PSHE Advisory Group, *Preparing Young People for Adult Life* (DfES, 1999), there was minimal reference to assessment. The report noted that some aspects of this area of the curriculum could lead to various forms of assessment that were available. These included the key skills that had been developed by the Qualifications and Curriculum Authority as a separate initiative.

I have been actively involved with the development and acknowledgement of learning in aspects of personal, social, health and citizenship education for nearly two decades now. My experience through, for example, the ASDAN award programmes suggests clearly that key skills can be developed in a way that significantly supports teaching and learning. This is especially true if the key skills are seen as complementary to – rather than duplicating – GCSEs such as maths (application of number) and English (communication). Indeed there are occasions when the key skill approach is more appropriate than the GCSE for certain learners. Now that the 'main' key skills (application of number, communication, information technology) are officially available, after much lobbying, to learners pre-16, it becomes possible to address the next stage of development, which is to recognize them in the schools' and colleges' league performance tables.

Status and political basis

By contrast to the PSHE Advisory Group, the deliberations on assessment of the Crick Citizenship Advisory Group at DfES were driven by a different focus but led to a similar conclusion to those of the PSHE Advisory Group. There was a similar spectrum of opinion represented, but the matter of assessment, since citizenship was to become a subject with Statutory Order status within the curriculum, was centre stage. The Group agonized over whether citizenship, as a statutory subject like any other, should be assessed in the same way as any other. If it were to be approached differently to other subjects, what would this do to its status alongside those others? What other assessment regimes might anyway be deployed if the subject area was thought to warrant a different approach?

The debate was influenced greatly by how the ontology of the matter was configured. What were the origins of the citizenship phenomenon, political and social? And what therefore, was its 'being', so to speak, its design and its purpose?

It seems clear to me from everything that Bernard Crick has ever said about the subject that the inclusion of citizenship in the curriculum for 2000 and beyond had always, at its heart, a social and political agenda (see Introduction and Chapter 1). This was about restoring a sense of community, responsibility and collective care through a process of heightened awareness and of involvement, and this is what had convinced and energized David Blunkett. The agenda was one of social inclusion and social justice. It seemed to be one of the attempts to be made by a Labour government to redress the balance of 18 years of a Conservative agenda in which such values had been denied, denigrated and discarded.

As such it appears to me therefore to be an arena in which it is not acceptable to adopt a pass/fail approach to assessment. Are we seriously to countenance failing people in citizenship by assessing them in the traditional way alongside other subjects? And moreover are we seriously to undertake this type of assessment because if we didn't then the curriculum area would subside into insignificance by comparison just because it wasn't thus traditionally assessed?

Mixed economy or divisive economy model

The arguments for allowing a range of current and traditional assessment options to be made available are at first sight convincing. After all, to provide GCSEs for the academics and NVQs for the more vocationally inclined, and then, additionally, progress file or some record of achievement for the rest, apparently allows for all abilities and aptitudes. In a sense – the market economy sense – it does do this. But what is left unchallenged, on this approach, is that the market economy model is itself a reflection of what some see as a divided and divisive national qualifications framework (if it is not also reflective of a divided society). These divisions of the qualification framework are themselves predicated on views of ability that are problematic in their rigidity: the academic as against the vocational, the practical as against the intellectual. What we never managed to achieve was what I think the fundamental agenda and the original political rationale for citizenship demanded. This was an inclusive and comprehensive, not a divided and differentiated, model, a differentiated model moreover masquerading as fit for the purpose through an approach that, so the public script goes, suits all varieties of needs (but that actually leaves all the divisions it upholds intact).

So sure enough, citizenship will be offered as a GCSE (but called citizenship studies in the belief that the mere insertion of the second word 'studies' manages to save us from the consequence of both failing and being seen to fail people in citizenship). I can't believe really that this sort of linguistic legerdemain and manipulation actually alters the social relationships and realities in which the language is located.

It will also be possible under the settlement finally agreed by the Citizenship Working Group for the awarding bodies to come up with lots of NVQ-style units in citizenship. And what else? Well, there are all the offerings of curriculum programmes that are developed by schemes such as ASDAN and CSV where the focus is on providing a set of challenging activities that may engage the learner, challenge assumptions and encourage exploration and involvement in relevant issues. These sorts of programmes provide curriculum input as well as offering a way for teachers in school to assess and reward the achievement of learners.[17]

Post-16: citizenship and PSHE in the post-compulsory phase

Let's turn to look at the situation of assessment post-16 beyond the statutory school-leaving age. Post-16, the development of citizenship is not so fettered with the necessities of Statutory Orders, and so decisions about assessment are not so complicated by that regulation and the operation of the associated reporting systems and requirements that go with it. Indeed the post-16 Crick Report, *Citizenship for 16–19 Year Olds in Education and Training* (DfEE, 2000), suggests a more active and experiential approach to learning and development in a broader matrix of contexts in which citizenship may be exercised and manifested.

Nevertheless in this context also, there is need for considerable care about the manner of assessment and the link to qualifications as a suitable or auditable output measure of the curriculum input.

Time will tell whether the Learning and Skills Councils (which have been remitted by the Secretary of State with the responsibility for the development of citizenship entitlement opportunities in the post-16 arena) will be able to get beyond the rather blunt instrument of output measurements defined by qualifications achieved. These outputs, far from liberating teachers' practice, often fetter them to aim for a qualification that is approved just because it is externally assessed and on the approved lists. It is another example of assessment, linked to funding, driving the curriculum.

Peer and self-assessment

The DfES has however recently expressed interest in the development of an assessment model that includes self- and peer assessment as well as linking to the wider key skills. The Award Scheme Development and Accreditation Network is working with colleagues from DfES on the feasibility of this sort of approach.

The key skills, both main and wider, are, at the same time, themselves the subject of considerable change and complexity. What are currently referred to as the main key skills (application of number, communication, information technology) have, in the process of their development by the Qualifications and Curriculum Authority, been subject to the inclusion of externally set and marked tests in order that they qualify as externally approved qualifications. The QCA has laid down eligibility criteria for the qualifications that it lists in its National Qualifications Framework. Ironically, this assessment requirement has itself led the Secretary of State, Estelle Morris, to request the current review of the post-16 reforms on the grounds, at least partially, of assessment overload. These post-16 reforms had included the main key skills as an additional component for A and AS level learners.

The results so far of this post-16 review include the conclusion that education and training providers in colleges may continue to offer key skills development for learners, but Learning and Skills Council funding has been decoupled from the necessity to achieve the key skills units of qualification as an outcome. This also means, in principle, that further education providers in the future will be able to seek the provision of citizenship as an entitlement without having necessarily to achieve a qualification outcome, although they will certainly have to provide evidence of a systematic approach to curriculum delivery for audit purposes.

Wider key skills

The wider key skills (improving own learning, working with others, problem solving) are not, in the same way as the main key skills, subject to external testing arrangements. This is for the good reason that such external testing is far less appropriate to the assessment of these units. Instead, assessment for the wider key skills is currently based on the production of a portfolio of evidence. However, for this very reason, the wider key skills units are regarded technically by the DfES and the QCA as somewhat less than proper qualifications. This is a great pity, since they represent at least some of the desirable learning outcomes encouraged by citizenship development. You will not find the wider key skill units on the specifically approved list of external qualifications in the relevant DfES circular. Instead there is a reference to their general, rather than specific, approval. This is precisely because, to be fully approved, qualifications must fit the QCA's stipulations for entry to the National Qualifications Framework; and these stipulations include the requirement of up to 40 per cent minimum of external assessment (as opposed to internal teacher assessment). This is so even if the judgement, on educational grounds, is that such external testing is not appropriate for some areas of personal, dispositional or skills development. This situation seems to me to be ludicrous. The authorities are now considering assessment methods that will be appropriate to the wider key skills and will at the same time fulfil the stipulations used nationally by the QCA and the DfES for admission to the Qualifications Framework. That is in the short term.

In the long term, the fundamental question of the appropriateness of these stipulations of external assessment for qualifications (that is to say before anything can be counted as a 'proper' qualification) needs, in my view, to be fundamentally reviewed and modified.

Centralist agenda

But for the time being, the circle has been squared, and the net seems to have been tightened to a rather centralist agenda. And that agenda appears to be to maintain standards by imposing a very restricted view of what can count as rigorous assessment. Allowing teachers for example to exercise their professional judgement does not play a very great part in the current preferred quality assurance model. And it is this that sets the qualifications and examinations agenda. If the recognition of such professional teacher judgement was admitted we wouldn't have to rely so heavily on the exam boards to administer the sort of tests and exams that government seem to think are the hallmarks of effective practice and high standards. These are the very assumptions and criteria that have steered, if not dictated, the model of assessment that has, in its turn, shaped the agenda in relation to citizenship assessment. Let's hope that we begin to see some shifts in this arena in the future. This is because we must get on with the real business, which is difficult enough, of developing a caring and just community with involved, committed, caring and educated citizens, and leave behind us the business of passing and failing people, at least in this context if not also in others.

An opportunity – and some guidelines

The case for formative assessment by teachers has been made by Dave Brockington in the foregoing section. This aspect of assessment should come from *discernment* and be based on portfolio evidence. This argument, of course, is part of the larger case to move the assessment of education towards recognizing those things that we value across the whole curriculum, rather than concentrating almost exclusively on those things that are the most easily measured. The tension is between two apparently conflicting priorities: world-class education (standards – summative assessment) and social inclusion (person-centred – formative assessment). At the moment, when it comes to decisions, particularly decisions about money, the standards squad are points ahead in the game. But there are whispers of change in the air and citizenship education could be at the forefront of fresh approaches.

Flexibility and choice

First, the government that brought us citizenship education brought us a broad vision of its purpose, accompanied by a deliberately 'light touch' Order and the insistence that GCSE short course examinations in citizenship studies are voluntary.

Second, the QCA citizenship team is encouraging educators to 'measure what they value' rather than value only what they measure. There could be no clearer invitation for teachers to devise fresh ways of recognizing student achievement.

Third, we are being encouraged by some senior educationists to recognize that most assessment – and the most useful assessment at that – is based on *discernment* rather than measurement. 'Discernment is rooted in the judgements of the professional teacher who has a significant experience of the student who is being assessed. We need to rediscover the legitimacy of the discernment of professional people as they support and enable young people to learn. The issue is about the use of *measured evidence* set alongside *other information* about a student' (Professor Bart McGettrick, Department of Education, University of Glasgow). Maybe our problem is that we have become so used to being told what to do, that we have almost forgotten what it is to do things on our own!

Before embarking on a brief exercise in creative assessment, it is important to have a quick look at the rules of the game.

Current guidelines for assessing citizenship education

At both key stages 3 and 4 requirements for assessing, recording and reporting citizenship are broadly the same as for all other national curriculum subjects. There are no requirements to submit school data.[18]

At the end of key stage 3, teachers will be required to assess pupils' attainment. This will be required for all pupils who complete Year 9 in the summer of 2004.

Throughout key stages 3 and 4, teachers will be required to report on pupils' progress in citizenship to parents as for other foundation subjects. This applies from August 2002 onwards.

Current differences

All national curriculum subjects and RE now have an eight-level scale of attainment used to report teacher assessment at the end of Year 9. Citizenship, however, simply has three *end of* key stage descriptions similar to those that were used to report in art, music and PE. Pupils will be assessed as 'working towards', 'achieving' or 'working beyond' these expectations.

At key stage 4 the method of assessment will be determined by the way subjects are taught in the school. There are no statutory reporting requirements, except reporting to parents.

Key features of assessment

Effective assessment in citizenship should not be different to effective assessment in any other subject. Key features it should include are:

- focused planning and teaching of the appropriate knowledge, skills and understanding;
- pupils having clear knowledge of the intended learning;
- a range of teaching strategies to meet learning needs of pupils;
- a range of assessment strategies to provide effective feedback including self-assessment, review and reflection; and

- a portfolio of evidence possibly linked to existing records of achievement.

Key stage 3

Reporting on citizenship education in KS3 poses a particular challenge. A discrete report is required. It is not sufficient simply to mention citizenship education in subject reports – valuable though that is – and to leave parents with the task of making sense of it all across the school. Some citizenship coordinators are understandably daunted by the prospect of consulting individually with all subject staff in order to put together a report. Even making coherent sense of a series of different subject references to citizenship education is probably one challenge too far.

Recording achievement

One feasible solution that honours the purpose of citizenship education is to support *the young person* in becoming responsible for her or his own portfolio of citizenship achievement. The pupil collects the evidence of development in citizenship and keeps it in a National Record of Achievement (NRA) or progress file. It is likely that over the next few years electronic forms of record keeping will be formally approved and encouraged at national level. This evidence may well refer to other records, artefacts, reports or events. CSV strongly recommends that class as well as individual folios should be kept for all community projects.[19]

The TREE programme

A growing number of schools use and value the TREE programme. (This programme has had a number of titles during the period of its development, and was earlier called the Pathways Project.[20] It is a cross-phase programme that links work in primary schools with continuing development in secondary education. It builds on the image of a tree with its roots, branches and leaves.) This is a programme designed to enable students and staff build up a consistent and dynamic record of their achievement. It provides not simply an account of what they have done, but a continuing basis for reflection and discussion. The student takes responsibility for keeping his or her own records and the (form) tutor ensures that there are regular opportunities to discuss progress, celebrate success and identify further learning needs and opportunities. It becomes the student's tool for managing his or her own lifelong learning. It fits well with what a growing number of firms are using in connection with Investors in People. It is also designed to help the student reflect on his or her education for active citizenship.

The TREE programme is built on the premise that there is an identifiable group of personal qualities or attributes (a combination of knowledge, skills, understanding, attitudes and values) that are essential for:

- the underpinning of effective learning, ie enabling individuals to take advantage of 'quality teaching' and all the other learning opportunities that the school and its partners provide, leading to 'raising standards';
- making well-considered, informed decisions about next steps in education, training, career planning and life in general (including the roles and responsibilities of citizenship);
- making successful transitions between phases of education, training and jobs (TREE operates in primary as well as secondary schools and can be used to make the transition between schools more coherent and supportive);
- obtaining and retaining employment in a rapidly changing 'world of work'.

Tanfield School – among those directly contributing to this book – has positive experience of using the TREE programme with students.

Award schemes

Award schemes such as ASDAN (accrediting key skills) and the Duke of Edinburgh award scheme are valued and used by many schools.

Key stage 4: optional examinations

One of the possible ways of delivering citizenship at key stage 4 is through the GCSE short course route. Currently the only available specification is from OCR and it can be accessed from their Web site. The other exam boards are working on their own specifications and they are likely to become available at various points throughout the coming year on their own Web sites.

It is important to stress that the short course GCSE is only one of a number of possible ways of meeting the requirements of delivering citizenship at key stage 4 and that the short course itself can be taught in a wide variety of ways. There are a number of examination options that are not finally approved at the time of writing.

Developing internal assessment

Internal assessment offers possibilities for monitoring, assessing and evaluating the citizenship programme, including those based on ALC. The following suggestions are offered as pointers:

1. **Consider the assessment options**
   These can be student- or school-focused. They include:
   - examinations;
   - research studies;
   - participation projects;
   - community service schemes;
   - work-experience-based initiatives;
   - student self-reviews.

   Is there qualitative feedback on these processes? How is comparable learning, eg through work placements, assessed?

2. **Plan ahead**
   Ensure too that the students think through their activities in advance and set out clearly what they hope to achieve in terms of:
   - The service or product, including the standards they intend it to meet.
   - The values involved. Consider the three core citizenship values for inclusion: rights/responsibilities; authority/democracy; freedom as autonomy. But encourage the students to add their own. Do the values apply to all involved in the project? For example, are the freedom and autonomy of the client group appropriately respected?
   - The skills to be learnt. Use key skills (including general key skills) as a starting point, but the student may identify other skills.
   - The attitudes required from team or project members.

3. **Link assessment with recognition, celebration and evaluation**
   - Encourage mutual recognition of student achievements including eliciting responses from the student, his or her peers and community partners (or clients), and the relevant teacher. Ensure that the class and student keep appropriate records.
   - Encourage students to make the connections (and distinctions) between assessment, recognition, celebration and evaluation).

4. **The impact of citizenship education on the whole school**
   Review the impact of active citizenship against whole-school data, including:
   - lesson attendance;
   - quality of work;
   - change of ethos.

Feedback

It is valuable to formalize feedback on the experience of activities in and beyond the classroom:

- school council;
- student feedback;
- teacher feedback;
- parent feedback;
- informal community or employer feedback.

Clarity about objectives

Clear, coherent and consistent objectives should run through the planning, development, implementation and review process at every level. When assessment is part of mainstream planning, provision and evaluation, everyone will necessarily be involved. As one adviser commented, 'This is a chance to wake up the sleepers among the staff!'

Variety of learning experiences

The assessment and evaluation of education for active citizenship is most effective when it draws upon a wide range of learning experiences, teaching strategies and styles. These experiences will come from all three dimensions of school life (see Figure 14.10).

Activities and experiences will include: group work, role-play, circle time, photographs, visitors, community projects and partnerships locally and at a distance (eg e-mail links overseas). Many will find the following checklist of assessment guidelines helpful.[21] It brings together key issues for both formative and summative assessment.

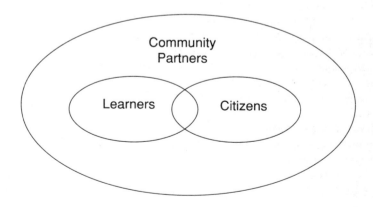

Figure 14.10 *The three dimensions of school life*

Guidelines for assessment: a summary checklist

'Assess what we value rather than valuing what we assess!'

- Assessment should be active and participatory, addressing progress in pupils' development of skills and participation as well as knowledge and understanding.
- The learning objectives should be shared with the pupils, helping them to clarify the outcomes and to recognize what the standard to aim for is.
- All pupils should receive feedback on their progress and achievement. Peer feedback is valuable besides that of the teacher in identifying new targets.
- Activities can provide opportunities for assessing more than one aspect of performance, including knowledge and understanding, participation and skills.
- Portfolios of work establish consistency of standards, drawing upon a range of activities and learning outcomes. Use photographs as well as pupils' work.
- Planning a talk or presentation, designing a display or Web site, leading a discussion or debate may provide suitable samples of work for a portfolio.
- Pupil self-assessment, peer assessment and the views of those adults other than teachers who are involved in PHSE and citizenship are part of the process.
- The formative and summative assessment process should provide pupils with opportunities to add to their own progress file or record of achievement.
- Schools should ensure that the progress and achievement of all pupils is recognized and celebrated. It must not imply that pupils are failing citizens or judge the work, personality or value of an individual or his or her family.

Developing the assessment process will require:

- **learning outcomes:** an understanding of clearly stated learning outcomes for the key stage (with reference to the aptitudes and abilities of the pupils);
- **social learning activities:** a view of the full range of social learning activities across the school and its local community (context for learning);
- **criteria** on which to make a judgement about progress achievement, ie what it might look like when the learning objective has been achieved;

- **access to a range of teaching strategies** to cater for and develop a range of learning styles of pupils (with particular emphasis on skills of reflection, inquiry, communication and participation);
- **pupils review their progress:** strategies to encourage pupils in reviewing their progress in achieving the learning outcomes, listening, observation, skilled questioning, quality feedback (what has been achieved) feed-forward (what the next steps might be).

Evaluation: the big picture

If we are to evaluate the impact of education for active citizenship, it is important never to forget the big picture. How far (and on what evidence) is citizenship education in your school contributing to a 'change in the political culture of this country both nationally and locally: for people to think of themselves as active citizens, willing, able and equipped to have an influence in public life'?

A question such as this might be the subject of a year-on-year research project by students working in partnerships with teachers, governors, parents and community partners. The 'portraiture' research model in Chapter 15 might be helpful here.

Student self-assessment

Lipson teachers encourage students to assess the quality of what they do for themselves. As in drama, they might also be asked to assess the quality of the work that others do and to discuss how they came to their conclusions. It is from these discussions that students get a tangible idea of what quality is and what has to be done to achieve it. Where there is a difference between the students' and teachers' assessment, effective teachers use this as a basis for discussion.

(Lipson College *Little Red Book*)

Involving students in school

Schools should not just build any kind of community, but democratic communities which value participation, equality, inclusiveness and social justice... The communities should start in the classroom in which pupils share responsibility for their own learning and for regulating each other's behaviour. Involving pupils and parents in decision-making, teaching and learning decisions... extend[s] these democratic principles further.

(A Hargreaves and M Fulham[22])

If we are to bring about 'a change in the political culture of this country both nationally and locally: for people to think of themselves as active citizens, willing, able and equipped to have an influence in public life', we need to ensure that young people leaving secondary school have already had real experience of democratic involvement in the life of their school and community. The programme of study for citizenship education lays down that pupils (in KS3 and 4) should learn to 'negotiate, decide and take part responsibly in school and community based activities'. Furthermore, the Crick Report is clear that schools must consider the extent to which their ethos is consistent with the aim and purpose of citizenship education:[23]

> The ethos, organisation, structures and daily practices of schools have a considerable impact on the effectiveness of citizenship education. Schools need to consider to what extent their ethos, organisation and daily practices are consistent with the aim and purpose of citizenship education, and provide opportunities for pupils to develop into active citizens. We believe that schools should make every effort to engage pupils in discussion and consultation about all aspects of school life on which pupils might reasonably be expected to have a view, and wherever possible to give pupils responsibility and experience in helping to run parts of the school.

The educational case for student participation

The value and importance of the active participation of pupils in schools goes beyond the immediate purpose of education for active citizenship. As far back as 1993 Bernard Trafford argued the case for sharing power with pupils in schools.[24] Trafford argued then – and his case remains relevant still – that there needs to be a new approach to involving students in having a say in the life and work of the school. He offered five reasons for sharing power with students:

1. **Quality of ideas**
   Children, as recipients of the teaching offered by the school, know better than anyone 'which teaching styles are successful, which techniques of learning bring out the best in them, and what the ethos of the school consists of'.[25]
2. **Education for citizenship**
   'Young people should leave school with some confidence in their ability to participate in their society, to resolve conflict and, if they oppose a course of action, to express that opposition fairly, effectively and peacefully... The development of social, planning, organisation, negotiation and debating skills is a major part of this scheme.'[26]

3. **A channel for complaint**

   As our present society becomes dominated by charters of various sorts, schools are becoming familiar with a greater willingness among their clients to complain. There is nothing necessarily wrong with this... It makes arguably good sense to make it easy for students (and their parents) to express any concerns they have.[27]

4. **Creative use of dissent**

   Empowering students is not merely a devious means of avoiding confrontation: a school that shares power with pupils may well avoid the problems that will inevitably come when authoritarianism becomes finally unacceptable in schools as in the rest of society.[28] Trafford makes a powerful case for recognizing and fostering courage in young people. He quotes from John Holt: 'With few exceptions, schools and school people do not value courage in children. Not understanding it and having very little of it themselves, they fear it, and do all they can to stamp it out. They think that children who are brave are hard to handle, rebellious, defiant, and that children who are scared will be easy to control.'[29] Things have changed over the past 20 years, but the point is still worth making.

5. **Motivation**

   At the heart of the quest for student motivation has to be an open, democratic atmosphere. Although the deliberations of the school council may well be concerned with the power to change things, the hidden agenda is more important:[30] 'If democracy in school is about anything, it is not so much about power... as the free exchange of ideas. Without that open, continuous debate, power sharing is pointless.'[31]

   Motivation is also about risk taking. Young people 'want to learn to govern themselves. They want to take risks – Lord, how anxious they are to be at risk, intellectually and emotionally, and how shameful it is that so many of them should find their teachers, the whole system of education, lacking in every kind of courage!'[32]

Sharing power

The desire to exercise power over students is the enemy of quality. As power is shared, students work harder. This is why the student council, mediation and circle time are vital at Lipson. What students want is a school where it is apparent to all that teachers are constantly trying to make things better. The strong 'we care' message is the foundation of quality education.

(Lipson Community College)

Recent research
School councils, participation and reduced exclusion

Recent studies underline the importance of student participation and motivation as a significant contributory fact to raising standards and quality. Professor Lynn Davies of Birmingham University,[33] working with School Councils UK,[34] identified a number of ways in which school councils could help reduce exclusions.

These ways include:

- direct impact through peer control or monitoring of children at risk of exclusion, and peer support or advocacy for individual children;
- semi-direct impact through: 1) generating codes of conduct and anti-bullying policies that are seen as owned by pupils; and 2) pupil-inspired ideas to minimize behaviours associated with exclusion;
- indirect impact through conveying to pupils and parents the powerful messages that: 1) children are listened to and treated with respect; and 2) children should 'look out for each other and be able to express grievances'.

Davies emphasizes that 'school councils cannot be seen in isolation from a number of other key strategies and structures in a school, and will interact with these in varied ways to promote inclusion. These include target setting, pastoral systems, and rewards and sanctions systems, less formal or official means of exclusion, equal opportunities, and other ways of encouraging pupil solidarity.' She further identifies the principles that emerged from her research as underpinning the work of all good practice schools. These principles include:[35]

- giving pupils a 'voice' and encouraging skills of self-advocacy;
- giving pupils a sense of 'agency', of their role in achieving change;
- giving pupils practice in decision making and choice, both in curriculum and in behaviour;
- maximum equity between staff and pupils, with pupils treated with the same respect as adults;
- inclusion for all with achievable targets and visible success.

Pupils have grown and matured as they have assumed responsibility to help and assist younger members of the school community.

(Craig Weaver, Teacher, Bettws High School)

(Source: CSV / Barclays New Futures)

The impact of participation on standards

The research by Derry Hannam with CSV (referred to previously in these pages) stressed the importance of participation upon standards.[36] The report, based on a relatively small sample of schools, gives a clear indication that, taking like with like, participative schools show fewer exclusions, better attendance and comparably better exam results than do schools with significantly less student participation.

'A few schools square the circle...'

Hannam comments:

> In my work as an Ofsted trained inspector I found that there are some, perhaps it would be more accurate to say 'a few', English secondary schools that are significantly more democratic than most. These schools seem to manage to 'square the circle' of authority and compulsion with real freedom and responsibility. They appear to be able to create an ethos where education for democracy is experientially possible and by so doing enhance the ethos in such a way that makes it progressively more possible. Very often superlatives such as 'excellent' or 'outstanding' creep into the normally staid 'Ofstedspeak' when relationships between students and between students and teachers are described by inspectors in their reports.
>
> These schools are to be found in leafy suburbs, in rural areas, and perhaps most surprisingly in socially deprived parts of cities. They are becoming models of successful education for democratic citizenship. In fact it is time that some of these schools gained 'Beacon' status for this quality. My impression as an inspector has been that although significant staff time is indeed devoted to supporting the activities that create the democratic ethos of these schools there appears to be no price being paid in conventionally measured attainment. On the contrary it appears that some students who might otherwise give up on school learning develop a renewed sense of purpose in an environment that raises their self esteem through the sharing of trust, responsibility and participation in decision making. This is most obviously the case for some less academic boys. Unfortunately the research evidence in this area is thin.

Varieties of participation

Typically there are four varieties of student participation within the life of the school:

- the school council;
- research project;
- peer learning;
- peer support.

The school council, often linked with year councils and class councils, featured strongly in many of the schools with whom CSV has been working over recent years.

School councils

Several schools in the CSV/Hannam study referred explicitly to their school councils in their prospectus:

- 'The school council plays a key part in the curriculum review process, discussing individual subjects, cross-curricular issues, school policies and procedures and the distribution of the school fund, as well as co-ordinating charity work and social occasions' (School H prospectus).
- 'The school council has as its aim to provide a forum for pupils' views to be discussed and for changes to be agreed. The school council has a powerful influence on many aspects of school life, from the pupils' statement on equal opportunities and bullying, to the school environment and school uniform' (School L prospectus).

  The School L school council constitution refers explicitly to the UN Convention on the Rights of the Child, stating as one of its aims: 'To monitor the school's implementation of Article 12 of the UN Convention on the Rights of the Child.' (*NB* The members of the school council who were interviewed *did* know what Article 12 says. This was clearly not tokenistic in this school.)
- Unusually one vice-principal wrote in a covering letter: 'the school actively encourages student participation in a number of ways but to my surprise much of this involvement does not feature in written school policy, philosophy or objectives'. In fact the school (School B) involved the students in many participatory decision-making processes and activities.

CSV comment – student councils

Jim Mulligan, CSV senior trainer and development worker, has visited a number of school councils. 'In our experience,' he comments, 'student councils have started to work well as they have been given real power. There are still very significant areas where students have no say and this must be made clear to young people. But if students can see that they are listened to, are given a budget, are allowed to advise appointment panels, are encouraged to attend and report to governors' meeting, they will give their time and energy to the student council.'

Student councils should be organized so that: 1) every student experiences it at feedback time in tutor groups; and 2) as many young people as possible during their six or seven years in secondary school should experience being a delegate. This is feasible at year council level.

A school can organize a mock election every time there is a general election, and so give every pupil the chance to experience at least one such event.

St Peter's Collegiate College, Wolverhampton

- **School council:** Growing in importance. Has been involved in discussions about feed and anti-bullying programmes.
- **Mediation:** Anti-bullying buddies programme.
- **Peer education:** Sixth form peer reading programme linked with Years 7, 8 and mainly with some Year 9 students who still need help. Sessions take place on one or two days a week. It is separate from the new buddy system. One or two of the sixth formers were people who had reading help themselves. Peer reading programme, Reading Together.
- **Sports leadership:** Junior sports leadership and community sports leadership awards linked with primary school children. Students organize gym and games with primary children. This can support higher standards because they have to report their learning, including in writing. 'Sensible schools should highlight these activities as part of citizenship education.'

Tanfield School, Durham – Citizenship Order

- **School councils**
  Pupils are introduced to the democratic process within the school council system. Two pupils from each tutor group are elected to represent their peers on the year council. In turn, two year representatives are elected to the school council. Important issues are discussed and all pupils are able to contribute to major decisions. The democratic process is taught through active citizenship.
- **Evaluation and research**
  The school has been involved in the CSV Lighthouse project, and is currently involved in the DfES Citizenship through the Creative Arts project. The main aims of both projects are similar, looking to identify and share good practice.
  School-based research includes investigation into peer-led education, ie peer tutoring, peer mentoring and peer mediation.

- **Mediation**

  A small group of pupils participated in the CSV Lighthouse Schools' visit to Fort Collins, Colorado in 1998. One of the initiatives that most impressed the pupils was the mediation work that contributed to the ethos of the US school. On their return, pupils looked into the possibility of introducing mediation into their school. The school contacted a number of bodies to identify the source of some means by which it might move the pupils' plans forward. The pupils approached Durham county anti-bullying service and were able to negotiate some initial training that would help them understand the basic principles of the mediation process.

  A group developed a suitable role-play based on the fairy story 'The Emperor's New Clothes'. This role-play was used as part of a workshop the group organized in every primary school in the area. This small group has received the Diana Princess of Wales Award in recognition of their work in raising local awareness of the principles of mediation and being involved with the training of new members of the group. The group has gradually grown and the service provided is now well established. The young people have attended social inclusion and good practice conferences and contributed to workshops on every occasion.

- **Peer education**

  There is a strong sense of community within Tanfield and older pupils have traditionally supported the learning of younger and less able pupils, both out of lessons and within the curriculum (group work etc).

  The peer reading scheme is well established. Pupils from Year 10 take responsibility for working with pupils on a weekly basis during lunchtime.

  The peer mentoring scheme is now part of the citizenship entitlement of Year 10 pupils who act as mentors to their mentees in Year 7. The match of mentor to mentee is made as far as possible by three common factors: 1) primary school; 2) gender; and 3) interests or hobbies. Although the scheme was initially introduced to support the younger pupils it was quickly evident that the scheme had a positive effect not only on their education but also on that of the mentors. The scheme was introduced in order to support the emotional well-being of Year 7 pupils and it was soon discovered that the initiative supported learning at both key stages.

  Peer tutoring has taken place during link courses with children with both mild and severe learning difficulties and also with children from local primary schools. Working in the creative arts, technology and PE led to recognition by Barclays New Futures. Peer tutoring was an important teaching and learning style employed during the JC2000 project.

Cross-phase peer tutoring took place during a half-termly placement when Year 10 pupils worked in local primary schools. Year 11 pupils following an ASDAN course have worked in a local special school as peer tutors.

Year 11 pupils have worked as peer tutors in the art department, helping a group of Year 7 pupils cope with the printmaking process.

Peer mediation is now a well-established service provided by a group of pupils trained in mediation techniques. The pupils deal with low-level disputes, leaving staff to deal with more serious incidents. The aim is to ensure that mediators are drawn from every tutor group and that petty squabbles can be dealt with even before an appointment for a mediation session is made.

Research projects

Many schools are increasingly inviting students either directly or through the school council to work on feasibility studies related to questions facing the school community. These might relate to the wider life of the schools (eg catering issues) or be focused on matters of curriculum, teaching and learning. Research projects can be initiated at the request of either students or staff.

Peer learning

Increasingly schools are enlisting pupils in peer learning initiatives. CSV has developed a paired reading scheme, CSV Reading Together. This has been used by university and college students offering reading help in schools, but has also been extensively developed within secondary schools and between secondary schools and their primary partners. Many schools have developed their own reading programmes on similar lines. Peer tutoring, however, is not confined to reading. For example, St Edward's School in Romford developed an extensive tutoring initiative with local primary schools.

St Edward's School

Pupil commitment is for two hours per week.

Work at St Edward's Primary

Eight students were involved:

- Subjects covered included IT, English, maths, science and art.
- Students were mainly involved in classroom support. The primary school was not always fully prepared for them. Students would have liked more autonomy over the activities rather than finishing off what the teacher had started.
- Three students worked in the nursery section.
- Main outcomes for tutors were greater tolerance of younger pupils and a boost to self-confidence.

Work with Trinity (PMLD) School

Three students were involved:

- work in hydrotherapy pool – very demanding;
- support for drama – issue of unpredictable behaviour;
- had learnt sign language to provide additional support.

'It gave us the determination to succeed... a humbling experience.'

Corbett's Tey (MLD) School

One student worked in this special school, providing help with IT.

In summing up his impressions Peter Seaden Jones, the CSV/Barclays New Futures adviser, commented, 'Very articulate students, many of whom are intending to go into teaching!'

Peer support (and peer education)

Many peer involvement activities include various kinds of mentoring and personal support. In some cases schools, like the Marlborough School in Oxfordshire, develop transfer or transition projects between primary schools and themselves.

Peer support and peer education initiatives often include 'sympathetic listening schemes' through which students listen to each other's problems and run anti-bullying initiatives. At Bettws High School more than 270 students were involved in Year 7 and 15 in Year 12. The school was an early winner of a Barclays New Futures award for promoting the large-scale anti-bullying project through student leadership, advice and support.

Year 12 and 13 students offered a peer advice and listening service (PALS). The aim of this is to deter bullying in the whole school and also to encourage Year 8 students in particular to discuss their experiences. Sessions are held during lunchtime three times per week. The scheme has extended to Year 7 students in the hope that starting school is no longer such a daunting experience. Parents have felt reassured that bullying is being effectively tackled by the school and teachers alerted to problems early on.

This is not simply a good project but has managed to put in place a peer help system that all schools should emulate.
(David Black, Barclays New Futures adviser, Bettws High School)

(Source: Barclays New Futures)

Students at Bow schools tackle conflict

Students, staff and parents from primary and secondary schools in Bow are learning conflict resolution skills and in turn becoming peer educators in schools. They help others to resolve conflict through peaceable means. Training residentials are held in schools by experienced consultants. Skills acquired are passed on to peers and colleagues, enabling schools to provide these skills without requiring outside support.

Curriculum challenge: involving students in school – the Marlborough School, Shipton Road, Woodstock, Oxon

'SSS – Secondary School Sussed'

The Marlborough School is located in the town of Woodstock approximately 10 miles north-east of Oxford. A large proportion of students are drawn from a variety of rural villages. It is a mixed comprehensive school (ages 11 to 18). There are nine primary schools in the partnership.

The transfer project is known as 'Secondary School Sussed' or 'SSS'. The project was devised by a group of Year 8 students from September 2000 to March 2001 and piloted in the summer term 2001. It is a project that enhances the induction programme that has been in place for some time. The project is designed to:

● help Year 6 pupils at primary school overcome any fears and anxiety about their new secondary school;
● help Year 6 pupils increase their confidence;

- support the parents of Year 6 pupils when their children may be anxious;
- offer advice about how to succeed in the new school environment;
- set up a 'buddy' system so that every new student has a particular friend who can provide advice and support;
- give information about the Marlborough and make the school an even friendlier place;
- encourage new and ongoing friendships and therefore reduce the potential for any bullying.

A large number of Marlborough students 'buddy' the new Year 7 group. This year the project has involved approximately 350 young people. Naturally, opportunities for personal development are an essential feature of this transfer work. All schools within the Woodstock Partnership are involved and any school beyond the normal catchment area that has children transferring to the Marlborough. No one was selected to be involved – all students were asked to volunteer. Their positive response was superb and the project has been a great success.

Evaluation

The project was the school's 2000/01 entry to the Thames Valley Partnership school in action competition. This organization is dedicated to promoting active citizenship. A panel of judges evaluated the work, which won the Equitable award with £2,500 prize money for the best sustainable project. The school hopes to repeat and refine the project each year. It has also conducted its own evaluation and asked for responses to a questionnaire from all participants including parents of the children involved in the project.

Contact details: Pam Maynard, Project-based coordinator; Ed McConnell, Head

PeerAID – a nationwide initiative with CSV and the Ibis Trust

The Ibis Trust has worked extensively with CSV over the past decade to support and train students and staff in secondary schools to develop peer education projects.

PeerAID began in 1991 as a nationwide initiative to enable young people in secondary schools to work together to tackle health and social issues through peer education projects. The initial focus was on the prevention of the spread of HIV/AIDS. The scope of the project has since broadened to include other issues.

The most effective learning comes when young people have to share with others what they themselves have learnt. Peer education enables young people to develop their knowledge, skills and values in a way that can be demonstrated and replicated. The approach works well with young people of all abilities.

The PeerAID initiative is now disseminated through a training programme, and is continuing to expand into new areas both geographically and in terms of the focus of the projects.[37] This includes:

- additional year groups volunteering to become peer educators;
- new sources of potential peer educators being developed;
- additional 'hard to reach' groups being involved;
- new challenges – drug and substance abuse, bulimia and bullying;
- GNVQ curriculum links
- university students taking part in PeerAID projects;
- the involvement of 'beginning teachers'.

Henrietta Barnet School in Hampstead went on to develop a 'two-tier' peer education project, building on the expansion of the work over three years. Year 10 recipients of peer education programmes run by the sixth formers were then trained (partly by the sixth formers themselves) to offer sessions to Year 8 students.

Maria Fidelis School in the London Borough of Camden chose a peer education approach to issues around bullying and peer pressure among Year 7 students, involving many of the sixth formers who have been running the sexual health programme to date.

Birmingham University students, as part of the CSV Learning Together programme, are working to assist PeerAID projects in a number of inner-city schools with a high concentration of Muslim pupils.

PeerAID involves young people in secondary schools in helping other young people deal with health and behavioural issues through peer education.

Refugee project

Hampstead School in north London developed a PeerAID programme for refugees.

The school serves a very varied area and has a particular specialism in working with newly settled refugee children who speak very little English. They have a high number of Bosnian and sub-Saharan African pupils, as well as those from the various Asian communities. A particular feature is the linking of participation in the project to a national achievement award scheme for young people, which is valued by employers and educational institutions. The main thrust of the work enabled younger pupils to produce a welcome pack for new pupils, to reduce racism and bullying and promote positive inter-community relations and more mixing among different racial groups.

Student survey

A number of schools such as Deptford Green School are actively consulting their pupils about citizenship and citizenship education. They frequently base this consultation on a survey. As students become used to setting up their own research, which can include interviews as well as written surveys, schools can create a regular momentum for student consultation, opinion taking and policy forming. Here again responsibility can be delegated to the lowest feasible level and linked with training in survey work and statistical analysis. Learning and democracy are powerful partners in this as in so much else.

Our student-led projects

The idea is to get students working with staff and each other developing essential skills that they can carry on into later life. I've seen children thrive and blossom working in this way. One student in particular, but only one among many was transformed. She became confident and a good manager of people and of her own resources. The children value the experience as they get older. They have the opportunity to meet people and manage money and resources. You don't get that in the classroom.

(Changemakers student at the Deanes School)

Involving students – beyond the school

Many curriculum initiatives lead to students volunteering to work on the project in their own time, often during lunch breaks and sometimes after school. The boundary between service learning in the curriculum and student initiatives beyond the curriculum is often, therefore, blurred. The arrival of citizenship education as a foundation subject will almost certainly increase the proportion of projects set up with deliberate curriculum links to assessment and accreditation. Nonetheless, there is already considerable evidence that students are increasingly taking a lead in heading up community projects beyond the gates of the school. They are increasingly taking responsibility for important decisions about why and how the projects are run.

Operation Library Outreach

Ysgol Gyfun Aberaeron is a bilingual comprehensive school in west Wales. There are 880 pupils between the ages of 11 and 18. The school aims to promote the widest possible range of educational and cultural experiences for its pupils; its roots are firmly embedded in the values and traditions of the community it serves.

Operation Library Outreach started in September 1995 with the assistance of a Barclays New Futures award (£8,000). The project aimed to establish a book loan service for senior citizens that caters for their needs and interests; there is a particular focus on the housebound and isolated in a scattered rural area. The financial support from Barclays enables the school to involve two local (feeder) primary schools in the development of the project.

School pupils were at the heart of the planning and implementation of the scheme. The school council and student librarians have taken advantage of the resources provided by the newly refurbished and updated library to establish a personal delivery service to the client group. The senior citizens were asked about the kind of materials they would like to see provided and there are plans to implement a talking book service, enlarged print books and a newsletter.

Some of the visiting students stayed and talked to, or read with, their clients. This developed their social and communication skills and helps to keep bilingualism alive within the community. Students recorded their learning and experiences from the project on their record of achievement.

The school featured in an article in *Governors' News* and there are already indications that this kind of project will be attractive to other schools in England and Wales that seek to provide a community service for local citizens.

The Nobel School: student participation in the community

Local

On activity days when the normal timetable is suspended students have: designed and painted a mural in the changing room; dug and planted the award-winning RE garden. Key stage 3 students have donated and delivered harvest to elderly local residents and the local homeless; painted scenery for a youth club pantomime; prepared work for a holiday club. Year 7 students have hosted and guided 120 children from a local primary school in the RE garden. Students have sung carols in homes for elderly residents; have had a sleepover to raise funds for the homeless. The string ensemble has busked to raise money.

National

Students have participated in Council for Education in World Citizenship conferences in London and in school to contribute to the national debate on citizenship, and some students devised a questionnaire for a selection of Nobel students to feed into this debate; some have contributed to the UN forum on human rights; other students made papier mâché corgis for the Herts Garden Trust for the Queen Mother's birthday parade; and one student is a member of the nascent Youth Parliament. Students raised over £1,000 for a meningitis charity when a fellow student died; Gary Younge, formerly of Stevenage, Assistant Editor with *The Guardian*, spoke to general studies students.

International

Students visit the Somme and Auschwitz with the history department and France and Germany with modern foreign languages. In the past they visited Russia and raised over £1,000 for victims of Chernobyl.

Global

Global links and activities have been set out above (The global dimension).

An inside challenge

Student visits to members of the community are not confined to older people. Katie Craig, an A level design and technology student from Woldingham School, has written to CSV about a challenging initiative involving two schools and a London prison:

Lower sixth students teamed up with their peers from Whitgift, a neighbouring boys' school, to work in harmony as a real life design team, developing solutions for a real client, in this case Holloway Prison, a women's prison in London. Mothers with babies from 0 to 9 months old reside in a

Mother and Baby Unit (MBU) so that they are able to care for and bond with their infants at these vital stages of life. A crèche is provided on the MBU to enable mothers to attend work or educational sessions, whilst their children are cared for by qualified nursery nurses. However the site of the old crèche was rather cramped and bleak; the area was also split into two areas with a busy walkway through the middle, and so the prison decided to re-site it. The Woldingham/Whitgift team was set the task to assess the needs of the mothers, nursery nurses and babies in the new crèche area and design and make suitable prototype products. Holloway had undertaken to decorate the walls and carpet the floor of the new crèche area, otherwise the room was bare. This project has involved a site visit, on 17 September, for the design students to get aquainted with the prison, interviews with the clients and thorough and detailed research into the development of young babies, security, health and safety issues.

Meeting with the Experts – On 1 February 2000 the design teams from both schools were visited by a team from Holloway prison, including the Health and Safety Officer, a Prison Officer and two Nursery Nurses. They had arrived to check up on how the projects were coming along and offer any advice they could, as well as make criticisms of the work where necessary. Although the projects were only partially completed they were able to offer the students some valuable advice on what improvements could be made to their work. Each of the team of 'experts' from the prison came around the workshop and talked to each student individually, detailing what was, and was not acceptable to the prison and clients in the crèche.

Testing – On 1 March 2000 the prison staff visited again, this time to see the finished products. They brought 7-month-old Kyle, one of the children in the unit, with them to test the new products on. It was a tense time as he went around each project and his reaction was gauged. However, he was very excited by all of the projects and was soon worn out from evaluating all the new products for the Holloway MBU crèche. From the positive feed-back and thanks received from the prison and lengthy articles in both the *Times Educational Supplement* and *Croydon Advertiser* related to the work, I think it is safe to say that the project was a huge success. The project with Holloway was an amazing opportunity for all students involved, who got first hand experience of working for a real client, and insight into the functions of prison life, a life far from our own.

The project has also attracted wider interest with the above mentioned newspaper interest and then, this year, the project was nominated for, and won the Barclays New Futures Award which will be used to fund the project for two years at both Whitgift and Woldingham. Further acknowledgement was gained when the project won an award at the Surrey University Young Entrepreneurs competition, leading to the selection of Woldingham as a representative for Surrey Schools to send one student to St James Palace to meet HRH Prince Philip, the Duke of Edinburgh, in May 2000 and explain the work done for the prison.

The project provided excellent experience for all those who took part, working in real life situations. Many had never designed and manufactured a product for a real client before. The whole experience was very satisfying. It was hard work and hopefully the collaboration between the prison and school will prove to be as successful in the future.

CSV Millennium Awards

For three years (1998–2001) CSV promoted a CSV Millennium Awards scheme throughout the UK. The aim was to enable young people to initiate and lead projects that brought schools and their communities together around a shared task. The scheme was a part of the larger programme of Millennium Awards promoted by the Millennium Commission. Each project received a grant, which depended on its duration and scale. The following examples demonstrate the range and imagination of what the students decided to tackle. The programme was open to young people up to the age of 24.

GT Music 2000 project (Matlock)

Liam Walker was a part-time college student studying mechanics when he won his CSV Millennium Award to establish and run a recording facility, GT Music 2000, for young musicians in the Matlock area. He also wanted to organize music workshops for young people with disabilities. He had the firm support of his parents, the head of music at the local comprehensive school, a local special needs music teacher and officers of the county council.

The centre was located in a disused bungalow and an adjacent small building that had previously been adapted for use as a recording studio. It was on the site of a local authority residential centre on the outskirts of Matlock and was fully accessible to people with disabilities. Liam secured their use after considerable negotiation with Derbyshire County Council.

Liam drew his inspiration for this project from a small music recording facility in Chesterfield where he had been involved as a volunteer helper. He had assisted with week-long music workshops for young people with special needs and therefore had some previous experience of the organization and planning involved. Chesterfield is a considerable distance away and inaccessible by public transport to young people who live in the rural community surrounding Matlock. Liam knew a large number of youth bands in the Matlock area and had done some research to confirm that they would use GT Music 2000.

Over 100 young people were eventually involved in the project. As a special needs teacher in a local school, his mother was able to help in identifying and recruiting young people with special needs to attend the music workshops. With a passion for music making, Liam demonstrated real determination and courage in taking on such a challenging project.

Liam noted in his evaluation:

> I learnt to be a bit more organised but I found the paperwork a bit difficult. I was more concerned about working with the people at GT Music 2000 than having to fill in lots of forms although I realise it was needed. I learnt that you don't have to be paid to get job satisfaction and that it is important to communicate with all the people involved in a project. I gave skills to some people that made them feel better about themselves. I am pleased that I can see something through; that I am able to commit myself to something I believe in. I will continue the project at a different location and hopefully it will carry on for a long time. Thank you.

The Ashminster House garden design project (Ashford)

As a Year 13 student at Highworth Grammar School, Ashford, Lucy won an Award to design and build a small 'low maintenance' sensory garden at a residential nursing home for the elderly. She recruited the support of a group of fellow pupils, who worked with the residents on the design of the garden.

The plot was approximately 30 by 25 feet and located by the front entrance of the home. It could be seen from the windows of the residents' rooms. The original plan was to work on the larger back garden but the residents suggested that improvement to the front area was their priority. They enjoyed spending time there just watching the world pass by. However, they wanted it to be an attractive and tranquil area. The garden would be 'on view', so that local residents and visitors to the home would be able to enjoy meeting friends and family in pleasant surroundings.

In designing the garden, the pupils considered the garden's appearance, fragrance and 'touch sensitivity'. This sensory element increased the variety of ways in which the garden would be enjoyed. The garden also included some raised beds so that residents, including wheelchair users, could be involved in planting and maintenance if they so wished. Lucy also developed contacts with other local voluntary groups to broaden the community involvement and increase the potential offers of help and support. The school made a commitment to the continuing support and maintenance of the garden, in order to foster an ongoing relationship between the home and the school.

All the volunteers gained new practical skills through their involvement with the sensory garden project. Gardening, design and building skills (including bricklaying) were all essential to the success of the project. The volunteers also had to recognize the special requirements of the residents and consider them in the processes of design.

Long Streets environmental attainment project (Belfast)

Chris Quinn was a volunteer youth worker at the Star Centre and studying part time on a youth leadership course. He had been unemployed since leaving school.

He wanted to improve the drab environment in the Long Streets New Lodge area of North Belfast. The area ranks as one of the most disadvantaged wards in Northern Ireland. More civilians have been killed in this square mile than in any other part of the country during the troubles. The project aimed to improve the concrete 'gap' between two housing terraces by creating a multi-active play area including a volleyball, basketball, badminton and football pitch. Chris Quinn, together with his project team, also painted murals on the gable end walls adjoining the play area.

The project team was drawn from two local secondary schools (an all-girls school and an all-boys school) that were very keen to see the project develop. The site was opposite the Star Neighbourhood Centre, a focus for local community initiatives.

There were no facilities for young people's play in the New Lodge area other than the streets. The 'gap' in the street, which parallels the peace line, had been vandalized and was an obvious eyesore to local residents. Chris recruited local young residents to his project team so the new play facility would be well respected. The fact that the project had the full support of the Star Centre also ensured its sustainability in the medium term. The residents of the area were consulted and were supportive of the project.

The housing was due for demolition in a few years' time but, in light of the deprivation and current political situation, the Award was considered to be money well invested. Chris and his project team had the opportunity to develop a range of skills including project planning and management, publicity and promotion, mural painting and creation of a playground as well as teamwork and event organization. Local builders, painters and artists provided the training in landscaping, painting and artwork. The volunteers learnt that they could play an active part in their community and benefit from the improvements. Chris was an excellent role model for local young people and diligent in his attempt to influence his community positively.

Project glimpses

Ideas for projects can readily be shared through very brief project descriptions, such as these:

- **Physical disability**
  GNVQ students are working with disabled students in order to help them to fulfil KS3 national curriculum design and technology requirements. Last year puppets were made and this year it is likely that a sensory garden will be developed.
  Student involvement: 13 in Year 12 and 5 in Year 13
  Tolworth Girls' School and Centre for Continuing Education, Surbiton
  (Source: Barclays New Futures)
- **Anti-smoking**
  Students were involved in organizing and delivering a campaign to local schools and community groups promoting awareness of the hazards of smoking to children.
  Student involvement: 82 in Year 7
  Lindisfarne County Middle School
- **Research project: health, rural access, environment, disability**
  The project involves enhancing access to hills and dales for visitors with disabilities and all members of the school's local community. The students will be involved in researching needs, finding solutions to problems, preparing and presenting findings to relevant organizations and supporting the development of an access project.
  Student involvement: 37 in Year 9
  Settlebeck High School
  (Source: Barclays New Futures)

CSV has a community partners Web site on which are a series of case studies that can be searched against relevant criteria. If you have a good case study for us, please leave us an e-mail on the Web site (Contacts). The Web site address is: Communitypartners.org.uk.

Curriculum challenge: students in the community

St Peter's Collegiate School

- **GNVQ in social care** involves students on work/study placements in care homes and schools. Social care placements are often extended to an afternoon a week. This work is written up and evidenced for GNVQ. Within GNVQ pupils present their learning to each other. Business placements also involve young people in giving presentations to each other.

- **Presentation of learning and citizenship education:** You can have an entitlement for young people to present to others – although the context and content may be very different. At St Peter's, sixth formers regularly present assemblies, as do other year groups and form/tutor groups.
- **'Our children are very, very busy.** They are heavily involved in a wide range of activities, many of which help with citizenship education.'
- **Barnardos – raising money.** 'Each year we select a local, national and international charity to help with our Lent Appeal.'
- **Placements:** In care homes one afternoon a week.
- **Partnerships** – with industry and church. One element of what the school will be doing is to stress increasingly the importance of telling potential partners about ways they can develop work on citizenship education. The young people work with the Brothers of the Good Shepherd to provide food and clothes for people who need them. The textiles class made a reredos banner for the chapel at New Cross Hospital. Members of staff are conscious that they wish to develop community partnerships further.

Students – Tanfield School

- **Political involvement:** Pupils have met with the local MP and MEP. A small group have also visited Brussels and contributed to debates.
- **Community projects:** Learning is one of the key issues in the development of the community.
- **Placements:** Work placements in the community.
- **Projects – direct action, indirect action and campaigning:** The introduction to active participation in community issues looks at three methods of involvement – fund-raising, direct action and advocacy – as means to address problems. Pupils in KS3 look at school community issues and move on to local community issues in KS4, usually through peer-led projects. Global issues are usually addressed in the form of a personal piece of researched project work.
- **Building partnerships:** The school has established partnerships with a wide range of bodies within the local and wider community. The 'Alarming' project where pupils were involved in installing intruder alarms into the homes of the elderly resulted in partnerships being formed with the local residents association, neighbourhood watch and Durham Constabulary. The school has strong links with parents, local business, the local primary schools, two special schools and the local tertiary college.

Summary – the curriculum

Planning

- **Planning** – the effective citizenship curriculum is planned against defined aims, objectives and outcomes in the context of the cycle of learning.
- **School objectives and citizenship objectives** can relate and be mutually and strongly supportive.
- **The audit should support these objectives** and be planned to meet them.
- **A project case study** on community care demonstrates the close links between curriculum planning and citizenship education.
- **Curriculum for global citizenship:**
  - The global dimension is an integral part of citizenship education.
  - The Anglo-European school offers a strong insight into how European and world citizenship can be integrated within the curriculum.
  - The national curriculum offers more opportunities than ever before for a global dimension to be incorporated into the life and work of schools. It includes, for the first time, a detailed overarching statement about the values, aims and purposes of the curriculum.

Creating learning experiences

Experiential learning is the bedrock of education for active citizenship. Experiential learning is a band within the broader spectrum of active learning (see Figure 14.11):

Experiential Learning

Description, reflection, speculation, discussion and deciding/rehearsal, role-play, mock events/ALC

⟶

Active Learning

⟶

Service Learning

⟶

Figure 14.11 *Experiential learning within active learning*

- **Reflective practice** is essential to education for active citizenship.
- **Learning theory:** Recent research into teaching and learning has produced a further crop of practical insights into how we can improve learning.
- **Active learning in the community** (ALC) is a methodology ideally suited to the challenges of teaching education for active citizenship.
- **Political literacy** starts with the processes of general literacy, communication and decision making and progresses through to action in the real world that meets real needs.

Assessment

- Assessment should recognize the achievement of all pupils.
- Teachers should be aware of the issues in the debate on the relative importance of formative and summative assessment.
- The key features of assessment include:
  - focused planning and teaching of the appropriate knowledge, skills and understanding;
  - pupils having clear knowledge of the intended learning;
  - a range of teaching strategies to meet the learning needs of pupils;
  - a range of assessment strategies to provide effective feedback including self-assessment, review and reflection; and
  - a portfolio of evidence possibly linked to existing records of achievement.
- Teachers should be aware of external assessment options, including short course GCSEs.
- Teachers should be aware of opportunities for internal assessment.

Student involvement

- **Reasons for sharing power with students** include developing: 1) quality of ideas; 2) education for citizenship; 3) a channel for complaint; 4) creative use of dissent; and 5) motivation.
- **Recent research:** Recent studies underline the importance of student participation and motivation as a significant contributory factor to raising standards and quality and helping to reduce exclusions. Principles of good practice include:
  - giving pupils a 'voice' and encouraging skills of self-advocacy;
  - giving pupils a sense of 'agency', of their role in achieving change;
  - giving pupils practice in decision making and choice, both in curriculum and in behaviour;

- maximum equity between staff and pupils, with pupils treated with the same respect as adults;
- inclusion for all with achievable targets and visible success.
- **Approaches in the school:**
  - the school council;
  - research project;
  - peer learning;
  - peer support.
- **Student involvement outside the school** comprises everything from environment projects to personal social service, and community newspapers and festivals.
- **Learning experiences:** All student services and initiatives need to be understood, developed and supported as learning experiences.

Professional development

Schools by definition are learning organizations. Teaching and learning is what they are about. There is, however, all the difference in the world between the culture, values and practice of an institution based on teaching and one that is rooted in learning. As a society we are moving away from a culture of teaching towards a participative, ever-changing culture of learning. Table 14.3 suggests some of the relevant distinctions between a teaching and a learning culture.

The culture of a learning organization

Several of the schools depicted in our portraits stressed their role as learning organizations. In this they are responding to the increasingly prevalent trend to regard schooling as part of the continuing process of lifelong learning. In a world where not only is information exploding, but the processes of communication are being transformed within the space of a decade or two, it is no longer possible to equate learning with traditional teaching. Furthermore, the democratization of politics and society is leading to the democratization of learning. The fresh approaches to pedagogy outlined above create further compelling reasons why schools in modern democratic societies must necessarily move towards becoming communities of learners.

Members of school communities – teaching and non-teaching staff and pupils – are bound together by their shared commitment to learning, and their commitment to learning involves a commitment to

Table 14.3 *Distinctions between a teaching and a learning culture*

Aspects	Focus on teaching	Focus on learning
Culture		
Context	Local/national	Global
Rate of change	Slow or moderate change	Rapid change
Knowledge	Print-based growth in knowledge	IT-based information explosion
Communication systems	Print and some telecommunications	Fast-evolving interactive IT systems
Culture	Monoculture – tradition	Pluralism – relativism
Politics	Oligarchies of right and left	Third way – a new consensus?
Enemies	Bipolar world (East versus West)	The politics of terrorism?
Values		
Culture	Tradition and practice	Individualism – diversity
Authority	Hierarchy – obedience	Autonomy – negotiation
Style	Oligarchy – school rules	Democracy – negotiated rules
Metaphysics	Religious worldview	Secular worldview
Professional practice		
Knowledge (content/process)	Teach a body of knowledge	Learn to process/transfer knowledge
Methods	Chalk, talk, books and libraries	Interactive/experiential IT-based
Differentiation	Little	Extensive
Interaction	Teacher as instructor	Teacher as facilitator
Assessment	Formal teacher assessment	Self-, peer- and teacher assessment
Discipline	Rules set by oligarchy	Negotiated rules – students take responsibility for managing their own learning and behaviour

foster active citizenship. 'Citizenship is a way of learning and a way of life,' say staff at Deptford Green School.

We are all learners

All schools have excellent teachers. More specifically, all schools have teachers who are wonderful exponents of particular aspects of classroom practice, whose expertise could and should be shared with others.

A learning organization must have learning as its core activity at every level. Therefore, the Principal sees his primary role as Head Learner. All members of the College community must be encouraged to have joy in learning – students are motivated by the open mindedness and willingness to learn of their teachers. The exponential growth of information means that there are no conceivable limits to this process and every need for each of us to become life-long learners if we are to be successful, happy and fulfilled.

(Lipson Community College *Little Red Book*)

Professional development

Against this background, professional development for practitioners of citizenship education means more than the occasional course or conference on the theory and practice of teaching citizenship. A school committed to citizenship education in its full sense will expect all members of staff to:

- understand the purpose and outline content of the Order;
- be clear about the contribution of their own subject specialism to citizenship education;
- understand and practise democratic and participative approaches to learning;
- model in their behaviour and relationships the values of the Order;
- support and promote organizational developments in the school that reflect the broader purposes of citizenship education.

Professional development in this context, therefore, includes: 1) knowledge; 2) skills; 3) attitudes; and 4) the capacity to influence the culture of the school. Professional development for citizenship education demands in teachers the *same* knowledge, skills and attitudes that are built into the programme of study for the pupils. Education for active citizenship requires a variety of techniques (including service learning), effective differentiation and a commitment to democratic values. Some of this can usefully be learnt through seminars and INSET days, but much of it will be learnt through peer support and mentoring, good supervision, creative study (including the use of new Web sites) and the development of reflection and feedback systems throughout the life of the school.

Several of the schools in our portrait gallery have the Investors in People award, which is relevant to professional development. The Investors in People process requires organizations to demonstrate a commitment to staff development at every level within the organization. It offers a framework around which good practice can be built and continuously improved upon.

Investors in People

The award:

- requires commitment at all levels:
  - top management;
  - every member of staff;
  which means that there must be clarity about everyone's contribution;
- involves each of us in:
  - understanding our part in the whole;
  - keeping a record of our learning and reviewing our learning needs;
  - annual appraisal and progress meetings;
- links the development cycle with the learning cycle.

The organizational development cycle involves:

- planning – against policy;
- acting – providing goods, services, publicity and quality control against targets;
- reviewing – against standards.

The personal learning cycle involves:

- deciding what we need to learn – against the plan;
- learning in a number of formal and informal ways;
- recording and reviewing our learning.

NB Organizations are free *within the framework* of Investors in People to decide precisely how to implement the programme. There is no require-ment, for example, to keep a learning log or progress file. For example, at

---

CSV (Education) we created a learning log on a database, which automatically analysed and produced a series of reports when required. The award's criteria are increasingly emphasizing outcomes rather than inputs.

The Investors in People framework looks at how learning is managed in relation to planning, communications, performance reviews, management effectiveness, and training and development (including induction and objective setting). The strength of the approach is that professional development is set firmly within the context of the life and work of the school. It offers an excellent tool by which CPD can be reviewed, evaluated and improved at the personal and the organizational levels.

The value of INSET events

In-service training days on education for active citizenship can be extremely valuable particularly where team building around new knowledge and practice is concerned. St Peter's Collegiate School, Wolverhampton deliberately linked the audit process with a short, lively INSET event.

Where possible CSV prefers to work with staff from the whole school rather than simply with those with immediate responsibility for PSHE and citizenship education.

A number of organizations (see the Appendix) are equipped to offer schools training on various aspects of citizenship education. It is important, however, that training is designed to promote shared responsibility for citizenship throughout the school. Some members of staff will be more enthusiastic than others. It is important that each staff member can make his or her distinctive contribution without feeling that intolerable additional demands are being made.

CSV has concentrated on developing training based on the principles of service learning and active citizenship. A typical training day is set out below.

CSV training programme on active citizenship

10.00	Session 2 – Introductions
10.10	Session 3 – Citizenship: the challenge
10.30	Session 4 – Whole school issues
11.30	Tea/coffee break
11.45	Session 5 – Departmental opportunities

12.30	Lunch
	Session 6 – 'The ideal citizen'/the good citizen is...
14.00	Session 7 – Community projects – making them real and relevant
14.40	Session 8 – Target setting
	Session 9 – Final comments
15.00	Course ends

Developing leading practitioners

Citizenship education is a fresh subject demanding a distinctive training and appropriate pedagogy. There is urgent need to develop a specialist cadre of leading practitioners who have the knowledge and skill to:

- develop fresh, relevant and innovative practice;
- offer training and support to colleagues who are specializing in subjects other than citizenship;
- provide students with training in democratic processes;
- develop informed community partnerships with individuals and organizations outside the school;
- develop and lead research on key questions concerning education for active citizenship.

The newly formed Association for Citizenship Teaching (ACT) will increasingly provide a forum for sharing good practice, research and professional development.[38] The Association has a journal and a termly bulletin for members.

Total quality learning

Lipson Community College has derived the following core values for total quality learning:

- We are all learners.
- We nurture a creative and innovative spirit within people.
- We are future-orientated, with the desire to shape our own individual and community identity.
- We are in pursuit of excellence for and from all, in an emotionally healthy manner.
- We are a 'family' of caring individuals.

Research through portraiture

One of the challenges to professional development is the urgent need for appropriate research methods that will enable staff and pupils to record, review and evaluate their citizenship programmes. In recent years US colleagues have developed a research methodology that increasing numbers of practitioners in schools and universities regard as ideally suited to investigating questions thrown up by citizenship education and service learning. The method is called portraiture and it is included under the heading of professional development because it provides an invaluable tool for citizenship facilitators and teachers. What follows, however, is equally relevant to the sections on curriculum, creating learning experiences and inspection.

Throughout this book I have drawn on the metaphor of the portrait artist. This has been deliberate as citizenship grows from vision, and vision is often better communicated through images rather than abstract concepts. Citizenship education has to be set against the backdrop of the big picture, and we need constantly to remind ourselves that citizenship is about people. When implementing a new foundation subject we must not lose touch with the faces and voices of the pupils and students concerned. The most dynamic young people's projects often have a strong visual content: a nature trail, artefacts for people with disabilities, learning games for children with special needs or a PowerPoint presentation on local history using pictures lent by older people. The images may sometimes be tougher and more challenging, for example in a campaign for a sustainable environment or on an issue of human justice. It is often the stories and images that move and excite us more than the statistics and lists of bullet points.

A flexible but powerful approach

Portraiture is about creating a careful word portrait of a project or set of projects. It invites us to pose a central (guiding) question and then systematically gather evidence in story form from the participants, so that we can come to a picture of the answer to our question. Portraiture can be as simple or as complex as the author or artist of the portrait wishes. It can be the basis for a major research project drawing not only on the voices of the participants but upon the facts and figures that underlie what has been achieved. Alternatively, it could be the framework for a class portfolio, a wonderful and sharply focused record of what has happened on a mentoring programme or a sports visit to Africa.

Wherever there is a need to tell the story of a project with the intention of helping the listener or reader to understand the critical issues involved, portraiture offers a disciplined and richly textured approach.[39]

Summary – professional development

1. **Learning organization:** CPD is most effective when part of a school is committed to developing the culture of a learning organization.
2. **Professional development:** A school committed to citizenship education in its full sense will expect all members of staff to:
   - understand the purpose and outline content of the Order;
   - be clear about the contribution of their own subject specialism to citizenship education;
   - understand and practise democratic and participative approaches to learning;
   - model in their behaviour and relationships the values of the Order.
3. **INSET:** Use INSET strategically in developing a commitment to education for active citizenship throughout the school.
4. **Developing leading practitioners** can be a powerful way forward.
5. **Portraiture** can be a good way of recording progress and reviewing learning and therefore future learning needs.

Management

Managing the whole-school strategy for citizenship education means ensuring that there are resources, people and systems to realize the vision and objectives that have been set for citizenship education. This means managing three related but overlapping aspects of school life: 1) learning (the taught curriculum); 2) behaviour and relationships within the school (the pastoral curriculum); and 3) engagement with the school's external communities. In this sense a school comprises three communities: learners, members of the school community (school citizens) and members of the wider community (community citizens).

The life, activities and learning of these communities should permeate the process of developing, managing and reviewing education for active citizenship (see Figure 14.12).

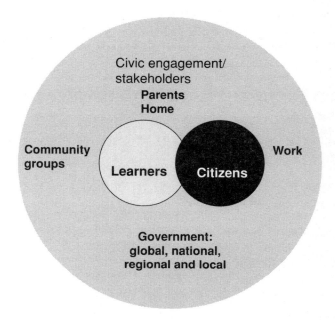

Figure 14.12   *The life, activities and learning of the three communities*

Each school will vary in the way it handles responsibilities for these three aspects of school life. The key point to note here is that there has to be the means to manage as well as encourage citizenship education in all three of these.

Democratic values

The democratic values[40] that are increasingly influencing the life and work of society and schools – freedom as autonomy, no authority without democracy and no rights without responsibilities – will also influence the way the school is managed and its work reviewed. Each student will be given as much autonomy as is feasible in developing her or his school career; the authority of both teachers and students will be rooted in democratic practice; and in matters of learning and behaviour, rights and responsibilities will for staff as well as students be related.

The school will in all three aspects of its life promote the knowledge, skills, values and dispositions of reflexive citizenship. Furthermore each aspect will impact on the other two. Positive behaviour and good relationships encourage learning; effective learning fosters responsible behaviour; and appropriate engagement with the school's local communities supports both behaviour and learning.

St Peter's Collegiate School, Wolverhampton – management

1. **Head** meets with Deputy Head and the Head of Careers and History to review policy.
2. **SMT:**
   - **Planning:** There is a strong planning base for the development of the whole-school curriculum.
   - **Context:** Technology college and Beacon School.
   - **Policy developments** are discussed in SMT. Staff know that SMT is clear and supportive over citizenship education.
3. **The citizenship team:**
   - **Citizenship coordinator:** Julie Lawton (Deputy Head), Head of Pastoral and PSHE/Citizenship.
   - **Meeting with Head:** Julie Lawton and Cicely Thomas meet with the Head, Hugh Bishop, to review and take forward progress on implementing citizenship education.
   - **Full team:** Julie Lawton, Leader/Deputy Head; Cicely Thomas, careers and history; plus one technology (Year 7 tutor); one English (new Head of English); two history; one business – GNVQ, sixth form tutor/upper sixth government and politics/Youth Parliament. Newly qualified teacher coming from maths with strong interest in citizenship.
   - **Team meetings:** Probably a team meeting each half-term. Staff given some time to meet.

The partnerships, agreements and activities with the outside community (including most importantly parents) will influence both the curriculum and the ethos and conduct of the school. As Terry Creissen, Principal of Colne Community School, commented, 'Students are given plenty of opportunities to have a positive impact, which means they are less likely to look for activities which have a negative one.' For example, where students are engaged in decision making, peer education and mentoring, anti-bullying programmes and project management issues of behaviour are tied directly to matters of curriculum and learning.

Citizenship teams

Managing citizenship education demands a wide range of skills and is frequently a team responsibility. See, for example, the case study above on St Peter's Collegiate School where a staff citizenship team has been drawn together from across the school and is chaired by a deputy head.

Schools are working on a range of team approaches, including:[41]

- Specialist PSHE/citizenship teams.
- Year group teams: carousel systems within year groups whereby teachers can specialize in a smaller number of areas.
- Subject links, for example citizenship is made part of a social studies course, especially in KS4, taught by specialists with relevant first degrees.
- Some schools have cross-functional teams to link the pastoral with the academic aspects of the school (see box below). Schools that have regular cross-functional working (by whatever name) have a built-in opportunity to relate citizenship education to all/most aspects of school life.
- ICT/RE: Information and computer technology is process-rich but content-free. Religious education allows for moral and philosophical issues to be explored and debated.

Cross-functional teams – Lipson Community College

We feel that everybody should have the opportunity to contribute to improving the quality of what we offer here at Lipson. As a result, all of us will be members of one of the cross-functional teams. These are:

- Accelerated Learning
- Primary Liaison
- Health and Safety
- GCSE Think Tank
- Public Relations and Presentation Evening
- Reporting and Assessment
- Staff Development
- Induction

(Extract from the Little Red Book)

Bridging the community of citizens and the community of learners

Citizenship education requires that the gap between the pastoral and academic life of the school is bridged. In terms of citizenship education we have thought of this as the bridge between the citizen and the learning communities of the school. The word 'academic' is too narrow to encompass the full meaning of 'learning' as used in this book, and the word 'pastoral' suggests care for students rather than care by students. This emphasis is also too narrowly personal and does not take on board the idea of school as a civil community with a role to play beyond its gates.

The staff at Lipson Community College have addressed this challenge through a pastoral system composed of vertical 'guilds'. All students have a personal tutor. The core task of the tutor is to 'be there' for his or her tutees, to nurture their learning and development and to act as an advocate for their students. The staff describe their approach in these words:

In order to foster this role and to allow students to involve themselves in solving their own problems, we have introduced 'circle time'. This is a technique whereby the group sits in a circle and discusses issues in an open, honest and respectful way. Only one person can speak at a time when in possession of a token, and all must abide by the rules. This technique allows all members of the group to contribute on an equal basis and without fear. The College year group councils take this concept one stage further and will be based firmly within the guilds from now on.

The year group councils elect the school council, which in turn is related to a city-wide student council (Voice of Plymouth Students – VOPS).

In this way every student has the opportunity to have her or his voice heard.

We don't give up on our students or community. In the past it has been all too easy to blame the social background of our students. We have enough energy creators on the staff now to ensure dynamic and imaginative leadership at all levels within the College.

Quality learning zones

The guilds are now arranged in zones associated with particular faculties and sixth form study groups and are led by a zone assistant principal. We see these as 'quality learning zones'. They will make regular meetings between academic and pastoral staff much easier and help us transcend the artificial academic/pastoral divide. Each term these quality learning zones will allow staff to talk through issues, working them through to good practice.

Guild teams will develop planned tutorial activities including opportunities for literacy, numeracy, circle time and assemblies. Guild heads will develop an effective programme of cross-age tutoring within the zones. Teams will decide on display areas and maintain the quality of the environment. They will work with students and parents to agree the ethos and codes of behaviour within their zone.

CSV comment: A guild system of this kind creates a management framework capable of bringing together a wide range of ALC citizenship initiatives both within and across the zones. They can also offer a basis for wider community involvement.

Nurturing creativity for active citizenship

Whatever management systems are in place it is important that they nurture a creative and innovative spirit within people. Steve Baker at Lipson College in Plymouth says:

> We recognize that joy in learning is to do with intrinsic motivation and that this in turn is to do with ownership of the learning process. People who are able to exercise their creativity and who are encouraged to innovate are far more likely to be intrinsically motivated and therefore to be effective learners... The ways in which we believe we can accomplish this even more successfully are laid out in the College Development Plan.
>
> As a learning organization, we are constantly reviewing the world our students are likely to inherit and the shape of their future needs. It is our assessment of this situation which forms the rationale for the future direction of the College.

The larger agenda for management

Management also, of course, includes creating and reviewing the framework of resources and responsibilities that link curriculum development with assessment, evaluation, pedagogy, continuing professional development and community partnerships. The carefully thought-through and strongly supported citizenship team at St Peter's Collegiate School and the cross-functional teams at Lipson both offer examples of such an approach.

Management of citizenship education – Tanfield School, County Durham

1. **The role of the Head**
   The Head totally values and supports the work. His vision has completely changed the ethos of the school.
2. **SMT**
   Fully support the work.
3. **Citizenship coordinator:**
   - has the support of the Headteacher and SMT;
   - has the responsibility for coordinating citizenship and not for teaching all of it;
   - will need to give advice and help other colleagues with planning;
   - will teach on the programme;
   - will monitor the whole programme.
4. **Citizenship team**
   - A development group consisting of the Headteacher and a number of teachers involved in school-based and extra-curricular activities has been established.
   - The group is chaired by a member of the senior management team.
5. **Audit**
   - An audit of activities has been carried out.
   - A curriculum survey will take place in order to identify elements of citizenship already existing in the present curriculum. Gaps in the taught curriculum will be identified and covered by the appropriate subject area.
6. **Planning**
   - All departmental development plans are expected to include evidence of citizenship, in line with the school development plan.
   - Learning objectives are central to the planning and evaluation of the programme.
7. **Monitoring, evaluation and review**
   All areas of study, including citizenship, are monitored, evaluated and reviewed on a regular basis within an established school programme.

Summary – management

1. **The management for citizenship education** involves allocating and monitoring responsibilities and resources across three distinct related but overlapping communities of the life and work of the school:

- learning: the school as a community of learners;
- behaviour: the school as a community of citizens;
- civic engagement: the school as a community among other communities (stakeholders).

2. **Several models of management** and coordination are offered from current practice in schools.
3. **Management provides an operational framework** for the relationship between curriculum, assessment and evaluation, pedagogy, CPD and community partnerships. It requires, therefore, some form of cross-functional team or consultation process.
4. **Bridging the gap:** Management of citizenship education also requires some way of relating the academic to the pastoral, or – in the terminology of this book – bringing together the citizen community with the learning community of the school. We give an example of a school that relates the student council movement to the guild system, which forms a bridge between the pastoral and academic concerns of the school.

Context

Logistics

It is now time to look out of the window at the longer-term strategic issues that will affect for good or ill the development of education for active citizenship. The development of effective citizenship education is a long-term process and affects all aspects of the life of the school and its relationships with the communities that it serves.

Funding

Throughout this part of the book much stress has been laid on the fact that citizenship education, at its best, makes a positive and clear contribution to quality and standards in education. In short, we cannot afford for social, political and academic reasons to ignore the central importance of education for active citizenship. All the leading schools in our portraits make this point, in one way or another. The team at Deptford Green has made the most direct case for the proper funding of citizenship education:

In a national context where so many secondary schools are tempted to treat citizenship as an initiative too far, the only way to promote this theme is to demonstrate how it can contribute to a school's success. We believe that it is absolutely essential that those schools who are well placed to pioneer aspects of citizenship education and provide tangible examples of manageable good practice are given the funding to develop citizenship education as a specialism.

Deptford Green has raised significant funds for its citizenship unit through seven-year commercial sponsorship from a bank, an Excellence in Cities grant, and the local Single Regeneration Budget 'Get Set for Citizenship'. The school has pursued its fund-raising strategy with intelligence and vigour, and has deservedly been successful. Wider questions arise from this achievement. How can other schools, equally committed and vigorous, have a similar opportunity to raise such necessary resources? Deptford Green has made the case for specialist school status for citizenship education. Government has not yet conceded that case, although the DfES is rapidly expanding the number and range of specialist school grants. Not every school has the opportunity to apply for serious long-term sponsorship from local business and it is hard for those schools to acquire the sponsorship that will attract other money.

Recommendations

- **Recommendation 1:** *The DfES should as a matter of urgency review the possibility of granting specialist school status for citizenship education.*
  Applicants would certainly need to show how they intend and expect citizenship education to contribute not only to the ethos of the school but also to raising standards of performance and school attendance (no rights without responsibilities!).
- **Recommendation 2:** *Basic grant funding should not be dependent on a school being in a position to find matching money.*
  It might still, however, be appropriate for supplementary grants to be made by government in cases where business provides additional support for an initiative. Business is often reluctant to support education unless there is matching support from government.
- **Recommendation 3:** *Resources are needed to support graded posts for citizenship education.*
  Small and medium-size comprehensives, in particular, are reporting difficulties over funding additional salary points for teachers taking fresh responsibilities for citizenship education. The quality of what is achieved in citizenship education will depend largely upon the quality of the staff who are leading and managing such a complex initiative. Introducing a new foundation subject involves schools in

allocating permanent new responsibilities to staff. It is not enough for government simply to provide start-up funding from the standards fund – welcome though that is (no responsibilities without rights!).

- **Recommendation 4:** *Schools as a matter of urgency should explore ways to share with each other in meeting the costs of developing community partnerships.*

A community unit (such, for example, as is being established at Deptford Green) might be set up and jointly funded by a group of schools. Indeed a community unit serving a group of schools in an area makes managerial as well as financial sense. Dick Atkinson argued in the mid-1990s that schools should cluster together and form networks of social regeneration and community development.[42] His thesis is as relevant now as it was then. He concluded by costing his proposal. 'If, in a group of 9 primary and one secondary school, each school contributed 2% of its income towards community involvement, they would raise on average £148,000. This would be enough for up to ten members of staff to be involved.' His figures need adjusting against today's prices, but the point is substantial and well made. The unhelpful competition that has grown up between schools in the market culture of the 1980s and 1990s has not helped Atkinson's cause. Now is the time to reopen the case.

Buildings and the physical environment

A rich, stimulating environment is the main factor in achieving full potential. Think about the classroom, corridors, the school as a whole – could we use more pictures, music, colours etc.

(Lipson Community College *Little Red Book*)

A large proportion of the most imaginative and enduring student projects are to do with buildings and the environment. Students set out not only to improve their own school buildings and make them more available for community use, but also to improve other physical environments in their community. This raises strategic questions for both schools and local government concerning the degree to which they consult and involve young people when considering rural and urban development programmes.

School environments

The schools with whom CSV has worked have a remarkable track record in developing projects to improve the school and local environment for the benefit of the wider community as well as pupils. These examples suggest that those concerned with environmental matters in and beyond the school should, as a matter of course, consider the part that young people can and should play in such developments.

Pupils from the Marlborough School and the Ormerod Special School worked together to design and construct a garden in a covered court-yard in the main Marlborough School buildings. The work on the garden was done in school time and the garden was deliberately designed as an environmental resource, offering opportunities for use and enjoyment to everyone, but with particular emphasis on those with *special needs*.

Woodland track

Girls at Lewis (comprehensive) Girls' School in the beautiful Rhymney Valley in the centre of Ystrad Mynach cleared a piece of heavily over-grown woodland to create a track for the enjoyment of visitors and local people. One enthusiastic participant commented, 'We really enjoyed the opportunity to work outside and were thrilled to see the results of our hard work... It was great to be involved in something that would be of benefit to so many people for a long time to come.'

At St Peter's Collegiate School in Wolverhampton, students are thinking of ways in which they can use their open-air amphitheatre for the benefit of parents and members of the local community. All the chil-dren in Year 7 write plays in teams and act them to each other on a Year 7 drama day. One member of staff suggested that these plays could take citizenship themes and provide an occasion for the public to visit the school and to join with the students in reflecting on community issues.

Buildings – Nobel School

- Hertfordshire Country Council is introducing a health qualification for school grounds, etc.
- The school has begun development with the award-winning multi-faith RE garden and has plans to develop the school grounds further.
- Sixth form facilities are currently being improved.
- The school has plans for a memorial garden in memory of three students and a teacher who died.

St Peter's Collegiate College

In drama, all Year 7 children write plays in teams and act them to each other in the open-air amphitheatre on a Year 7 drama day. The children could take citizenship themes, and invite people from outside to join in. Parents would be interested in joining in.

> The environment garden was designed in part by the young people. A science project is a pond that collects rainwater, pagoda, etc (lower school, KS3). The local authority visited with the environment bus.

Rural isolation

The STAG (Sutherland Teenage Action Group) youth café was the brain-child of a small group of highly motivated young people in North Sutherland. Anne and her young colleagues won a CSV Millennium Award, and set about establishing a youth café as a meeting place in this rural community where recreational facilities are almost non-existent. In addition to being a place where young people can relax with friends, it aims to provide private study facilities. The group also plan to run small discussion groups examining issues of direct relevance to them and to run activity taster days throughout the summer months. As a result of their initiative to date, they have been donated a portacabin, which will be sited adjacent to a permanent building owned by a community group for young mothers.

It is difficult for those who have not visited the area to conceive of the isolation experienced by its young people. This establishment of a youth café will therefore have a profound effect on the lives of the local youth population.

Pimlico estate

Rosa Ernst is a Year 12 student at Pimlico School in London. With her CSV Millennium Award she set out to improve facilities for the residents of Churchill Gardens Estate, a large council housing estate in Pimlico, by planting a recreational garden. Pupils from Pimlico School acted as the project team and the school will adopt the maintenance of the garden as a long-term project. There is currently some tension between the school pupils and the local community so improving the pupils/community relationship is one of the prime aims of the project. The site is secured within a boundary wall and was chosen because it would make an ideal community area as the flats overlook it. Development of the garden required design work, construction, planting, creation of seating areas and possibly a designated children's area. Rosa has already received written support from the landlords. The Award provided funding for plants, gardening equipment and materials, training and advice from garden experts, publicity for the garden and an opening ceremony event.

Studio refurbishment

Alan was a 17-year-old pupil at Tain Royal Academy, Ross-shire when, before commencing media and cultural studies at Edinburgh University, he won a CSV Millennium Award to refurbish and develop a drama studio with a removable stage within an existing joint-use school/community building. He and his team aimed to transform the facility so that it could be used for producing a play with 1st year students on prevalent social issues (eg bullying and 'fitting in'). The next stage in the plan was to travel to all rural feeder schools to perform the play on site, and recruit 10- to 13-year-old pupils to attend a summer club, which would operate on a twice-weekly basis. Initially the play was to be presented to the community in the refurbished centre in Tain but subsequent events were planned to be staged in eight rural locations during the summer. The summer drama club gave Primary 7 and 1st year students the opportunity to gain experience in creative writing, singing, dance, musical studies, stage management and production, set construction and stage make-up. An awards ceremony was planned to celebrate the completion of the project where certificates would be presented to the participants.

Sensory garden at a residential nursing home

As a Year 13 student at Highworth Grammar School, Ashford, Lucy Turton won a CSV Millennium Award to design and build a small 'low maintenance' sensory garden at a residential nursing home for the elderly. She recruited the support of a group of fellow pupils, who worked with the residents on the design of the garden.

In designing the garden, the pupils considered the garden's appearance, fragrance and 'touch sensitivity'. This sensory element increased the variety of ways in which the garden would be enjoyed. The garden also included some raised beds so that residents, including wheelchair users, could be involved in planning and maintenance if they so wished. Lucy also developed contacts with other local voluntary groups to broaden the community involvement and increase the potential offers of help and support. The school made a commitment to the continuing support and maintenance of the garden, in order to foster an ongoing relationship between the home and the school.

Eco-centre

Mickey, Mark, Carrie Ann and Marc were pupils at St Christopher's Special School in Wrexham. With the support of staff, the group created an environmental centre for use by schools in the area.

Tarmac plc gave the school an ex-RAF hut on a sand and gravel site that was eventually to be turned into a country park. Tarmac also gave the school considerable support in kind. The group helped to refurbish the hut, order equipment and promote the centre as an environmental action and information centre. The aim was to create a meeting place for local community groups and offer courses in practical environmental management for local volunteers and schools.

Pupils were referred to St Christopher's from junior and secondary schools throughout north Wales so the group were able to use these links to promote the centre. The school and its pupils also had a record of success in securing media coverage for previous projects they had initiated and therefore the group were able to capitalize on contacts to attract press support for the eco-centre project.

Carrie Ann was positive about her experience: 'I am very proud of what I did for the local community and for the local schools. What I enjoyed most was working with the computers and helping kids to go on the Internet.'

Shared buildings and resources

Community schools and colleges (such as Sawtry, see Community schools and colleges, below) often enjoy a much more dynamic partnership with their local communities over buildings and property. Libraries, theatres, swimming pools, and conference and training facilities are, for the most part, most effective when shared. The school of the future is likely to see a much more radical and productive pooling of community resources.

Recommendations

- **Recommendation 1:** Schools should as a matter of course consider their own premises as well as the environment beyond their gates as a learning resource.
- **Recommendation 2:** Local government should as a matter of course consider involving schools in its environmental programmes.
- **Recommendation 3:** Plans for new buildings and significant conversion of education buildings should as a matter of course have concern for developing shared facilities between the schools and their local communities.

Governance

The link between the school and the world beyond its gates is crucial for the effective development of education for active citizenship. In this the role of the head and the governors is critical. The aims and objectives of the Citizenship Order need to be a regular item on the governors' agenda in relation to:

- funding (see above);
- forming, developing and promoting the vision and mission of the school;
- building programmes;
- community partnerships (see Chapter 16).

Student representation

Although under present rules students cannot be members of the governing body, they can be represented at governors' meetings.

Professional associations

The continuing and active involvement of governors' professional associations and supporting bodies is needed to disseminate and encourage good and innovative practice.

Partnership with local government

Local government is seeking to promote the active involvement of young people in decision making, and has announced its standards-based initiative, Hear by Right (see Chapter 16 for further details).

Building community partnerships

Partnerships between the school and the local community provide the framework and support for lively education for active citizenship. Those schools that have given attention to forming such local alliances have demonstrably reaped the benefit in the extent and variety of placements and projects that they are able to offer to their students. Almost every project in the community described in the foregoing pages has involved a partnership of one kind or another.

The partners

Partners vary, but most will be drawn from one or more of the following:

- **Other schools**
  Probably the most popular community partner is a local school.

Secondary schools have been enthusiastic to involve students in helping to build strong links of all kinds between themselves and their primary 'feeder' schools.

- **The local authority**
  The local authority has a major role to play as a partner in young people's education for active citizenship. The Hear by Right initiative is creating a culture in which local government is increasingly interested in involving young people in aspects of its planning and work. The Yardleys community care project (see earlier in this chapter, under The curriculum) enjoyed strong support from Birmingham City Council and CSV. The city-wide student council in Plymouth likewise enjoys the backing of the City Council. The story can be repeated in almost all parts of the country.

- **Public services**
  Increasingly projects are enjoying the support of public services such as health, the police, the magistrature and the fire service.

- **Commerce and industry**
  Schools have been used to working with employers on work placements, some of which have a clear citizenship dimension. Some firms have, through their community units, been keen to support citizenship initiatives of many kinds. CSV's work in schools has enjoyed support from many major companies, including Barclays, BP, National Power, British Telecom, NatWest Bank, Royal Mail, News International, Deutsche Bank, and Rio Tinto to name only a few. In Chapter 16 we explore the attitude of big business further.

- **Community and voluntary sector organizations**
  Many schools have already well-established partnerships with local and national voluntary sector organizations that can be invaluable in providing help, particularly in the form of published material, for project activities.

The Children's University project

The programme is run by a team of 12 students from Queensbridge School, Birmingham. They organize Saturday classes for primary school children. The team makes all the arrangements including recruiting children and teachers and they work as classroom assistants.

This programme is great for the primary school children but it is even better for the students. They develop their self-esteem by working in a context where their knowledge can be shared with younger pupils. They determine what would appeal to a nine-year-old on a Saturday morning and what skills there are among Queensbridge staff, parents and other adults that they can exploit.

The Children's University happens every term for four weeks on Saturday mornings from 10 till 12. It operates on the Queensbridge School site and Clifton Junior School site. Classes vary from term to term but typically include maths, French, IT, art and design, design and technology, sport, orienteering and German. The team aims for eight classes with 20 pupils in each, one teacher and two classroom assistants. The teachers and classroom assistants are paid expenses.

'This project enables us to put a value on the students' skills and knowledge. They operate beyond what they thought they could do, they have responsibility beyond what they have previously had and they have relationships with professionals which is as near to equality as it is possible to get in a school' (Roger Brewster, Deputy Head).

Accreditation is done by the Duke of Edinburgh award scheme.

I did two PE courses and music when I was at primary school. They teach you basic skills. They recognized music was my talent. Now I just love to teach children who are smaller than me how to learn and make the best of school. I like to show them school can be fun, show them what those Year 1 students showed me. It's hard work to fit everything in but homework is my priority.

(Year 9 student)

In my last year at primary school I did an IT course. I didn't know anything about computers. I didn't even know how to switch one on. When I left I was brilliant. I was so good my Dad bought me a computer. In the summer I came to Queensbridge School and carried on and now I am an IT mentor so I can help students learn to my standard. I don't mind giving up Saturdays. I'd only stay in bed anyway. My parents are keen because it keeps me out of trouble. When I go to college I'll come back to pay back what I've been given. My parents think I've got good aims and I should be able to fulfil them, not go dossing on the streets like some people.

(Year 9 student)

CSV Community Partners Web site

CSV has set up a community partners Web site to help schools link with appropriate national and local partners. The address is www.communitypartners.org.uk. The site offers an extensive list of relevant organizations, particularly at a national level. It allows schools to search for appropriate partners against particular criteria (year group, subject, topic, etc). It also includes some guidelines for good practice. We invite readers not only to use the site but to contribute further examples of valuable partners, particularly local partners, through the e-mail reply service.

School policy

Schools such as Deptford Green have built up their local partnerships as a matter of school policy:

> Essential to developing citizenship at Deptford Green has been our growing understanding of ourselves as a community school. In broad terms we define this as a school linking very closely with the local community to provide an education that is inclusive for all local pupils, provides support to parents in that community and is seen as a force for achievement within the local community.
>
> We aim to be more than a school, providing support for the range of circumstances that emerge in our inner-city environment. Through working with a wide variety of outside partners we hope to combat some of the inequalities that are a barrier to young people being included in school and society. If young people feel excluded then there is little chance of them feeling any commitment to being good citizens.
>
> Key to our development as a citizenship school is our work with a range of community workers and learning mentors. Working closely with our sophisticated pastoral systems they provide the bedrock for inclusion.
>
> The school works in partnership with the Children's Society in a DfEE-funded project. The Children's Society started working with the school in September 1999, funded until March 2002. The workers brought with them experience from the very successful Genesis Project that they had run at Warwick Park School in Southwark. Within the community department they coordinate the work of a number of different projects with funding from different regeneration sources.

Deptford Green has been quite explicit about its community aims, which form a useful checklist for any school interested in strengthening its community links around clear education purposes.

Community aims – Deptford Green School

The school has the following community aims:

- To develop ways of working with local secondary and feeder primary schools to promote citizenship education in the local area.
- To extend and deepen working relationships with local businesses and community organizations through projects related to citizenship education.
- To develop facilities and practices that encourage adults in the local community to make more use of school facilities, both to promote adult literacy, numeracy and communication skills and to strengthen our working relationship with the local community.

- To fund and facilitate a local community newsletter, which is written and produced by our school students in cooperation with members of the local community.
- To engage in joint citizenship projects with local primary and secondary schools.
- To develop a facility as a homework centre and to encourage the use of the premises for Saturday schools.
- To work in partnership with specialists in the local area to offer a range of events and activities to promote learning in the community about aspects of citizenship, including courses and seminars on capacity building, local history and environmental issues in the local area.
- To promote the use and status of community languages in addition to English at school and in the local area.
- To work collaboratively with our sponsors to develop our work in citizenship education.
- To twin our school with schools in Europe, Vietnam and South Africa and to develop ongoing communication and mutual support with these schools.
- To support local primary and secondary schools in developing effective school councils.

Specialist focus on community

Specialist schools are encouraged to link their particular focus on activities that benefit the wider community, as has been evidenced by Lipson College's community aims, for example, which include a commitment to:

- provide our partner schools and our community with facilities, tuition and expertise in the performing arts;
- develop our ICT capability so as to deliver to our partner schools and other organizations specialist tuition, training, shared resources and other services;
- develop a regional, national and international role through enabling staff and students to work with and share the cultures of artists, teachers and students in other schools, areas and countries;
- widen participation and achievement in the arts by our students, students from partner schools and adults from our community and beyond through development of the Community Arts Centre;
- build links with sponsors and other partner organizations in order to strengthen the operation of the College in its specialist role.

Volunteers in schools

CSV has developed a number of programmes and training packages to involve students, employees, retired people and community members in schools as mentors and tutors.[43] In Pennywell Secondary (Community) School in Sunderland, CSV has supported an adult volunteering project that has worked with a peer support programme in the school. The aim of the programme is, in the words of the Deputy Head Sandra Smith, to 'provide a school environment in which all children can feel safe and secure, can learn effectively, and achieve their maximum potential. I consider that we are nearing our goal'.

Peer support in Pennywell School

Pennywell students have extended their training programme by training others, including teachers, business partners, parents and a range of professionals and young people. They have done this locally, nationally and overseas.

Imagine the impact on self-confidence and self-esteem if at 14 years of age you are asked to:

- organize and deliver a training session for 80 teachers;
- deliver a seminar at the North of England Education Conference;
- prepare a peer support plan detailing a year's targets, which are incorporated into the school development plan;
- travel overseas to train peer supporters;
- host an international conference on raising achievement.

Pennywell pupils have done this and more.

Good practice in partnership building

CSV's experience suggests a simple set of good practice guidelines that are worth noting when schools and partners seek to work more strategically together.

When you are developing community partnerships be clear about:

- what you are looking for from your community partner;
- purpose;
- duration;
- staff commitments – lead contacts;
- expected outcomes;
- management/finance/administration;

- child protection issues;
- emergency procedures;
- the benefits that the partnership will bring *both* the partner and the school;
- the contribution you will each make to the project.

It is also important to agree management, monitoring and reporting procedures at both ends of the partnership. These mean that you need to be clear about:

- **Contact person:** Who is the lead contact person with the partner organization/with the school?
- **Financial arrangements:** What are the financial arrangements (if any), including financial support or sponsorship from a third party?
- **The role of other people**, eg community volunteers/people from other organizations.
- **The monitoring, evaluation and reporting arrangements:** These need to be set up from the start rather than brought in at the end.

It is also important to make the most of your project and ensure its findings and activities reach the widest relevant audience. For example, an oral history project with senior citizens might end with a publication/exhibition/PowerPoint show/assembly etc that can involve the immediate partners, members of the school and other people from the community.

Citizenship days

It is increasingly common for schools to organize and promote annual citizenship days with members of their local communities. These are opportunities for schools and their communities to come together and to identify shared concerns that can lead to action and mutual support over the coming year. Such days provide an excellent starting point for partnership or further opportunities to develop fresh initiatives where partnerships are already in place. They provide students with a range of relevant and important responsibilities in the organization. Such occasions also require review and follow-up.

Community schools and colleges

For many years, particularly in counties such as Cambridgeshire, there have been community schools and colleges that have set themselves at the heart of the life and learning of the community. These institutions have much to offer education for active citizenship and in significant respects they prefigure the ways in which future schools are likely to develop.

Sawtry Community College, Huntingdon

Sawtry Community College has a long history of serving its local community. The school buildings are shared with the village, including the theatre, library and swimming pool. Sports events, drama and adult learning are points at which school and community come together. Sawtry is not a school that simply makes its facilities available to the community; it is a school that from cradle to grave is an integral part of the community. School and community policies overlap and draw from a shared agenda of interest, opportunities and concerns. In this sense Sawtry and colleges like it offer a model of the way in which community education and education for active citizenship come together.

Sawtry Community College – senior citizens project

Year 8 students working on this intergenerational project are building on a long-standing Sawtry tradition of providing a feast supper (each June) for senior citizens in the community, in partnership with CARESCO, a care in the community group.

The staff citizenship coordinator required the student team to produce an action plan to claim the first tranche of funding from Barclays New Futures. The Y8 student council assembled – 12 pupils – and discussed their ideas for taking the project further.

In the Christmas term, they prepared a number of decorative hampers and delivered them, via the school minibus, to senior citizens in the community. An attractive display of photographs and letters of thanks was mounted. The pupils ran a competition for the most attractive hamper. Discussion produced the following ideas:

- An 'adoption' scheme: Building on their expertise in IT, the pupils would teach the use of e-mail and the Internet on a one-to-one basis. The College is involved in a pilot of laptops for pupils' initiatives, and 50 per cent of Y8 have possession of a laptop.
- Compiling a local history of Sawtry, Alconbury and Stilton with the help of the senior citizens.
- Concerts and plays, linked to the feast.
- A day trip, which could involve shopping and visits to places where the seniors used to work.

CSV comment: One way of getting a lot of young people involved – maybe every young person in a year group – is an activity such as this example from Sawtry. The activity lasts for a couple of hours but the planning takes a long time if it is used wisely. This can give young people insights into the needs of the elderly.

'It is not just "Come on, Year 8, let's give the old folk a treat",' comments CSV senior trainer, Jim Mulligan. 'The built-in reflection will enable young people to become caring citizens. Many curriculum areas can give lesson time and the quality of the learning will improve because the young people are committed to it.'

Partnerships

St Peter's Collegiate School

- **Link with Barnardos** through an ex-parent who is involved as a professional charity worker.
- **A youth council** exists in Wolverhampton and the students will be voting for a representative young person to join it. This needs to be established as part of a regular involvement; it is important to get the timetables in sync with each other.
- **Magistrates' courts:** There is a PSHE/citizenship curriculum link over three consecutive weeks.

The Nobel School

What should education at The Nobel School look like in 2004: spaces in and out of the building which support formal and informal learning... more collaborative working with other institutions, closer to the community...

(Developing the Vision)

Tanfield

We seek consistently to develop flexible and permeable boundaries within and beyond school.

It can be done and is being done

There can be something daunting about case studies that give the impression that everything is perfect. It is good to know not only that something can be done and is being done, but that it is being done by people who understand that we can learn from what goes wrong, and that we are still learning. Marshfields Special School in Peterborough is a wonderful case in point. It has achieved great things, but it has taken time to do that. And it has not always been plain sailing.

CSV has worked with the school over a number of years, particularly on the CSV Lighthouse Schools project (see Chapter 13).

Marshfields School: CSV commentary

The walls come down

Over 10 years ago the school was cut off from the community. Young people were bussed in and spent the day contained in the school, and were then bussed out again. By the time CSV had become involved there had been a fundamental change. The invisible walls were down. Young people were going into the community and local people were coming into school. But was this community involvement enhancing learning? Yes, in places. Were all the teachers committed? Probably not. Jim Mulligan from CSV worked with the school for three years, encouraging planning and helping teachers make curriculum connections to the community activities. He also ran a staff INSET day, which included:

- exploration of typical examples of active learning in the community;
- an audit of what was being currently undertaken;
- discussion about and identification of the next steps to be taken.

The results of the collaboration are there for all to see.

The mission of the school over the seven years to 2001 has been summed up in the words, 'we strive to be at the heart of the community'.

Marshfields took part in the CSV Lighthouse Schools visit to Colorado in 1998 to learn more about the US approach to service learning in the community (see above, The curriculum, The global dimension).

The portrait is included for three reasons:

1. **From fortress to open house:** The school has consciously and deliberately opened itself up to the community to create its distinctive and highly successful programme of community involvement.
2. **From suspicion to trust:** The shift from the siege mentality of previous years to the trust and openness that is now so characteristic of the school ethos took time.
3. **Service learning and special needs:** The methodology of service learning (active learning in the community) is described in detail earlier in the chapter (The curriculum, Active learning in the community – a methodology). It is an approach that is suited to pupils of all abilities. The success of Marshfields underlines its value when used with children with special needs and learning difficulties.

Marshfields School and its community partners

Marshfields is a purpose-built special school catering for 157 students aged 5 to 18 years. All the students have a statement of special educational need, which identifies their moderate learning difficulties. In addition, many students have their learning difficulty further compounded by social, physical, communication, sensory, emotional and/or behavioural problems.

The school is situated within the Welland Estate in Dogsthorpe, Peterborough. The estate is recognized as an area of high social deprivation and it has attracted funding from both the European Commission and the Single Regeneration Fund to improve its community facilities. Only 10 per cent of the school's population actually live on 'the Welland', as the school caters for students from the whole of Peterborough and beyond.

In recent years the school has won a number of curriculum awards and received highly favourable comments from OFSTED inspections.

Young people – a resource to the community

The students placed in a special school often feel remote and withdrawn from the main thrust of the community.

Living and learning 'at the heart of the community'

Marshfields School strives 'to be at the heart of the community' (see Figures 14.13 and 14.14). This commitment is worked through in the daily life of the whole school community. Staff, students and parents at Marshfields recognize that the whole-school commitment to learning in and through the community enhances learning, raises self-esteem and equips students for everyday life when they have left the school.

Teaching is made easier and more effective when the teacher can draw on the real-life experiences of the children. For example, mapping skills are learnt from work on the wildlife garden instead of just looking at an atlas.

Each year all classes are asked to raise money for local charities. Year 4 children have raised £280 to buy two cows to feed a settlement in Bunooma, Kenya. The teacher used this activity to enhance her mathematics teaching.

Community wildlife projects

- Year 9 students have helped with a community wildlife garden in Paston. They have improved the condition of the heavy clay soil.

- Year 10 have laid concrete for walkways.
- Year 11 have laid patios on site.

Animal projects

Year 9 students have been involved in the construction of barn owl boxes as part of the Welland Valley barn owl project.

Year 9 students made 20 dormouse boxes and are surveying the distribution and populations of the dormouse in Cambridgeshire woodlands.

Bus shelter featured on the BBC

The art department painted a drab bus shelter, working locally in conjunction with Dogsthorpe Residents Association. The resulting mural was featured on BBC television's *Look East*.

Across the generations

Personal, health and social education is enriched by the students working in local playgroups and this forms an important module of their childcare course. Besides working as play leaders, the students produce toys, made in design technology, for the children who attend the playgroup.

Summary – context: recommendations

- **Recommendation 1:** Headteachers and governors should ensure that community partnerships and education for active citizenship feature systematically on their agenda.
- **Recommendation 2:** Headteachers, governors and partners should review the use of their grounds and premises and seek opportunities to maximize the educational and community benefit of the school's environment.
- **Recommendation 3:** All schools should ensure that they are in touch with their local authority (not just the education department) in connection with the Local Government Association's Hear by Right programme (see Chapter 16), which seeks to increase young people's democratic involvement with and through local government.
- **Recommendation 4:** All schools should reflect on their long-term development as centres of learning and community regeneration and seek appropriate partnerships with government, business and community organizations (see Chapter 16).

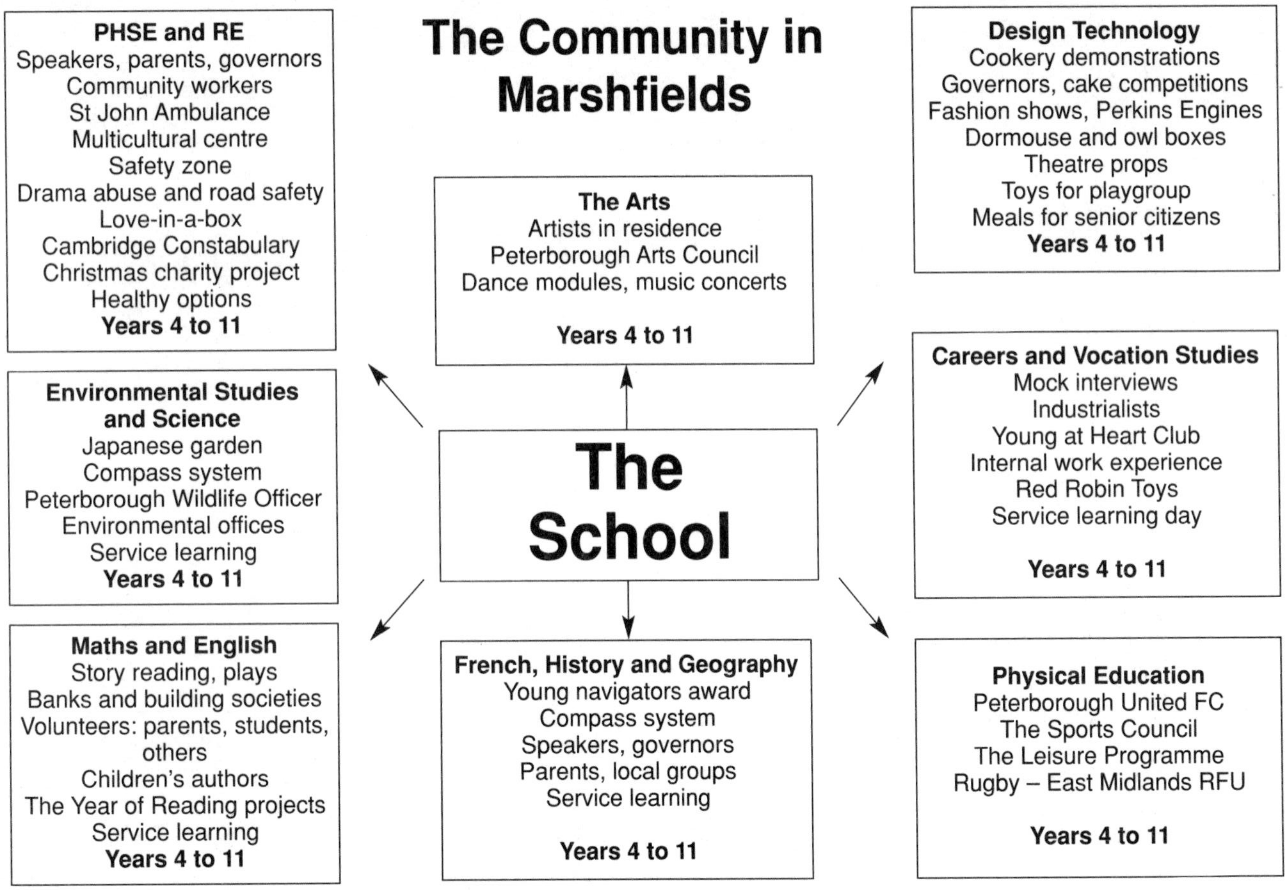

The Community in Marshfields

The School

Design Technology
Cookery demonstrations
Governors, cake competitions
Fashion shows, Perkins Engines
Dormouse and owl boxes
Theatre props
Toys for playgroup
Meals for senior citizens
Years 4 to 11

Careers and Vocation Studies
Mock interviews
Industrialists
Young at Heart Club
Internal work experience
Red Robin Toys
Service learning day
Years 4 to 11

Physical Education
Peterborough United FC
The Sports Council
The Leisure Programme
Rugby – East Midlands RFU
Years 4 to 11

The Arts
Artists in residence
Peterborough Arts Council
Dance modules, music concerts
Years 4 to 11

French, History and Geography
Young navigators award
Compass system
Speakers, governors
Parents, local groups
Service learning
Years 4 to 11

PHSE and RE
Speakers, parents, governors
Community workers
St John Ambulance
Multicultural centre
Safety zone
Drama abuse and road safety
Love-in-a-box
Cambridge Constabulary
Christmas charity project
Healthy options
Years 4 to 11

Environmental Studies and Science
Japanese garden
Compass system
Peterborough Wildlife Officer
Environmental offices
Service learning
Years 4 to 11

Maths and English
Story reading, plays
Banks and building societies
Volunteers: parents, students, others
Children's authors
The Year of Reading projects
Service learning
Years 4 to 11

Figure 14.13 *The community and Marshfields*

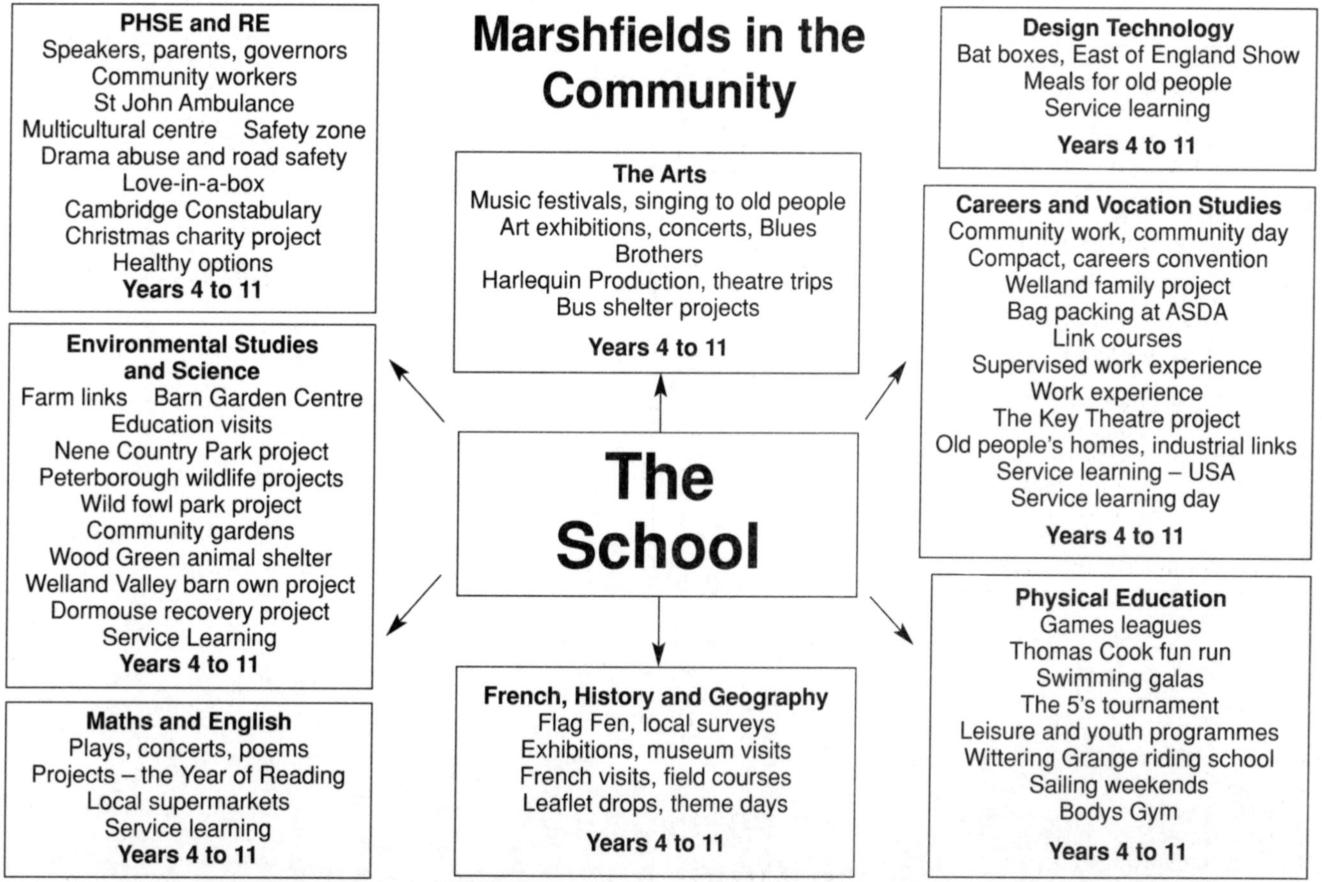

Marshfields in the Community

The School

Design Technology
Bat boxes, East of England Show
Meals for old people
Service learning
Years 4 to 11

Careers and Vocation Studies
Community work, community day
Compact, careers convention
Welland family project
Bag packing at ASDA
Link courses
Supervised work experience
Work experience
The Key Theatre project
Old people's homes, industrial links
Service learning – USA
Service learning day
Years 4 to 11

Physical Education
Games leagues
Thomas Cook fun run
Swimming galas
The 5's tournament
Leisure and youth programmes
Wittering Grange riding school
Sailing weekends
Bodys Gym
Years 4 to 11

The Arts
Music festivals, singing to old people
Art exhibitions, concerts, Blues
Brothers
Harlequin Production, theatre trips
Bus shelter projects
Years 4 to 11

French, History and Geography
Flag Fen, local surveys
Exhibitions, museum visits
French visits, field courses
Leaflet drops, theme days
Years 4 to 11

PHSE and RE
Speakers, parents, governors
Community workers
St John Ambulance
Multicultural centre   Safety zone
Drama abuse and road safety
Love-in-a-box
Cambridge Constabulary
Christmas charity project
Healthy options
Years 4 to 11

Environmental Studies and Science
Farm links   Barn Garden Centre
Education visits
Nene Country Park project
Peterborough wildlife projects
Wild fowl park project
Community gardens
Wood Green animal shelter
Welland Valley barn own project
Dormouse recovery project
Service Learning
Years 4 to 11

Maths and English
Plays, concerts, poems
Projects – the Year of Reading
Local supermarkets
Service learning
Years 4 to 11

Figure 14.14 *Marshfields and the community*

Inspection

Inspection is not one of the challenges of *initiating* education for active citizenship. It is rather a matter of providing OFSTED with the relevant evidence that the challenges are being tackled effectively. Of course, one of the reasons behind making citizenship education a statutory requirement was that it would guarantee that the subject would be taken seriously. In other words it would be inspected throughout the school and assessed at key stage 3. The evidence at the time of writing is that OFSTED is committed to the spirit of the Order as well as to the specific requirements of the programme of study.

Hold to the purpose of citizenship education

The purpose of citizenship education is to bring about 'a change in the political culture of this country both nationally and locally: for people to think of themselves as active citizens, willing, able and equipped to have an influence in public life'. This cannot be achieved on the back of an examination, however well conceived. We have already seen how young 'Angie' from Yorkshire would be likely to fail such an examination, and yet she was a demonstrably remarkable citizen. Examinations should serve the goals of citizenship, not the other way about. Happily OFSTED understands this clearly. HMI has set about devising a framework for assessing the contribution of citizenship to young people's education that respects the intentions of those who conceived and fashioned the Order on to the statute book.

Encouraging good practice

The OFSTED assessment framework aims to help teachers and inspectors evaluate how well schools are doing in helping young people gain the most from their entitlement to citizenship education. In this sense the framework is formative. It is to support and encourage good practice. The framework also sets out to develop standards against which formative and summative judgements can be reached and comparisons made between one school and another. Unless the reader believes that all attempts at summative assessment are misconceived, OFSTED's response to the undoubted challenge of inspecting citizenship education is instructive and encouraging.

A new kind of subject

The challenge of inspecting citizenship education raises three distinct but related issues. In the first place, citizenship education is not only new but, in assessment terms, unprecedented. There is no existing canon of good practice on which to draw, as there is in the case of, say, inspecting a new language. In the case of citizenship, inspectors, teachers and pupils are entering virgin territory and must work together to make the best sense of it. In this sense, OFSTED like the rest of us is working out the rules as it goes along. It is open season for those who want to influence how things happen. It is doubly important that our best teachers bring their skills, experience and commitment to developing effective strategies for evaluating citizenship education. It is clear that OFSTED recognizes the importance of teachers doing this and it speaks of the need in these circumstances for teachers to place 'greater weight on [their] own judgements or standards from direct observation'.

Teachers are more likely to 'own' the evaluation of citizenship education where they have had a direct hand in shaping the way it is done. This issue of ownership is important if teachers are to reclaim their professionalism after years of being told what to do by external agencies. Furthermore, the teacher who owns his or her work is the teacher who will help young people own theirs.

The ethos of the school

Secondly, citizenship education touches on the ethos, values and behaviour of the whole school. It offers young people a unique entitlement to learning through engaging with the life of the school and its communities. The *culture* of the school is central, not incidental, to citizenship education. The school ethos is not as elusive as some would suggest. It may in certain respects be hard to measure on a scale of 1 to 10; but in many respects it is the most palpable dimension of school life. It is also one of the most permanent. The contents of the curriculum will vary from day to day as will the headteacher's diary; but the ethos of the school will be the constant backdrop for the daily drama that is the life of the school.

Mission and core values

Schools will describe their ethos in different ways but the essential spirit of an institution stems from its core values and the way those values are interpreted in practice. Most schools have relatively full mission or vision statements. A good mission statement can lead to a simple set of core values for which there will be simple but powerful indicators. These indicators focus on the way individuals are valued and the way in which learning is valued and understood. This provides visitors to the school including other young people, parents and inspectors with first-hand evidence about the things that the school holds dear. Some schools, as we noted earlier, are devising citizenship manifestos that set out clearly and imaginatively for pupils and parents precisely what is on offer from the school. This development could prove helpful for everyone and is worth monitoring over the immediate years ahead.

Clearly stated citizenship aims

Schools like Deptford Green crisply announce the importance of education for active citizenship in the taught and whole curriculum: 'At Deptford Green citizenship is a way of learning and a way of life.' Members of Lipson College staff describe the school's mission as aiming at:

1. excellence for all and from all;
2. being a learning organization where everyone is searching for continuous improvement;
3. stretching each individual's talents by making Lipson a 'College for every future'.

They explain what lies behind the idea of being a College 'for every future'. 'We aim to promote cultural, physical, moral and spiritual development, enabling young people to become *active participants in society and responsible contributors* to it. Lipson will be a College for every future.' They add that they will ensure that the College 'operates effectively and efficiently at the heart of the community, offering equality of opportunity for all. We promote excellence at the heart of the community.' In other words, the critical connection between quality, learning and community is made from the start and becomes a vital element in the ethos of the school.

Student participation

For the average visitor it is easier to detect the ethos of a school than it is to collate and interpret the numerical measurements of achievement. It is easy to respond to the general atmosphere of the school. Are people welcoming, confident and helpful? How do students and staff relate to one another? What is the general feel of the place? Is it calm, relaxed and purposeful? Or is it frenzied, confused and tense? Where is the discipline coming from, from within or without? How participative are the students as learners, as citizens and as members of a local community? Most inspection teams are alert to these issues and comment perceptively upon them. See, for example, the OFSTED comments on Marshfields (see earlier in the chapter, Context), and the Deanes School, reproduced below.

The Deanes School: OFSTED report (1999)

In 1999 a team of OFSTED inspectors visited the school and looked in detail at what was going on. They reported approvingly on what they found:

- Students have very good attitudes to work and are eager learners.
- Relationships among students and between students and teachers are very positive.
- Students' social development is very good.
- Extensive community links provide a very good enrichment of students' learning experiences.
- A very wide range of extra-curricular activities extends provisions very effectively. Of parents who responded to the OFSTED survey, 92.5 per cent believe the school encourages children to get involved in more than just their daily lessons.
- Of parents who responded to the OFSTED survey, 85 per cent believe that the school's values and attitudes have a positive effect on their children.

Increasingly members of inspection teams will learn to adjust their questions to recognize and encourage those aspects of the school ethos that relate most directly to citizenship education: values, responsible action and democratic participation.

Students own their learning

Third, the focus of citizenship education must be on the extent to which each student owns her or his learning. Citizenship education, like personal and social education, is about more than knowledge and skills or even understanding. It is about the thread of meaning that links the individual to society. In citizenship education we need to discover creative ways of recognizing and valuing our distinctively human trait of making meaning. Our current obsession with categorizing attributes that are (or appear to be) measurable against clear objective standards has blunted our readiness to foster and celebrate other more numerically elusive qualities.

The example of the work at St James Middle School, Bury St Edmunds on design and technology is especially relevant here. It was singled out for especially favourable comment by HMI: 'I have visited 39 secondary schools and your middle school. Nowhere else have I found the variety and excitement in technology that is displayed here' (Mr Wheeldon, HMI). The Year 8 students were designing and making learning games for children with special needs. They were working on a subject that required accurate measurement (and the use of maths) for its technical success. They were also engaged with young children with serious learning difficulties, where empathy (not physics or design) was vital to the quality of their relationship. The project would only be truly successful when these two dimensions – the technical and the relational – were fused in a single experience.

A Year 8 student from the design and technology project commented on what he had learnt:

> I think it's a good project. It gives the children at the special school some fun but it also makes me feel good. I feel I've done something for other people and I feel pleased that they can play with the toy I've made. Even if we do something wrong it makes us all the more determined to get it right and finish it. I think it's a great opportunity because if we didn't do this we might never meet a person with disabilities. I think it is really good the way handicapped children get on with their lives as normally as possible, and that they don't let their disabilities get in the way of anything. It really makes me think hard about the smallest things in life that I take completely for granted. It wasn't until I did this project that I realized how lucky I am.

St James Church of England Middle School, Bury St Edmunds

CSV has enjoyed a partnership with St James School through work on the Barclays New Futures design project whereby Year 8 children make aids for children with special needs in the community. The case study gives a remarkable insight into what can be achieved through a focused initiative of this kind:

St James is the only Church of England voluntary aided middle school for pupils aged 9 to 13 in Suffolk. It has 500 pupils. The site is very attractive, on the edge of Bury St Edmunds with the Abbey Gardens on one side and open fields on another. There are large playing fields and ample hard play areas.

The school aims to value and respect individuals for what they are and tries to develop the sense of the spiritual dimension of life through membership of a Christian community.

In academic terms we are pursuing quality. We live in a world where results matter and good results usually stem from hard work. Nothing worth while is achieved without effort. Our social aim is to enable our pupils to take their places with confidence in society, to accept its rules and to try to help solve some of its problems.

(P Elstone, Headteacher)

Designing and making for children with special needs

As part of the national curriculum design and technology course, all Year 8 children at St James design and make aids for children with special needs in the community.

Design problems for the children to solve come from occupational therapists, REMAP, teachers and carers from special schools, child development centres and local opportunity groups. Often the problems are telephoned in to the technology department directly and are added to a design opportunities list, which is given to the new technology groups when they have their first session of the nine-week technology course.

Children work in groups of two or three and start with a brainstorming session to sketch some initial ideas and possible solutions to one of the challenges from the list of problems after they have listened to a talk, watched a video and seen examples of previous projects.

One member of the group makes a visit to meet the child with a special need and discuss the problem with the therapist, teacher or parent of the child. The design groups write a design brief and prepare a working sketch, which enables them to start making.

All the members of the group using a range of materials make the device or toy in the school workshop.

The students make another visit to the school to test the finished product and see if any modifications are needed, using advice from the expert who set the challenge or from observations of the child using the product.

Successfully completed products qualify for a CSV certificate.

Pupils are highly motivated especially after visiting children with disabilities and they stay on task well throughout the nine sessions of 160 minutes. Design teams know that the benefits to the child with the disability will be directly attributable to the success of the project. Underachieving boys seem to latch on to the notion that it is cool to succeed because the need is so real. They enjoy working in teams using the strengths of each member to achieve the quality needed for a successful design.

Children with special needs benefit not only by receiving a special aid or toy for the next stage of their development but also by meeting other children in the community. Some of the young designers continue their association with the children with disabilities by providing music concerts for them or doing more design projects when they move to upper school.

'The overall experience offered in design and technology is a strength of the school. The project linking pupils with a special school, designing aids for real needs, produces work of a very high and sometimes outstanding standard.'

Examples of projects

- A device with a musical reward to encourage simultaneous control of both hands in a hemiplegic boy.
- A slow eye-tracking device for a child with poor eye control.
- A farmyard to teach children with learning difficulties the names, shapes and sounds of farmyard animals.
- A device to hold paper so that a hemiplegic child can use scissors.
- A jack-in-the-box to be operated and reset with one hand for children with coordination difficulties.
- A device to encourage recognition of parts of the body for children with learning difficulties.

(Ricky Wilkinson, Technology Coordinator)

Ricky Wilkinson, the Technology Coordinator, commented on the way pupils traditionally have undertaken design briefs:

It seems to me the whole class is usually given the same design brief. They are all working on the same thing and I find that boring. The way we work might appear to raise difficulties with assessment. You can't compare an eye-tracking device with a hemiplegic device; but I assess on the *criteria of the national curriculum* and it has never been a problem. Our students achieve *well above the national average* but there is more to this project than getting a grade in a curriculum subject. Initially the students can be taken aback by the severity of the handicap. They find it strange to see someone the same age as them who is virtually a baby. And they see challenging behaviour. But usually our students are excellent. At this age, 12 to 13 years, they can identify with the children in an adult way but they are also young enough to play with them. They are not inhibited.

Evidence from a range of sources

The project has all the ingredients of good citizenship and good learning. It is also eminently open to inspection and assessment. There is a further dimension that will not have escaped the notice of OFSTED. The evidence of the value of the activity comes from outside the school as well as from within.

A parent of one of the children with special needs wrote appreciatively to the (former) headteacher:

Dear Mr Thackeray

I felt I must write to express my gratitude for Mark's wonderful chair. He has certainly enjoyed the social side of mealtimes since he has been able to sit at the table with the family. I think life must be somewhat limited if your world is restricted to floor level. This limitation would have continued for Mark without the offer of help from your technology department.

Please pass on my thanks to the children for their marvellous idea and the superb execution of that idea. They have certainly helped to make it easier to care for Mark and enabled him to enjoy mealtimes more.

Yours sincerely

Val Howe

Critical success factors

Ricky Wilkinson has given systematic attention to the factors that make for quality learning in his subject. He points out in his paper on good practice in his field that research has identified four critical success factors in teaching and service learning of this kind.[44] They are:

- collaboration and problem solving in 'design and make' activities;
- sustained motivation – including among underachieving boys;
- the development of a successful pedagogy;
- quality outcomes.

The need for research practitioners among teachers

These factors are likely to apply equally to service learning methods in other subjects. They give both inspectors and practitioners a clear basis for gathering and evaluating further evidence that will prove fruitful in planning, teaching/learning, assessment and inspection. These same factors need then to inform pedagogy and professional development. Nowhere is the presence of the teacher as research practitioner more valuable than in the service learning classroom. In this way in citizenship education – as in other parts of the curriculum – the bridge between the high ground of academic teaching and the swamp of classroom practice can be bridged. OFSTED have a vital role to play in encouraging and servicing such initiatives through their unique access to collecting information about what does and does not work in schools.

A relatively new form of action research technique, 'portraiture', offers a valuable tool for teachers to use within and beyond the school to investigate the broad-brush questions that demand more textured research techniques than those that rely almost exclusively on statistical analysis alone. Portraiture is also a technique that can be used by students in evaluating their projects, and as such would provide accessible, interesting and pertinent data for outsiders (including inspectors) who are actively interested to know more about the impact of education for active citizenship on its participants.

An inspector calls

Schools preparing for an inspection will shortly have access to the OFSTED framework for the inspection of citizenship education. At the time of writing this is not yet published.

The following guidelines offer a quick checklist of points worth noting. It is already clear from what OFSTED have said that inspectors will wish to talk and meet with students as well as staff. They have also pointed out that schools must keep appropriate evidence from projects and other citizenship activities. This is particularly important where significant learning is taking place at times other than during the inspectors' visits. The section on assessment earlier in the chapter offers further suggestions about the kinds of evidence that are important for assessment, accreditation, evaluation and inspection.

A quick checklist of points to remember

- **At key stage 3**, there *will be a requirement for end of key stage assessment* in citizenship. This will take effect following the introduction of citizenship as a national curriculum subject in September 2002.
- **At key stage 4**, as with other national curriculum subjects, there will be no statutory arrangements for assessment and reporting.
- **Previous reports on your school's achievement:** It is worth relating achievements in citizenship education to *what has previously been achieved* – and reported on – regarding pupils' attitudes, values and personal development. Always look for value added.
- **Collect and keep the evidence of achievement from a variety of sources** – pictures, videos, recordings, as well as written work.

- **Pupils** should keep track of their citizenship learning in and beyond the classroom. This can be linked to the progress file or its equivalent.
- **Class portfolios** for group activities and learning are also an invaluable source of information for participants and visitors, including inspectors.
- **Reflection:** It is very important that individual pupils can reflect and comment on their citizenship experiences.
- **Analysis:** It is helpful systematically to review learning among:
  - average pupils;
  - more able pupils;
  - less able pupils;

  with a view to identifying improvement opportunities.

  NB It can also be useful to compare achievements between boys and girls.

Notes

1. Figure 14.3 is from an address by Professor Bart McGettrick to the Four Nations Conference on citizenship education held in Glasgow, 27–29 September 2001.
2. Pendre High School, Gurnos Estate, Merthyr Tydfil, South Wales.
3. J Sacks, *The Persistence of Faith: Religion, morality and society in a secular age,* Weidenfeld & Nicolson, London.
4. Peter Mitchell (1999) *A Curriculum Framework for Citizenship and Social Education,* CSV.
5. QCA (2000) *Citizenship Education: Interim guidance,* QCA, London.
6. The following notes are extracted from DfES *Guidance on Global Citizenship.* See DfES Web site, www.dfes.gov.uk.
7. Send off for *A Curriculum for Global Citizenship: A guide for teachers and education workers* (short version) to Oxfam Supporters Communications, 274 Banbury Road, Oxford OX2 7DZ, UK. Visit www.ontheline.org.uk. It includes many resources for schools.
8. Donald Schon (1987) *Educating the Reflective Practitioner,* Jossey Bass, San Francisco.
9. HMI (1985) *The Curriculum from 5–16,* Curriculum Matters 2, The core document in HMI Curriculum Matters series.
10. Peter Mitchell (1999) *A Curriculum Framework for Citizenship and Social Education,* CSV.
11. Eric Midwinter (1971) Curriculum and the EPA Community School, in *Curriculum, Context, Design and Development,* Oliver and Boyd, Edinburgh.
12. National Research Council (2000) *How People Learn: Brain, mind, experience and school,* National Academy Press, Washington, DC. I refer here particularly to pp 234 ff.
13. National Research Council (2000) *How People Learn: Brain, mind, experience and school.*

14. From the Institute of Service Learning, Philadelphia. CSV is indebted to Dr Harry Silcox, then of the Global Institute for Service Learning, for his generosity and help in the early stages of the projects.
15. Developed and written for CSV by Francine Britton, the Global Institute for Service Learning, Philadelphia. The toolkit is published by Hodder & Stoughton, London (October 2000) and is available from Bookpoint.
16. The quote is taken from David Kerr's address on behalf of the QCA, given at Dawlish on 20 March 2001.
17. See for example:
    - service learning challenge: developing key skills through community service, ASDAN/CSV;
    - key decision citizenship and PSHE, ASDAN;
    - sex and relationship education, ASDAN and the National Children's Bureau;
    - drug education, ASDAN and the National Children's Bureau;
    - conflict resolution (example: confronting conflict), ASDAN;
    - global assignment, Action Aid and ASDAN.
18. These guidelines for assessment are based on a seminar workshop by Alun Morgan of the Shropshire and Telford and Wrekin Advisory Service (September 2001).
19. CSV (2000) *Active Citizenship – A toolkit for teachers*, Hodder & Stoughton, London.
20. TREE has been developed by an ex-head, Malcolm Brigg, who subsequently worked as an adviser to the then DfEE and worked closely with the business sector in drafting the programme.
21. Drawn from a seminar presented by Tony Breslin, Chief Executive of the Citizenship Foundation, and John Lloyd, Education Adviser, Birmingham City Council.
22. A Hargreaves and M Fulham (1998) *What's Worth Fighting for in Education?*, Open University Press, Buckingham.
23. Crick Report, para 9.1.
24. Bernard Trafford (1993) *Sharing Power in Schools: Raising standards*, Special Report for Education Now, Ticknall, Derbyshire.
25. C. Cullinford (1991) *The Inner World of Children: Children's ideas about schools*, p 2, Cassell, London.
26. Commission on Citizenship (1990) *Encouraging Citizenship: Report of the Commission on Citizenship*, HMSO, London.
27. Trafford, p 11.
28. Trafford, p 11.
29. John Holt (1982) *How Children Fail*, Penguin Books, London.
30. Trafford, p 13.
31. J. Watts (1989) writing in *The Democratic School*, Education Now, Ticknall.
32. E. Blishen (1969) *The School that I'd Like*, p 14, Penguin Books, London.
33. Centre for International Education and Research (1998, 1999) *School Councils and Pupil Exclusions: Research project report*, School Councils UK, London.
34. See the Appendix for further information on this organization.
35. Centre for International Education and Research (1998, 1999) *School Councils and Pupil Exclusions: Research project report*, para 8, p 4.
36. Derry Hannam/CSV (2001) A pilot study to evaluate the impact of the student participation aspects of the Citizenship Order on standards of education in secondary schools, Report to the DfEE.

37. These and other case studies are set out in *The PeerAID Book* by Amanda Brodala (Ibis Trust) and Jim Mulligan (CSV), CSV, London, 1999. Copies available from CSV (Education).

38. Contact ACT, c/o The Institute for Citizenship, Queensbridge Building, Albion Drive, London E8 4ET.

39. A summary of the method is available from the author on e-mail (potteryb@aol.com).

40. See Chapter 10.

41. These and some other notes are drawn from the Coalition for Citizenship presentation on Preparing for Citizenship (2001).

42. Dick Atkinson (1994) *The Common Sense of Community*, Demos booklet.

43. Melanie Elkan and Mandy Greenfield (1998) *Absolutely No Limits: A handbook for community volunteering in schools*, CSV, London. Pennywell School (2000) *Raising Standards through Peer Support*, CSV, London. Further information about CSV's volunteering in schools initiatives, contact CSV (Education) (tel: 020 7278 6601; e-mail: education@csv.org.uk).

44. See the paper given to the international conference on design and technology, IDATER 99, by Ricky Wilkinson MBE. The full title of the paper was: Key factors relating to good practice in the teaching and learning of Key Stage 3 Design and Technology. The author offers detailed insights into quality practice that are likely to be of relevance and interest to design and technology teachers in other schools.

PART IV:

Community matters

Community matters in education for active citizenship. In this part we explore themes that schools and communities share in common and which are crucial to the developing work of citizenship education:

- **Chapter 15: Volunteering and a citizenship culture**
  Volunteering is one critical element in the culture of active citizenship, and in recent years our understanding of volunteering has also changed.
- **Chapter 16: Going for partnerships**
  The government is encouraging partnerships between local government, the third sector, business and education in order to foster a welfare society.

These twin themes will be a necessary element in schools' planning and work on community matters over the years immediately ahead.

15

Volunteering and a citizenship culture

One of the best ways of putting the theories of citizenship into practice is through voluntary work in the community. Young people often display a spiritual and material generosity towards others which can disappear by the time adulthood is reached.

(The Lord Chancellor, quoted from the Crick Report, para 11.1)

Aims
- Volunteering is one critical element in the culture of active citizenship but must not conflict with entitlement.
- There is a distinction between philanthropy and activism.
- Volunteering can contribute to building social capital.
- Community volunteers can enrich the life of schools and foster citizenship education.

Citizenship education has a mixed ancestry. On one side of the family, it is the child of voluntarism and grass-roots politics; on the other, it is born of student-centred and experiential education. Voluntarism itself springs from two very different traditions in British social history: philanthropy and political radicalism. The philanthropic tradition is chiefly about ameliorating the plight of the unfortunate, while political radicalism aims to remove the causes that occasioned their plight in the first place. Crudely it is the difference between a soup kitchen and, say, a trade union.

Two approaches to volunteering

The tensions between these two approaches to volunteering and voluntarism are already being played out in schools and colleges, and are likely to feature increasingly as citizenship education raises the profile of volunteering and community action in schools.

Philanthropy

In Liverpool, young people at St Mary's College worked on the Seal Street project with the nuns in feeding and clothing homeless men and women on the margins of society. The students accepted considerable responsibility in this work through taking control of a number of activities. The project enabled young people to learn active citizenship at first hand through building a more caring society. 'Helping at Seal really is a highlight in my week; if I have a bad day at school, working with these people really makes me see how lucky I am,' said one student.[1]

Political activism

On the other side of the world Jennifer, a trainee teacher in California, responded very differently to a similar situation where she had been asked to help on a poverty programme in the Bay Area. Looking back on the experience, she said:

> I had a freak out! I used to work on poverty issues. The 'Bay Area Support Services' – they call it BASS – represented to me – have you heard of 'poverty pimps'? It's an expression in activist circles for organizations that individualize the problems of poverty and they don't look at it in social justice terms or in larger structural perspectives. They've created lots of jobs for themselves. They're into helping individual people, but not into ending poverty and don't see their job as trying to put themselves out of business. They want to make the social service sector bigger and bigger without changing the roots of the problem – which is a big debate I struggle with because, of course, I want people to have help right now, but I don't want it to be just about help right now... so I heard that name, BASS, and it reminded me of that orientation to poverty... [and I just freaked out].[2]

For the most part community involvement projects in British schools have been philanthropic rather than political. In any event they have tended to avoid explicit political campaigning. The reason is obvious. Most teachers are anxious not to be accused of political bias and are reluctant to engage in overtly political activity while in school. However, the clear requirement in the Citizenship Order that students should be encouraged to reflect on the political implications of their activities will almost certainly lead to growing political awareness around volunteering.

Volunteering versus course work

Reflection links community involvement with learning and, by association, with the requirements of the citizenship programme of study. This connection between curriculum and volunteering sparks another debate about the place of volunteering in citizenship education. Some people argue that the essence of volunteering is that it should be kept quite separate from activities that are required parts of course work. In the early 1990s CSV started Learning Together, a tutoring initiative that enabled university and college students to support teachers by offering pupils support in their studies. In some places the programme was assessed. Students would reflect on their tutoring experiences and give a formal presentation based on their experiences to a group of other students. They were marked on the quality of their presentation and its supporting evidence. These students had chosen to do tutoring – rather than some other activity – but their choice was within a course requirement. It was, in that sense, a part of their work and strictly speaking not volunteering at all. In other places students went into classrooms for a morning or an afternoon a week as, a purely voluntary activity.

Early in the life of the programme the debate about volunteering versus course work arose at a CSV Learning Together conference.[3] The exchange is instructive and the argument continues, in one form or another. A student who had been a CSV Learning Together volunteer said, 'It is essential that tutoring is and remains a purely voluntary activity. Tutoring is a gift. It's something the students bring to the children. I work with Jimmy because I want to work with him, not because I'm trying to improve my marks or lengthen my CV.' He clearly enjoys the support of others round the room.

A student who has done tutoring as part of his course work counters the point:

> But don't you see, I'm just as keen to help my students as you are. But I value the additional opportunity to reflect on what I have got from the experience. The fact I had to do a presentation on my tutoring really made me think about what I had gained from it. When I started I thought I was doing the kids a favour by helping them with physics. I did experiments with them and we made burglar alarms and bugging devices. We had a great time. If I had simply been a volunteer I would have left it at that. But

when I came to prepare my presentation I realized that I'd learnt a lot about getting my act together and about explaining things clearly without being patronizing. And yes, I do like having some course marks for all that effort. And yes, I have put it on my CV. I'm hoping to do a PGCE after I've finished my physics degree!

He, too, was supported by those who had shared a similar experience.

Volunteering versus entitlement

The situation in schools is, of course, different. Citizenship education is a statutory requirement as is community involvement. But there remains a debate between those who stress the value of volunteering, which can be encouraged by a school and counted as part of citizenship education, and those who value active learning in the community in the formal curriculum.

In many ways, however, the argument is rooted in a false premise based on a narrow definition of volunteering. Volunteering is, in this context, defined as unpaid, freely chosen, formally recognized activity through which people associate with each other around a mutually agreed social purpose. Usually, but not always, the purpose of the activity is underpinned by a concern for the common good.

It is immediately obvious that this definition provokes almost as many questions as it resolves. Does it include those numberless acts of good neighbourliness that are freely but informally undertaken? Does it include the staggering number of hours given by family members in support of people who are sick or in some way seriously incapacitated? Does it apply to motherhood or fatherhood or to the myriad acts of voluntary kindness undertaken by people at work who so frequently step beyond the bounds of their job descriptions? Was, for instance, the Good Samaritan a volunteer? Or, even more provocatively, was it simply the fact that Judas Iscariot was paid 30 pieces of silver for betraying Jesus Christ that stopped him from being called a volunteer? Volunteers largely staff political parties. Are those who volunteer to support the National Front, even to the point of committing violence, to be welcomed into the company of community volunteers? Clearly the notion of volunteering can be problematic. We therefore need either to abandon the use of the word volunteer or to redefine it. Which course of action we take will probably depend on circumstances.

Citizenship education and community involvement

In citizenship education volunteering is set firmly in the context of 'community involvement'. The Crick Report was clear about the importance of young people developing the habit of participating in their local and wider communities: 'learning about and becoming helpfully involved in the life and concerns of their communities, including learning through community involvement and service to the community'.[4]

In many ways, therefore, when dealing with citizenship education, it is simplest to avoid the use of the word volunteering and to speak instead of 'community involvement' and community action. There is, of course, a further dimension to community involvement that is not necessarily about volunteering. In citizenship education activities are designed to foster democratic values and to offer participants the opportunity to contribute to the way decisions are made and acted upon.

In summary, therefore, the community involvement strand of citizenship is 'voluntary' in the sense that it offers participants the opportunity to:

● exercise free choices within the limits of what the school can offer and allow;
● give freely of their time, experience, effort and good will;
● contribute to a definable community benefit;
● reflect on and learn from their experience;
● celebrate their experience.

It is certainly true that volunteering must be undertaken willingly and must be free from all forms of coercion; it is equally the case that in citizenship education it is the civic function of volunteering that is of most interest to those who are so keen to encourage it. The wheel has come full circle and we are back with the thesis that volunteering more than any other kind of activity can contribute to the nation's 'social capital'.

Volunteering as investment in 'social capital'

Robert Putnam, the father of theories of 'social capital', argues that in the United States 'something has happened in the last two or three decades to diminish civic engagement and social connectedness'. He then shows how volunteering can help us replenish the depleted stocks of communal trust and good will. He identifies three possible causes for the erosion of social capital in the United States:

- *The movement of women into the labour force.* Over these same two or three decades, many millions of American women have moved out of the home into paid employment.
- *Mobility: The 're-potting' hypothesis.* Numerous studies of organizational involvement have shown that residential stability and such related phenomena as homeownership are clearly associated with greater civic engagement. Mobility, like frequent re-potting of plants, tends to disrupt root systems, and it takes time for an uprooted individual to put down new roots.
- *The technological transformation of leisure.* There is reason to believe that deep-seated technological trends are radically 'privatizing' or 'individualizing' our use of leisure time and thus disrupting many opportunities for social-capital formation. The most obvious and probably the most powerful instrument of this revolution is television.

The notion of social capital is taking hold in Britain

There is little doubt that the notion of social capital is beginning to take hold not only in the United States but also in other parts of the world including Britain. Sporadic rioting in places such as Bradford, Burnley and Oldham is cited as an example of the breakdown in community relations. Government think tanks and voluntary sector agencies are actively exploring the implications for policy and practice. Commentators on the left are quick to point out that the most powerfully destructive cause of community conflict is the unequal opportunity faced in the job market by black and Asian people.[5] These critics are suspicious of the government intentions to create 'centres for diversity' in places like Bradford where 'they want jobs, not playgrounds'. Nonetheless, the social capital argument is arguably strengthened rather than destroyed by a more overtly political analysis of the problems. Central and local government are developing and trying out a number of strategies to promote community regeneration (see Chapter 16). We wait to see how effective these will prove to be, but it is at least a genuine attempt to address the social infrastructure of local communities. The notion of corporate citizenship has also spread to the business sector. Companies such as Shell are talking about the 'triple bottom line' where social investment is set alongside capital investment and investment in staff.

Volunteering and social 'connectedness'

In this context the proponents of citizenship education see volunteering as one way to strengthen the quality of local life through fostering a sense of 'connectedness'. The huge popularity of the Vermeer exhibition at the National Gallery during the summer of 2001 might in part be explained by the fact that so many people are hungry for a way of life that holds together harmoniously, a world where everything works and has a human scale.[6] We began this book with an imaginary portrait of the protagonists behind the big picture of citizenship education. These characters are politicians and thinkers, along with teachers and their students. Beyond the great hall in which these busy people are briefly assembled a woman in white headscarf, yellow jacket and full-length, brick-red skirt pours milk from a terracotta jug into a bowl. In this portrait of *The Cook*, Vermeer van Delft has captured precisely the serenity and mellow connectedness of a world that we have lost in our headlong rush into the second millennium. It is possible that the artist's world was nowhere as safe and wholesome as he made it appear; it is certain that we cannot turn the clock back 350 years. We can, however, create fresh opportunities to connect with and reflect upon the people and things about us. And this, in significant part, is the wider task of citizenship education. A special school creates an amphitheatre in a nearby wood and invites the neighbours and parents to share in their stagecraft; a secondary school builds sculpture to decorate an older persons' ward in the city hospital; and an IT class meets with adults to share their computer skills. And throughout the country older students assist younger pupils with their studies as tutors and mentors.

Slowly the fractured connections are remade through countless small but vital acts of volunteering, informed by shared reflection and a readiness to learn.

Volunteering and schools

CSV's experience is that community volunteers in schools, particularly in primary schools where they can be organized relatively easily and effectively, achieve three things, each of which contributes to the social capital of the school and the local community:

1. They model responsible and caring behaviour between adults and young people. Many children have little or no experience of responsible adults with whom they can have a positive relationship.
2. They contribute to the quality of learning through tutoring and mentoring.
3. They contribute positively to the ethos of the school. CSV developed a pioneer volunteering project with Winton Primary School in inner-city King's Cross. Visiting inspectors commented on the significant impact that this had on the behaviour of the children and the general atmosphere of the school.

CSV has produced a full account of this and related work along with guidelines and practical advice on good practice.[7] CSV also runs a nationwide programme involving retired people as volunteers in schools and, in selected places, employee volunteers in schools. Employee volunteers can be a powerful and effective way of meeting the training development needs of staff and the need of young people to enjoy the support of an adult mentor.

CSV's experience of working with Pennywell School helped us all understand how community volunteers can contribute significantly to young people's own community involvement. At Pennywell, adults supported the students in developing their anti-bullying programme in the school.[8]

It is always proved more difficult to involve significant numbers of community volunteers in secondary schools. CSV's London-wide volunteering programme with Deutsche Bank has proved both effective and rewarding, and shows what can be achieved when there is good will on both sides and some resources to ensure effective coordination. It is this additional need for support that is the stumbling block to progress in so many places.

Volunteer coordinators

CSV's work on community volunteers has included a partnership with the LEA in Southwark where CSV was employed to provide a group of schools with the support of a pool of local volunteers. This model works well and offers a way forward. In Chapter 14, Context, we recommended Dick Atkinson's idea that schools should band together, perhaps in association with their local authorities, to appoint coordinators to develop local community partnerships. The impact of volunteers, particularly in secondary schools, is unlikely to be significant unless there is further help of this kind. The Community Unit at Deptford Green School in London's New Cross is another example of what can be achieved by an individual school. Here again the school has successfully found the resources for the additional coordination and community development.

Recommendations

1. The school's citizenship manifesto could usefully set out a range of volunteering opportunities that will be offered to students in the school and community.

2. The student progress file (or TILE record should contain a section for recording volunteering.
3. The volunteering achieved by students in the school should be celebrated, perhaps by some annual event in partnership with community organizations. Students should take a leading part in organizing and leading such an event.
4. Schools should consider working with local government, business and the voluntary sector to establish some kind of community forum to promote partnership activities around citizenship including volunteering.
5. Volunteering activities should annually be reviewed by students and reported on to the school governors.

Notes

1. CSV/Barclays New Futures project.
2. Quoted from *Struggling to Learn Better*, Service Learning 2000 Centre, San Mateo, Citizenship Association (2001).
3. CSV worked closely with BP, which organized the early national conferences on student tutoring. BP's contribution to the development of student tutoring was a significant example of how a major company can make a major impact on citizenship education.
4. Crick Report, para 2: 11b.
5. *New Statesman*, 16 July 2001.
6. Will Hutton, *The Observer*, 8 July 2001.
7. Melanie Elkan and Mandy Greenfield (1998) *Absolutely No Limits: A handbook for community volunteering schemes in schools*, CSV, London.
8. Pennywell School/CSV (2000) *Raising Standards through Peer Support*, CSV, London.

16

Going for partnerships

Aim: This chapter shows how schools can develop further partnerships with local government, business and the voluntary sector.

Community partnerships in Britain

In Britain there is a move by national and local government to involve the voluntary sector[1] in sustaining and renewing local communities. In addition, local government is actively seeking young people's views on its services and policies.

There is a growing trend to create partnerships between local government and community voluntary organizations. This trend has significant implications for citizenship education, youth work and community development. Jack Straw, when he was Home Secretary,[2] described the change in attitude among local authorities towards voluntary sector organizations. He pointed out how Labour administrations in particular felt that the public sector should provide comprehensive public services, particularly in health and social care. Councillors and local council staff might engage occasionally with voluntary organizations, and even see them as supplementing social provision here and there, but they did not view such organizations as equal partners in sustaining and developing the quality of community life. All this has now changed, and partnership is the name of the game. This has significant implications for youth work and by association for citizenship education in schools.

Fresh approaches to partnership

Nicholas Deakin,[3] a specialist in the field of local government, points out that the necessary conditions for a change in the attitude of central and local government to civic engagement are now in place. New Labour has a strong majority in Parliament and therefore enjoys the political strength to pioneer fresh approaches. Under Gordon Brown, the Treasury has accumulated significant reserves and imposed a tight discipline over spending departments. The urgent need now is to fill the gap between the conception of policy at the centre and its implementation at the grass roots.

Effort to create joined-up policies

Government ministries are making significant efforts to create a 'joined-up' approach to social exclusion, urban regeneration and child poverty. Ministers, however, sometimes grow frustrated at the lack of progress at the grass roots and Blair has talked about 'banishing the pervasive culture of conservatism in local government'.

The question therefore arises: how can the access to effective public services best be promoted? The traditional view is that these services should be provided either directly through the state or through the market place. The old left, particularly in the form of the trade unions, is campaigning on behalf of public provision. The neo-liberals claim that private sector provision is the most efficient and is also ready to take risks.

Third-way approach

The third way, however, offers a possible further option through which the voluntary sector can meet (some of) the needs that the Government is seeking to satisfy. In the 1980s, agencies such as the Manpower Services Commission were used as a channel to fund additional voluntary sector services. Now, however, it is no longer simply a question of finding additional money for voluntary sector organizations. The new vision is that the voluntary sector might be significantly involved in *shaping* as well as providing community and social services. This approach is in line with the concept of the social investment state discussed in Chapter 5.

From the mid-1990s local government has been involved in implementing partnerships through the Single Regeneration Budget. For the most part voluntary sector organizations have been the poor relatives in this development, although they have been subcontracted to assist in delivering services. At the time of writing there is some uncertainty about what is going to happen next.

Councils as community leaders

Councils are in the process of reforming themselves to develop their role as community leaders. Whilst community leadership has always been part of what local authorities have done and been expected to do, it is now firmly established in statute. The Local Government Act 2000 has, for the first time, enshrined the community leadership role in law. It gives local councils a new power to promote the well-being of their area as a whole and encourages councils to look beyond immediate service delivery responsibilities to the wider economic, social and environmental well-being of their areas. This requires councils to work together with local groups to develop a strategy for their community. The Local Government Association has identified the key elements of community leadership as:

- involving and learning from local communities;
- building vision and direction;
- working effectively in partnership;
- making things happen;
- standing up for communities;
- empowering local communities;
- accountability to communities; and
- effective use of community resources.

Involving young people

Young people are key members of all local communities. It is essential, therefore, that in exercising their own leadership role, local councils consider the needs and aspirations of young people and that they involve them in decisions that affect their lives. In this context local government is working with the Local Government Association, the National Youth Agency and other organizations to promote the active and democratic involvement of young people in local matters that concern them. Benchmarks have been drawn up in the form of a set of standards against which councils can measure their progress. This programme for action is set out fully in *Hear by Right*, an important document that makes specific mention of schools and citizenship education.[4]

In assessing themselves against the standards, councils should look not just at those activities they are undertaking aimed specifically at young people, but also at those that include young people as part of their wider community leadership role. And while the standards deal only with the involvement of young people, many of them can be applied to other groups.

Which young people?

Young people are not a homogeneous group. They do not stay the same – they are continually changing. They could be profiled in many ways, for example: by age, gender, ethnicity and locality; by issues and problems such as education, homelessness, drug users and young offenders; by personality; or by socio-economic and psychological characteristics. General public policy and equity considerations suggest that an authority should be concerned with enabling all young people to take an active part in local democracy – if they wish. Not all young people will want to be involved at the highest level all of the time, so it is important to have a wide variety of opportunities for involvement, catering for the diversity of young people's interests, talents and needs. Young people must also have the right not to get involved.

With the right support from a council young people can be involved in a huge range of council activities and local democratic processes. These activities may be directly in relation to the work of the council or they may relate more widely to what is going on through other organizations in the community.

As the *Hear by Right* report points out:

> Young people involved in such activities may well find themselves coming into contact with the local council, for example, through campaigning for a political party at election time, through attending a council meeting to lobby on a specific issue, or through being consulted on a council plan as part of a local group. It is essential that young people, indeed all those concerned, find this contact a positive and useful experience.
>
> Looking at the local authority as an organization, there are many areas in which young people could be involved. With effective training and support for young people and for members and officers, young people can be and are actively involved in tasks in: planning and organising; doing and delivering; and checking, reviewing and learning. Councils will need to think carefully about which tasks they choose to involve young people in and what forms of engagement to use.

Opportunities for schools

Clearly this move by councils towards involving young people will open up opportunities for schools to work with their local authorities on the community involvement strand of education for active citizenship. There is a whole spectrum of potential involvement from consultation, representation and decision sharing to decision making and initiating projects.

The framework of practice outlined in the report will make an excellent basis for school–council partnerships.

Young people will, of course, both as part of school-based projects and their other activities be involved from time to time in activities that involve strong elements of political literacy. This is particularly the case with respect to campaigning of various kinds.

Building on existing success

Councils are, under existing legislation and practice, already involved extensively in consulting the public. It is now a matter of building on good existing practice.

Quality Protects

Quality Protects was launched in September 1998 and is now a five-year programme. It aims to transform the management of children's services and ensure vulnerable children get the very best in their life and in their futures. One of the key objectives of the programme is to improve participation of young people in the day-to-day decision making and service planning. The programme stresses that local authorities must listen to and involve children and young people in policy and service development and individual care planning. The Department of Health has a team of regional development workers who work alongside councils to ensure delivery of the Quality Protects programme.

The Local Government Association and Department of Health have produced a councillor's guide to Quality Protects. A set of training materials on ensuring children's rights and participation in care, *Total Respect*, has also been published. These provide practical advice on listening to and involving young people.[5] These materials may be of interest to students and teachers who are working together to develop democratic values within the school.

Best Value

Under the Best Value programme introduced in 1999 all councils are required to consult with the users of their services. Young people use many council services in their own right, especially services such as leisure centres, libraries and museums. Those children who are looked after by the authority will also receive support from social service departments.

The *Hear by Right* report, however, invites councils to think about the wider range of services they provide and to consider asking young people for their views on those. Adults are not the only people who live in council housing, and they are also not the only people affected by dirty streets or litter. Young people have views on crime, environment and regeneration – and should be part of the solution (linking with Home Office guidance to the Crime and Disorder Act). Young people can provide invaluable detailed feedback as front-line users of a vast range of council services and also provide exciting, innovative challenge to current ways of delivering services. Best Value reviews on such areas would benefit greatly from inputs from young people.

Connexions

'Taking account of the views of young people – individually and collectively' is one of the eight key principles for its design. The Connexions service planning guidance (October 2000) stresses that young people must be involved in the governance, design and delivery of the service, in addition to being consulted about innovative ways to deliver it.

The Children's Fund

The Children's Fund is funding preventative services for 5- to 13-year-olds at the risk of social exclusion. The Fund has a strong emphasis on involving children and young people. The Fund will ensure that children and young people are fully involved from the outset and an ongoing dialogue is established with them at local level throughout the design and delivery of the programme.

The Fund is encouraging children and young people to be members of the local partnerships that will decide what should be included in their proposals for the Children's Fund. It makes sense for schools to be in touch with the Children's Fund staff and to explore ways in which democratic initiatives of this sort can be linked with citizenship education.

Youth services

Youth services have long been in the forefront of developments involving young people in decision making and democracy and many schools are already actively involved – directly or indirectly – with their local youth services in forwarding new initiatives.

Voluntary and community groups

In many areas across the country both schools and councils are involved with local voluntary and community groups working with children and young people. Too often, however, there is no coherent liaison between the parties concerned and the chance is often missed to make the most of opportunities on offer.

An increasing number of schools like Deptford Green (see Chapter 14, Leadership) have already well-established liaison with local groups. Other schools, like Anthony Gell in Wirksworth, are discussing opportunities with governors who are well placed to help them build further links through groups such as Rotary.

Community development and neighbourhood renewal

New Labour's national current strategy for neighbourhood renewal is involving local authorities in creating local strategic partnerships. In this context local government is charged to develop a local community strategy. Every priority neighbourhood has to have a local strategic partnership, which can include schools. The Government's Central Neighbourhood Renewal Unit monitors this initiative.

The Government calls the national strategy for neighbourhood renewal a priority initiative, but in fact it absorbs only 2 per cent of national government expenditure, and is therefore very small in comparison to the purchasing power of the large spending departments, such as education, health and social services. Over the next five years the most effective neighbourhood renewal strategies will be those that are able to involve mainstream spending departments in aspects of the work of community renewal. Schools should be aware of these possibilities where they exist and seek to make the most of them.

Partnership: the challenge for the voluntary sector

'Partnership' is the fashionable term for these approaches; but partnership can mean a variety of things according to its context. It can range from major projects – under the general banner of Public Private Partnerships (PPP) and Public Funding Initiatives (PFI) – to a routine stress on community participation through token voluntary sector representation on local decision-making bodies.

Two things are clear. First, the voluntary and community sector should in future play a much more significant role than in the past. Second, if the voluntary sector is to be at the heart of new policy developments, it faces three distinct but related issues:

- terms of engagement;
- style of operation;
- impact on core values.

Each of these issues will affect the context in which schools seek to promote community involvement through partnerships with local government and other organizations.

Terms of engagement

Clearly schools are in an unusual position in that they are, at one level, part of local government and yet they are also community organizations responsible to their own governors. The next few years will prove very interesting in terms of the opportunities that schools will create to make the most of partnerships between themselves, voluntary organizations and local government initiatives (other than those taken by the LEA). At the moment, local organizations are for the most part proceeding with caution over partnerships with local government. It is, however, clear that the Government's national compact with the voluntary sector offers interesting opportunities to developing partnerships around compacts at the *local* level.[6] A number of these partnerships could create exciting new opportunities for shared work on citizenship education. CSV is interested in hearing from schools, voluntary organizations and local government with a view to disseminating good practice. (The reader is invited to contact CSV through its Web site communitypartners.org.uk and send an e-mail.)

Monitoring and evaluation

No less than 10 per cent of the £3 billion budget on urban regeneration is being spent on monitoring and evaluation. It is unlikely that schools will be expected to be responsible for the success or otherwise of the partnerships programmes with all the attendant questions about where the risk is parked. However, if schools were involved in projects where there was money for evaluation, it would be important to ensure that the evaluation served the purposes of the students as well as those of the partnership managers.

Style

Institutions have their own distinctive styles of working and these can cause conflict and problems for the partners. The style of a school encouraging young people to take part, for example, in a community care project may be different from the style and culture of the neighbouring social services department. In turn, this style may be different again from the style and culture of, say, the local Age Concern group. The minister responsible for neighbourhood partnership schemes, Lord Falconer, called for 'a major cultural shift' in the attitudes and approaches of stakeholders. Each stakeholder will tend to want the other partners to adopt their own language and style. Again, schools should proceed with caution. The benefits of becoming a member of a community partnership could be considerable. Such partnerships are capable of opening up a whole range of project opportunities from social care to environmental and community development. The important thing is that each partner, including the schools, should be clear about their own needs and expectations and understand how these can fit with the needs and expectations of the other players.

Core values

The culture of an organization also includes its core values. Schools are increasingly clear and often explicit about their core values. Many organizations have developed values statements as part of their recruitment procedure. These will include statements about the way that young people's roles are understood and developed. For example, there may be a 'standard' to ensure that the views and ideas of young people are actively sought in relation to the community placement or project. (The *Hear by Right* report offers helpful guidance on such issues.) Schools will need to be explicit about the values and standards to which they are working.

Who is in charge?

In local strategic partnerships it is important to know who is in charge. There does, however, need to be generosity about sharing leadership in ways that respect the status and contribution of local groups and of schools.

There are a growing number of examples of effective partnerships between schools and their local councils. The Yardleys School community care project, for example, was based on a partnership between the school, Birmingham City Council and CSV. The initiative would not have been possible without the strong support of the council. (See Yardleys School – project case study, Chapter 14, The curriculum.)

The direction of government policy suggests that there will be further, widespread opportunities for schools to enter local partnerships that will enable students to take part in opportunities to learn through meeting real community needs. The success of such initiatives will depend in large part on the extent to which the needs of schools and students can be taken into account. Student involvement should involve the minimum of bureaucracy alongside positive opportunities to:

- engage directly with client groups;
- contribute to decision making;
- record and evaluate the salient aspects of the work.

In other words students, as well as teachers, must be treated as genuine partners in the enterprise.

Partnership with the corporate sector

A growing number of businesses are excited about working with schools, and some of them are interested in helping schools develop education for life, work and citizenship.

Student tutoring with BP, Royal Mail, BT and NatWest Bank

CSV has been pleased to work with major national and international companies on education projects and sponsorships. In the early 1990s BP initiated a UK-wide student tutoring programme, whereby university and college students went into schools to support children and young people in their studies and other activities. The idea had much earlier been fostered by CSV's founder, Alec Dickson, and the first successful project had been set under way by Dr Sinclair Goodlad through a group of engineering students at Imperial College. CSV not only worked to build up projects on the ground, but also brought on board a further range of national commercial sponsors including Royal Mail, National Power, NatWest Bank and British Telecom.

A duty to contribute

The argument then, as now, was that major companies see it as part of their duty to contribute to the quality of education, which has so profound and direct an effect on the quality of life and, by the same token, the strength and stability of markets. It was significant that none of these companies was immediately concerned with selling their products and services directly to children and young people. They did, however, recognize that no company faces a vibrant future in a society where education fails to equip young people with the knowledge, skills, attitudes and experience to develop and maintain a prosperous, healthy society.

Example 1: Barclays Bank

Three years later Barclays Bank approached CSV through a sponsorship agency[7] about the possibility of developing a joint project around community projects. From this fruitful beginning the long-standing Barclays New Futures initiative was born. The programme offers more than £1 million in cash, resource materials, professional advice and support to schools who bid successfully for the prestigious Barclays New Futures awards. Over the first six years of the initiative Barclays New Futures made more than 500 awards to secondary schools across the country for projects that address key aspects of citizenship education through active learning in the community. In addition to the award-winning schools there have been a further 500 or so schools drawn into the programme through partnerships set up by the award winner. In all, over 1,000 schools have been directly influenced and encouraged by the scheme. A large proportion of the portraits and case studies in this book are drawn from CSV's work with Barclays New Futures.

In many ways the programme anticipated the government's move to make citizenship education a statutory requirement within the secondary curriculum. Barclays New Futures has, therefore, helped prepare schools for the entitlement to community involvement that they will soon be expected to offer *all* students aged between 11 and 16.

How Barclays New Futures came about

The story behind what led to the Barclays New Futures initiative is instructive. Barclays Bank decided towards the start of the 1990s to revise its programme of charitable grant giving, which until then had been made available to a very wide range of bidders asking for help on an equally broad spectrum of activities. Barclays staff were consulted and it was clear that they were interested in two things: 1) the quality of life in local communities; and 2) the quality of education. In response to these concerns the corporate affairs team, in consultation with the sponsorship agency, Kallaway, and CSV, came up with the idea of a long-term grant programme to help schools encourage young people to learn through tackling real community challenges.[8]

Companies are not interested only in sponsorship; they are also interested in involving their employees in community volunteering. In his report on *Volunteering in the 21st Century*, Gavin Mensah-Coker explores the issues behind corporate volunteering.[9] 'Consumers', he argues:

> will look not only at prices, quality of services and merchandise but also at the social investment policies and practices of companies. Consumers will have greater access to more information and will assert their power through spending habits and value-led personal choices.
>
> Employee volunteering will be carefully managed and controlled by companies in order to maximise the return on their investment. Analytical models will establish the links between community involvement schemes and the profit margins of the company involved. Companies will recognise the benefits of volunteering for employee retention, team building, profile raising, encouraging innovation and the testing of new managers. With the 'pick and mix' approach to career development replacing the 'job for life' attitude, employers will have to work much harder to build employer loyalty. Part of that work will be giving employees the opportunity to volunteer in company time without penalty, supporting the community in the ways that they choose. This will include offering volunteering sabbaticals to employees.
>
> Companies will be much more concerned about the work/life balance of their employees. Current evidence suggests that employees with a well-balanced lifestyle are more effective workers. Employers will use employee-volunteering initiatives to give employees the chance to correct that balance and to view the workplace as a more holistic environment.
>
> Technological developments will mean that employee volunteering opportunities will not be limited to the local and physical. Virtual volunteering will allow employees to support communities that are physically distant, but perhaps in a key market for their company.

Community involvement – a central plank in marketing

Community involvement will become a central plank of the marketing mix for businesses, informing PR and marketing campaigns, and even being used to spearhead particular campaigns. A stronger link will be established between the type of volunteering undertaken and the products and services of the company involved, as they seek to gain the maximum value from their investment.

Developments in sponsorship may lead to companies with well-known brand names leading campaigns on key social issues. For example, Glaxo Wellcome may become the lead voice on cancer research and care, while Amazon.com may become the champion of the library system. Companies will mobilize volunteer action directly rather than through a voluntary sector partner. Businesses will expand on employee volunteering schemes to run consumer volunteering initiatives, using volunteering opportunities to build customer loyalty.

CSV's experience is that companies are particularly interested in offering their employees opportunities to volunteer as tutors and mentors in schools. In this way schools can increasingly look to forming partnership with business as well as with community organizations and local authorities.

Barclays, in addition to sponsoring Barclays New Futures, also encourage their employees to volunteer. Chris Swales from the Bank describes – in the following section – the mentoring programme undertaken by staff from the Barclays Sunderland call centre.

Barclays education mentoring project (Sunderland)

Now in its second year, the business education mentoring scheme has grown from 12 mentors to 118 working with 148 disaffected children throughout Sunderland.

Mentors visit each child for one hour each month on a one-to-one basis to build trusting relationships and provide non-judgemental support and guidance.

They are currently working with nine secondary schools, including two special needs schools, and four primary schools. Many of the children come from poor backgrounds and have low aspirations and lack self-confidence.

Mentors work with the children to improve identified areas. They have also built up a strong network of professional services to call on for advice and help, including child protection services, health care, family planning, drug abuse council and the police authority. This group is highly motivated, enthusiastic and highly regarded by Sunderland Education Authority: 'The pupils look forward to their mentor's visits with positive anticipation.'

The case for business support

'Business has always had a long-term commonality of interest with wider society,' argued Vernon Ellis in his New Statesman lecture on the role of international capitalism:[10]

The acceptance of this can be traced as far back as the medieval Guilds, which sought not only to promote skills among their members, but also to create a stable, prosperous, strongly governed society in which those skills could flourish.

Then it was recognised by pioneers of the co-operative movement, such as Robert Owen, in the late 18th and early 19th century, and by the car maker Henry Ford in the 20th century, who observed famously that mass production requires mass consumption. I believe that this idea of enlightened self-interest is a key element of what corporate citizenship is really about.

But it is not the only element – it also implies a recognition and acceptance by business of societal obligations and expectations. Business, although sometimes initially resistant, has constantly evolved to meet society's goals and fuse them into its own interests. In this way, society's interests come to form part of the business case for making particular decisions.

He later goes on to argue that 'it will no longer be sufficient to be seen as a good corporate citizen just in one's home country. The recent controversy over the selling of generic anti-Aids drugs in South Africa shows the importance of business working with, not against, such broader societal expectations.'

Example 2: Deutsche Bank – mentoring and training

CSV's experience is that, while many companies remain reluctant to engage in corporate citizenship, there are a small number of major firms that have a clear vision of their responsibility to work with the grain of local communities not only in their country of origin but also in those countries with which they work across the world. This international message is reinforced by CSV's recent experience of Deutsche Bank, which has provided employee mentors and sponsored CSV active citizenship training in a group of London schools. It is promoting similar support for schools in Edinburgh.

At a convivial event in the Merchant Taylors' Hall in London mentors and students told the assembled company of teachers, students and bank staff of their pleasure in mentoring. One student said how much her friendship with her mentor meant to her by way of encouragement, intellectual stimulation and sheer enjoyment. One teacher described how the students waited for their mentors, their noses pressed to the window in anticipation of the chance to talk with and enjoy the company of a sympathetic adult.

Build partnerships with local firms

CSV strongly encourages schools to build partnerships with local firms where there is interest in mentoring and employee support for pupils and students. Wherever possible these partnerships can be used to promote and foster citizenship education. In forming community partnerships schoolteachers often remind themselves that most firms are led and staffed by fellow human beings who are interested in the world about them and who are, within the limits of their time and resources, prepared to consider ways of helping. Employers often resent simply being asked for money, money that they will often consider they do not have. Personal help is always a better starting point and, in the case of the examples given here, one good thing can lead to another. If employer-school partnerships of this kind are really to take off, however, it would greatly help smaller and less affluent firms to have their efforts recognized by government through some form of tax concession on the time and money they spend in working with their schools and local communities.

Too few per cent

Corporate commitment to social investment remains erratic and uneven across the board. Alison Benjamin, editor of *Corporate Citizen*, commented:[11] 'Without any commitment to maintain corporate community involvement, companies have carte blanche to close their community affairs departments and slash their community contributions at any whiff of financial trouble.' She further points out that among the FTSE 100 companies the average level of giving (0.4 per cent of pre-tax profits) is significantly *below* the 1 per cent recommended by the Per Cent Club – a 200-strong group of companies that promote a benchmark of 1 per cent of pre-tax profits.

Not all companies axe their community giving at the first sign of financial trouble. Per Cent Club member Marks & Spencer maintained its giving around the 1 per cent level in spite of its severe financial problems. Other companies, in spite of significant profits, failed to invest anything in the community. 'Logica's refusal to divest any of its £136m profits to charity is unacceptable and if it is serious about encouraging staff to fundraise, it should take a leaf out of its competitors' books,' commented Benjamin. She adds, 'The carrot most employees respond to is a pledge by employers to match, from corporate coffers, any money raised by staff.'[12] CSV, in its work with Barclays, has valued the £1 for £1 scheme run by the Bank for its staff community fund-raising activities.

There is a move among the more progressive givers to encourage benchmarking, not only of percentage giving, but also around standards of good and effective practice that includes employee and company support for their communities. In the mid-1990s half a dozen lading companies formed the London Benchmarking Group. They designed a template against which to 'better define the measures of efficiency and effectiveness of all types of community involvement activity by using benchmarking techniques'. Fifty companies now use this template.

Some companies, such as Lloyds TSB and Northern Rock, have set up semi-independent foundations as shareholders in the companies and to undertake responsibility for investing the relevant profits into charitable and community ventures.

It is clear that the potential for corporate community involvement is considerable, but that at present it is for the most part limited and vulnerable. If the Government is serious about encouraging active communities a more robust approach is needed. Organizations including schools and voluntary sector organizations are becoming used to the idea of Kite marks for quality practice. Investors in People, for example, is a Kite mark that may increasingly be treated by government as a necessary condition for receiving government grants or contracts. Investors in Community Kite mark could equally well serve a similar purpose. As part of the bidding process for government contracts (or grants) companies and organizations should be in a position to demonstrate their bona fides as corporate citizens. Such a Kite mark might also have some practical benefit in terms of tax concessions or benefits. This approach would have a double advantage for schools. It would open up further possibilities of funding and support to community involvement; but, perhaps more importantly, it would make it clear that all organizations – not simply schools – were being expected to play their part in promoting a citizen culture.

Summary and recommendations

1. **Social investment:** Government is gradually moving towards investing in community partnerships that foster community development and youth involvement.
2. **Youth involvement:** The *Hear by Right* report (LGA/NYA) sets out the possibilities for involving young people in local government initiatives.
3. **Local government will build on existing practice:** Quality Counts, Best Value, Connexions, Children's Fund, youth services, work with schools.
4. **Community development:** Local government has responsibility for promoting community development and neighbourhood renewal. This also opens up opportunities for schools.
5. **Commercial and business support:** There is a powerful case for businesses to support community involvement projects and in a number of cases they are doing this through working with schools.

6. **Recommendation:** There should be an Investors in Community Kite mark for companies that meet a simple set of benchmark requirements. This Kite mark should carry practical and financial benefits regarding government contracting and tax concessions/benefits.

Notes

1. The phrase third sector, universally used in Scotland, describes non-government organizations more appropriately than does the term voluntary sector, which suggests that all non-government organizations are involving volunteers.
2. In an address on the Human Rights Act to an audience in St Paul's Cathedral (October 2000) on the occasion of the publication of the study guide to the implications of the Act under British law (Home Office/General Council of the Bar, 2000).
3. Nicholas Deakin has worked as a civil servant and subsequently in local government. From 1980 to 1998 he was Professor of Social Policy and Administration at the University of Birmingham and is now a visiting professor at the Centre for Civil Society, London School of Economics.
4. *Hear by Right* (LGA, London, 2001), a document produced jointly by the LGA and the NYA, sets out these standards. It is available on the LGA Web site. This section of the present chapter draws on the contents of the document.
5. They are specifically for councillors and front-line staff. Copies can be obtained from CROA (Children's Rights Officers and Advocates) or the Department of Health.
6. Gary Craig et al (1999) *Developing Local Compacts: Relationships between local public sector bodies and the voluntary and community sectors*, YPS for the Joseph Rowntree Foundation. A summary of this is available on the Joseph Rowntree Foundation Web site, http://www.jrf.org.uk/home.asp.
7. Kallaway Ltd.
8. For further information about the Barclays New Futures award scheme contact either CSV Education for Citizenship, 237 Pentonville Road, London N1 9NJ (e-mail: education@csv.org.uk) or Barclays New Futures, Kallaway Ltd, 2 Portland Road, Holland Park, London W11 4LA (e-mail: barclaysnewfutures @kallaway.co.uk).
9. *Giving Time, Volunteering in the 21st Century* by Gavin Mensah-Coker, Researcher, Demos. This is a CSV report in association with Demos, June 2000. See Chapter 16.
10. Enterprise or exploitation: can global business be a force for good? by Vernon Ellis, International Chairman, Accenture, in the New Statesman lecture, 11 July 2001, published by the *New Statesman*.
11. *The Guardian*, Society, 31 October 2001.
12. *The Guardian*, Society, 31 October 2001.

Endpiece

The future of citizenship education at the time of writing (Spring 2002) hangs in the balance.

At worst this latest attempt at citizenship education may suffocate and die under the weight of fresh and apparently unconnected initiatives such as the Key Stage 3 Strategy.

At best, however, citizenship education provides a fulcrum for social, political and educational reform. It could genuinely lead to the change in our 'political culture' so eagerly sought by the Crick Report. It could also enrich standards through encouraging a generation of students to learn, work and live through informed reflection on real experience.

Future schools may build their curriculum around citizenship education.[1] Such schools will be very different from what they are now. They will be centres of life-long community learning, working with all sections of their communities in a shared quest for improving the quality of their own and others lives. The 21st Century Education Project in Dudley is one among several projects committed to creating, testing and evaluating a model school for the future.[2] There will be new and more stimulating ways for young people and adults to record and review, report and evaluate their learning.[3] There will be a fresh sense of personal and public pride and confidence among members of the teaching profession. The upcoming generation of students and pupils will work with us to cherish the best in our received traditions of voluntarism and community involvement. They will also set about the urgent task of finding new and more appropriate ways to meet the challenges of life in the 21st century.

Notes

1. *See Citizenship Schools: A practical guide for citizenship and personal development by Titus Alexander.* (Campaign for Learning/UNICEF, London 2001.)
2. This innovative project is based at the 21st Century Education Project, Ward House, Himley Park, Himley, Dudley DY3 4DF. The Project Director is Tony Hinckley BSc, MA, FRSA.

3. 'Portraiture' is a research method particularly associated with the name of Sarah
    Lawrence Lightfoot. (*The Art and Science of Portraiture*, by Sarah Lightfoot and
    Jessica Davis, Jossey Bass, San Francisco, 1997.) The author of this book
    (potterjb@aol.com) would be pleased to e-mail details of the approach to inter-
    ested colleagues.

Appendix: resources

The CSV Community Partners' Web site is designed to help teachers, pupils and their community partners to develop opportunities for citizenship education through community involvement. See www.communitypartners.org.uk. The Web site comprises:

1. **A directory of community organizations**
   An extensive list of organizations – both national and regional – that offer support to schools tackling citizenship education through community involvement.
2. **Guidelines for good practice**
   A set of general principles based on the experience of teachers and their community partners. The guidelines include references to the national curriculum.
3. **Case studies and project ideas**
   The case studies and project ideas are drawn from projects that have already been tried by teachers and students in secondary schools. The case studies can be searched against a simple set of criteria linked to project theme, key stage and subject. The project ideas are short descriptions of community projects.

Visitors to the site are invited to comment on what is offered and to suggest further information and ideas.

CSV Education for Citizenship works with schools, colleges and universities to involve young people in learning through positive community action. CSV Education for Citizenship is part of CSV, which creates opportunities for people to play an active part in the life of their community through volunteering, training, the media and education.

Disclaimer: CSV is not responsible for the contents or reliability of the linked Web sites and does not necessarily endorse the views expressed within them. Listing should not be taken as an endorsement of any kind.

Here are a few of the useful contacts that you can find on the Web site:

Association for Citizenship Teaching
The new professional association for those involved with citizenship teaching.
www.teachingcitizenship.org.uk

CSV Education for Citizenship
237 Pentonville Rd
London N1 9NJ
Tel: (020) 7271 6601
e-mail: education@csv.org.uk
www.csv.org.uk
www.communitypartners.org.uk

Hansard Society
St Philips Building
LSE
Sheffield Street
London WC2A 2EX
Tel: (020) 7955 7459
Fax: (020) 7955 7492
e-mail: hansard@hansard.lse.ac.uk

Parliamentary Education Unit
Norman Shaw Building (North)
London SW1A 2TT
Tel: (020) 7219 5521
e-mail: edunit@parliament.uk

Personal Finance Education Group (pfeg)
Centurion House
24 Monument Street
London EC3R 8AQ
Tel: (020) 7220 1735
Fax: (020) 7220 1731
e-mail: info@pfeg.org

School Councils UK
57 Etchingam Park Road
Finchley
London N3 2EB
Tel: (020) 8349 2459
Fax: (020) 8346 0898
e-mail: jess@scocon.demon.co.uk

The Citizenship Foundation
Ferroner's House
Off Aldersgate St
London EC2Y 8AA
Tel: (020) 7367 0500
e-mail: info@citfou.org.uk
www.citfou.org.uk

The Institute of Citizenship
62 Marylebone High St
London W1M 3AF
Tel: (020) 7935 4777
e-mail: ics@citizen.org.uk
www.citizen.org.uk

Useful organizations and agencies

Department of Education and Skills and QCA Web sites

www.dfes.gov.uk
www.qca.org.uk/subjects/citizenship
www.standards.dfes.gov.uk

Libraries

Libraries are often the holders of a database for local community organizations; this may be in hard copy format or on their Web site.

Local Government Association

www.lga.gov.uk

National Grid for Learning

www.ngfl.gov.uk

The Regional Arts Council

The Regional Arts Council database has information on the local and regional arts organizations, many of which often have innovative ways of introducing issues to students: www.arts.org.uk. Most of the regional arts councils have their own Web sites.

Volunteering

Citizens Advice Bureaux	www.nacab.org.uk
Councils for Voluntary Service	www.nacvs.org.uk
Education and Business Partnerships (EBP)	www.national_ebp@ compuserve.com
National Association of Volunteer Bureaux	www.navb.org.uk

Youth information

An extremely useful Web site with lots of organizations, issues and ideas is:
www.youthinformation.com

Other organizations both public and private

Timebank	www.timebank.org.uk
Learning Through Landscapes	www.ltl.org.uk
National Centre for Volunteering	www.volunteering.org.uk
Active Community Unit – Home Office	www.homeoffice.gov.uk/acu
Citizens Connection	www.citizensconnection.net
National Youth Agency	www.nya.org.uk
Connexions (the UK Government's strategy to ensure every young person gets the best start in life)	www.connexions.gov.uk
An Internet project for citizenship education in primary schools	www.timeforcitizenship.com

Index